BUCK FEVER

BUCK FEVER

*The Deer Hunting Tradition
in Pennsylvania*

MIKE SAJNA

University of Pittsburgh Press

Published by the University of Pittsburgh Press, Pittsburgh, Pa. 15260
Copyright © 1990, University of Pittsburgh Press
All rights reserved
Baker & Taylor International, London
Manufactured in the United States of America
Second printing, 1991

Library of Congress Cataloging-in-Publication Data

Sajna, Mike
    Buck fever: the deer hunting tradition in Pennsylvania / Mike Sajna
    p. cm.
    ISBN 0-8229-3645-3. — ISBN 0-8229-5436-2 (pbk.)
    1. White-tailed deer hunting — Pennsylvania — Warren County.
2. Deer hunting — Pennsylvania — Warren County. 3. Deer.
I. Title.
SK301.S217 1990
799.2'77357 — dc20   90–30615
                                                              CIP

In memory of
Richard John Sajna
1953–1976
You were always a better hunter

CONTENTS

PREFACE

The writer and naturalist Edward Abbey, who also grew up hunting deer in Pennsylvania's Allegheny Mountains, once wrote in an essay entitled "Blood Sport": "What can I say about hunting that hasn't been said before? Hunting is one of the hardest things even to think about. Such a storm of conflicting emotions!"

While I have long been vaguely aware of my sometimes contradictory feelings about hunting, the truth of Abbey's statement never really struck me until I tried writing in depth about the sport. At times while working on this book, I loved hunting as much as I have ever loved anything and hoped I might have the strength to continue hunting right up until the end. At other times, though, I was sad and ashamed of being a hunter, and wondered if I should quit. What right do I have to take the life of a creature as magnificent as the white-tailed deer? I asked myself.

I still don't know the answer to that question, nor can I say in any absolute way exactly what I feel about hunting. Except, I believe, no thinking hunter is completely at ease with killing.

One thing I hope this book shows in some way is the complexity of the hunting experience, the world that exists between the much publicized extremes on both sides of the issue. I also hope that knowledgeable hunters will ovelook any talk of hunting techniques and whitetail behavior they don't agree with or believe to be incorrect. This is not meant to be a guide to hunting the whitetail—there are more than enough of those on the market. This is nothing more than a look at a single deer camp during a single season. But I think scattered within this particular story are a few things other hunters may identify with and nonhunters might be surprised to learn.

For any success I might have had in my endeavor, there are

many people to thank. First, of course, are my deer hunting companions: my dad, Mike Sajna, Sr., who taught me how to hunt; Bob Burnett, who invited me to hunt out of his camp several years ago and became a valued friend through hunting; Garth Indyk, for the humor he always brings to camp; and Mike Burnett, for his youth. They all allowd me to write about them without reservation.

Ted Godshall, chief of the Pennsylvania Game Commission's Information Division, and Paul Brohn, public affairs officer for Allegheny National Forest, were indispensable for the background information and guidance they provided. Critics of the Game Commission and the U.S. Forest Service, and there are many, both hunters and nonhunters, may suspect that I was led to write certain things by those two agencies, but Ted and Paul never pressured me in any way. We talked. They told me what they knew and I checked what they said against other sources. In the places where they are quoted at length, I did so mainly because what they said appeared to be true and I liked the way they said it.

Brad Nelson, a biologist and the wildlife program director for Allegheny National Forest, was important for the information he provided about the whitetail in the national forest where the story is set. Likewise, Dan Shaffer must be noted for telling me about New Bethlehem's Big Buck Contest and the business that hunters bring to his town. Then there is Dr. James Adovasio, of the University of Pittsburgh's Department of Anthropology, who took time out of his very busy schedule to talk about Pennsylvania's stone-age hunters and the whitetail of prehistoric times.

Finally, I cannot say how much I appreciate Frederick A. Hetzel, director of the University of Pittsburgh Press, and Catherine Marshall, my editor. Though Fred is not a hunter, he had the foresight to be raised in the country, in an area full of deer hunters, so he understood what I wanted to do from the beginning. Catherine is simply outstanding. Her judgment and intelligence impressed me greatly. She kept me on a tight, straight course and did wonders for my spelling.

BUCK FEVER

I

Winter Memories

The deer loped through the snow-covered clearing in the slashings and was gone again. From across the gully it appeared almost like a shadow. For a moment, I had to wonder if I had even seen a deer. My eyes strained to catch another trace of movement in the saplings around the clearing, something to reassure me it was not pure imagination. But the deer had vanished as completely as if it had never existed. Dad had always told me, "People who don't hunt say, 'A deer's so big. How can you miss a deer?' Well, you let me take them out in the woods and show them how big a deer looks and how quick they can hide behind two little trees. Then let them try to shoot one. People who talk like that have never seen a deer in the woods."

For another fifteen minutes, I scan the thin places in the slashings, hoping, but not really expecting, to catch another glimpse of the deer. It is the third day of the buck season, our last day in the mountains for the week, and not the best of times for a hunter. By Wednesday, the number of hunters in the woods moving the deer is probably only a quarter of what it is on opening day. In Pennsylvania, where upwards of a million hunters are in the woods on the first day of buck season, that translates into roughly 250,000 individuals. Of that number, maybe another quarter, about 65,000, have the entire week off and are still in their hunting camps in the state's traditional northern deer country. If 65,000 hunters are scattered over 6 million acres (actually most of them would be

3

near roads) there's an awful lot of room for a white-tailed deer to sneak past.

The bucks remaining in the woods on the third day are a lot smarter, too. They are the survivors. On the first day, I stopped counting after seeing twenty-five deer. The second day, rain mixed with fog cut that number to seven. Now, the one that crossed through the clearing was my first of the day—after eight hours of hard hunting. On such lean days it is tough to forget about a single animal, especially if you do not know whether it was a buck or doe.

Once convinced the deer has gone for good, I leave my stand on the rim of the gully and follow my wet tracks through the snow back up the hill to the decayed tram road we had walked in on. Three years earlier a tornado had cut a path from Tionesta to Tidioute on the Allegheny River and on toward the center of the Allegheny National Forest. One of the spots where it had touched down was the mountain on which we were hunting. Stacks of uprooted and broken trees still lay scattered in unbelievable tangles. Among them, quick to take advantage of a light that seldom shines in the big woods, were patches of blackberry, goldenrod and countless other types of browse. Except for a few high places, the combination made it impossible to see, let alone move, more than twenty yards in any one direction. It was the heaviest cover any of us had ever hunted. We were in it because Bob and Eddie felt it was where the deer would be hiding.

On the tram road, I walk to a vague cul-de-sac of briers and brush and step into a triangle formed by the snapped trunks of three small pine trees. With my boot, I clear away the snow and debris from the base of the trees down to a quiet footing of moss and loam, then lean my shoulder against one of the trunks to wait. In his novel *At Play in the Fields of the Lord*, the naturalist Peter Matthiessen writes of a tribe of Indians who require young braves, as part of their manhood ritual, to travel alone into the wilderness. They may take with them only a jug of water and must sit for four days and four nights on a rock. One day and one night facing north. One day and one night facing south. One day and one night facing east.

And one day and one night facing west. They are to do nothing but watch. No one tells them where to look or what they are expected to see. Yet afterward they always return to their villages with a much deeper understanding of the earth and their place in its scheme.

While obviously nowhere near as intense an experience as the Indian ritual, three hours spent in the same spot on a deer stand usually leaves a hunter with at least some hint of greater things. Every year millions of people rush to the woods to escape the stresses of life in the high-tech age. But very few of them ever simply sit and watch. Their picnics, hikes, bird outings, and bike rides are typically little more than a down-shifting of the speed at which they live their daily lives. The deer hunter on a stand, though, must bring his life much nearer to a halt if he is to succeed. He must put all but the task at hand out of his mind. A trophy white-tailed buck is the end result of centuries of breeding under constant pressure from man. He is the most elusive big game animal on the North American continent. This is especially true in Pennsylvania, where the whitetail has become so adept at avoiding humans it can live virtually unseen within the city limits of Philadelphia and Pittsburgh.

From deer stands over the years, I have watched skunks playing together as innocent as children, porcupines luxuriating in the flavor of a seedling, flocks of turkeys scratching for acorns, and a red fox running with his tail flying. Twice, ruffed grouse have landed near enough for me to touch. One came so close I could have nudged it by moving the toe of my boot another four inches. The other entertained me by plumping up its breast feathers and displaying its tail. It was tough to bring myself to move and end both visits, but it had to be done before a deer appeared that might have been warned by the birds' drumming flight.

Trees and rocks become individuals after hours on a deer stand, too. Bends and twists speak of the opposition some trees have faced in their lives. Peeling trunks, the light and shadow of bark, forever changing with the day, reveal colors, tones, and textures neither human art nor science could hope to duplicate. Deep breaks and crumpling fronts show the victory of time over hard sandstone boulders as large as houses, and curving lines the path the water took to do its work.

But tucked between the pine trunks I am thinking only that it will soon be too dark to hunt and tomorrow we are going home. The thought disappoints me. The rhythm of the mountains and the hunt is still building, growing better all the time. Then I hear Bob and Eddie calling to each other from deep in the gully. I guess they must have jumped something and I stare off in their direction, but without much hope of seeing anything. A deer would have to walk up to me before I could see it through the brush piles separating us. I tell myself it probably would be better to concentrate on the tram road where I might catch something crossing, and I turn to see a deer standing in profile on the edge of the road.

The sight of the deer so surprises me that for a few seconds I don't quite know what to do. Or if I am even seeing a deer. My eyes could be playing tricks. At seventy-five or eighty yards, it seems almost to be part of the blow-down beside it. Then it turns its head to check up the road and I know for certain it is a deer. I carefully pull my binoculars from my coat and steady them against one of the trunks. I think I see antlers. But then I am not sure. I wait. Three more times the deer turns its head to check the area, but only once glances in my direction. It does not see me hidden behind the trunk and feels safe. And then I make out the curve of his antlers and the difference in their color from the branches next to him. I drop the binoculars back inside my coat, slip my rifle off my shoulder and bring it up against the trunk. The buck looks in my direction once more, but still without haste or nervousness. He's mine, I think.

Reminding myself the old .35 Remington I use shoots about four inches high and to the right at a hundred yards, I press my cheek down low on the stock and work its iron sights over to a spot low behind the buck's front legs. The heart. Then I hold my breath, fighting to keep the sight at the end of the barrel steady on the deer's chest, and touch the trigger.

The deer goes down with the explosion. Straight down. His

legs cut out from under him by the suddenly dead weight of his body. I pump another shell into the chamber and wait, braced against the tree, to see if he might get back up. But I do not expect it. A .35 Remington bullet weighs 200 grains. It is among the heaviest bullets used for hunting deer in Pennsylvania. Certainly, some luck has been involved, but I have never seen a deer hit with it take another step. Still, I hold my rifle ready across my chest as I start forward. Every hunting camp has stories of deer leaping to their feet after being knocked down and bounding off into the woods and the sights of another hunter.

When I reach the buck, he is lying on his side between two broken trees. Blood is running from a hole where an antler had grown, and his legs are still kicking. But it is only nerves releasing the electricity of life. He was dead before he hit the ground. I think of the old Indian prayer a friend told me about years ago, "I am sorry, brother, that you must die." But I don't repeat it. Instead, I look at his head and feel disgusted with myself. The careless attitude I've shown the target range in recent years is plainly evident. A white-tailed buck is too beautiful and magnificent a creature to ever shoot in the head. I am angry with myself for doing it. But things could have been far worse. I could have missed in the other direction and hit him in the stomach. A gut-shot deer can run for miles, and if he can't be trailed or doesn't run into another hunter, he dies slowly.

Stepping around the downed trees, away from any kicks that might be left in the legs, I lift the buck's head by its remaining antler. There are four points on it. In all probability, he had been an eight-point. A small eight-point, the biggest tine falling short of four inches, but not bad for the mountains of northern Pennsylvania. A sense of relief begins to grow in me.

By the time Bob appears from out of the blow-downs I am almost finished field dressing the deer and starting to miss the sharpness of the day. My hunting season is over. The story of how I got the buck still has to be told, and will be fun the first couple of times, but getting it will separate me from the others in camp. Anyway I look at it, the best is over. Life is becoming ordinary again.

II

North Country Trails

The war had been over for better than a year by the time his enlistment was up. Three years he had spent fighting in the South Pacific—New Guinea, the Philippines, a half-dozen smaller islands. A gunner's mate, he had served on destroyers, minesweepers, and PT boats. In New Guinea, he picked up a Japanese battle flag and then malaria and yellow jaundice. In the Philippines, he saw what happened when the Japanese packed people into a school in Manila and set it on fire. In his photo album were snapshots of Hiroshima after the bomb was dropped. "You were lucky if you saw three bricks standing on top of one another," he once said.

When he got back to the States, the big parades he had heard so much about were over. All that was left were a few banners and waves. He landed in Seattle and then went to San Francisco in time to watch, through the sights of his ship's five-inch guns, a group of prisoners trying to blast their way off Alcatraz Island. Then it was back to Seattle and finally a naval school in Washington, D.C., to wait for his discharge papers. He was glad it was Washington and not Norfolk. He had gone to boot camp at Norfolk and always remembered the signs: "Sailors and Dogs Keep Off the Grass."

Since he had thirty days' leave, he was able to go home a month before his discharge date. Pearl Harbor Day. He went back to Helca, the coal-mining patch in Westmoreland County, Pennsylvania, that was his home. His father had died when he was twelve and his mother when he was nineteen.

He was the youngest of the family. His two older brothers and one sister were married with young families, so he stayed with his two unmarried sisters.

As soon as his brother Joe heard he was back, he asked if he wanted to go deer hunting. Before the war Joe had hunted deer in Warren County with friends from Smock, a coal patch in Fayette County where he lived and worked. Having grown up in the country, the younger brother had hunted as a boy, but only small game—rabbits, ringnecks, squirrels. Without money to travel or a father to lead the way, and then the war, he had never had a chance to hunt deer. He was not even sure he wanted to go when his brother asked. He didn't have a rifle. The only hunting clothes he owned were a canvas small-game outfit. No heavy red and black Woolrich. It was hardly clothing for sitting in the freezing cold and snow of northern Pennsylvania's mountains in December.

But the older brother would not hear any excuses. He said he would get him a rifle and came up with a .22 Hornet, a gun only a step up from the tiny .22 caliber single-shot with which he had learned to shoot and hunt small game. It was hardly enough gun for deer, but it broke his resistance. He agreed to go. To try to keep warm, he decided to wear a pair of woolen baseball pants under his small-game clothes. He had once been quite a pitcher. Good enough for scouts to consider before he had to drop out of high school and go to work. The pants were left over from those days.

At Wildwood Resort, the collection of cabins up the Allegheny River from Tidioute where they stayed, everybody laughed when they saw him. The laughed at his small-game clothes. His baseball pants. And especially his rifle. "What're you gonna do with that peashooter?" they teased him. Their laughter was joking, not mean. But he did not like it. His pride was hurt. He did not say much, but took it as a challenge.

When they walked into the woods below Sandstone Springs in the dark of the first day it was snowing. It continued to snow all that morning and into the afternoon. It fell until it was a foot deep under the bare trees. But throughout it all he never moved from his stand. For five hours he sat in one spot, only occasionally standing and working his muscles to keep the blood flowing to his numb hands and feet. He saw hunter after hunter wander along the trail below him. But not a single deer. Then at two o'clock he glanced down the mountain and saw the buck standing about seventy yards away. A rack spread high and wide. A neck the size of his waist. Having rehearsed in his mind all day what he would have to do to bring down a deer with the .22 Hornet, he brought the rifle to his shoulder and took careful aim at the buck's head and fired.

The first shot hit the buck between the eyes. He shook his head, but did not fall or run. As everybody had predicted, the .22 Hornet was a peashooter without enough power. Quickly, he worked another shell into the chamber, lowered the sights to the neck, and shot again. This time the deer dropped where it stood, its neck broken.

Almost at the same time he reached the buck, an old hunter who had been posted nearby was next to him. Together, they stood in awe and amazement over the deer. It was a ten-point, a perfectly balanced and shaped ten-point, with a spread of sixteen inches and ramrod straight tines rising a full six inches above the beam of the rack. The old hunter helped him field dress the buck, and he began dragging it out of the woods, fighting to hold it back on the steep, snowy slope, until he saw it was a useless waste of energy and let the animal have its way. He rode it halfway down the mountain.

In the evening, when the other hunters returned from the woods, the buck was hanging in a tree behind the cabin. One after another they inspected it and could not believe what they were seeing. They couldn't believe it was his first deer. They couldn't believe the size of its rack. They couldn't believe he had sat so long in one place. They couldn't believe it weighed a hundred and eighty pounds field dressed. But most of all they couldn't believe he had shot it with that little .22 Hornet. "Now, you guys laugh," he told them.

■

Among the earliest and most vivid memories of my childhood is the mount of Dad's ten-point. It hung in the corner above our twelve-inch Zenith black-and-white console television. My mother called it a "dust-catcher." But to my brother and me it was nothing less than pure adventure. From hiding places behind the rocker and alongside the couch, or a barricade of pillows on the living-room floor, wearing our Davy Crockett caps, we hunted that deer on a hundred Saturday mornings, bringing it down time and again with our official Mattel buffalo guns. That deer made us into frontiersmen living off the land and traveling where no other white man had ever dared. Most of all though, it made us into Dad.

The pressure on the buck was especially heavy in late November during the deer season. Like young bird dogs, my brother and I would circle Dad as he packed to drive "Up North" with Uncle Joe. Our senses flooded with the sweet, musky earth smell of his Woolrich big-game outfit and burnt gunpowder from the .30/06 cartridges he recently fired to sight-in his rifle, we would prance around him, touching everything until he had to order us to settle down. Then we would sit and watch quietly for a few moments as he stuffed long underwear and wool socks and flannel shirts into the old navy duffle with his serial number still stenciled on the side.

Our behavior would remain under control only while he was in sight, though. As soon as he went back upstairs to find some overlooked item, we would immediately begin fingering his big, leather-handled knife in its sheath and trying on his red hunting cap. By the time he returned to the living room, his coming announced by the creaking stairs, we once more would be perfect innocents. Never touched a thing. Then one of us would run for our buffalo gun and begin a stalk of the buck that would continue, off and on, for the next several days until Dad finally returned from the mountains.

As we grew older, we carried the hunt from our living room to the fields behind our home in the former mining patch of Standard Shaft. Devastated by the H. C. Frick Coal and Coke Company, those fields probably had not seen a deer since before our grandfather began his fifty-four years in the mines at the turn of the century. But we would put on the hunting hats our parents had been forced to buy us and venture out with our friends among the crumpling foundations and blackberry bushes of Shanty Town, a Hooverville relic of the Great Depression, returning only when our excitement had been dampened by empty stomachs, and frozen fingers and feet.

While the buck was clearly a symbol of manhood for my brother and me, though no more than playing baseball and football, there was never anything *macho* about hunting in our eyes. Neither of us would even hear the word until I went to college and the women's liberation movement turned it into an expletive. For us, like most other country boys, hunting was a natural act. We lived with finding half eaten animals in the woods, cats proudly bringing home mice and young rabbits, farmer's complaining about fox and weasels killing their chickens, and the continuous sound of shotgun blasts every fall during the small-game season. Nearly everyday we were given glimpses of the natural world and accepted our place in it. The way we saw it, the animals around us expected to be hunted. That's why they avoided us and, as we were taught in parochial school, had avoided man since he was driven from the Garden of Eden. To them, we were another predator to escape. To us, their deaths were a part of life. When we ate the game that Dad brought home, that we cleaned and our mother cooked, we learned that meat did not grow on cardboard trays, wrapped in cellophane in supermarkets. In a way, we came to accept death as a part of life.

If the buck was a symbol of growth to us, though, its size left us with a somewhat distorted image of deer hunting. There was nothing unusual about the trophy in our eyes, which kept us from appreciating how difficult it can be to take a white-tailed buck. Moreover, Dad brought home a buck for ten years in a row. When he missed for two years, we wondered what was wrong. Then he hit another streak of five bucks in five years. The stories he told us of hunters going for twenty and even thirty years without getting a buck seemed unbelievable in the light of what he was doing. We wondered what was wrong with those hunters. Then, when I was fourteen, Dad decided it was time to take me Up North. Though there was a four-year gap while I was at college, it would be another ten years before I got my first buck.

■

Pete Palcsej found his way Up North from Dravosburg along the Monongahela River about the time Hitler's armies were beginning their march across Europe. He came to fish, not hunt, which seems only natural for an old towboatman who, after eleven years of retirement, still carries the habits and language of the river. Nobody simply backs up a car or truck in Pete's presence. They "ease it on in" or "slip it along-side." And if a hint of light penetrates his coffee, the brew is worthless and has to be poured down the sink. Rivermen need real coffee to help them through their twelve hours on.

During those early fishing trips Up North, Pete and his friends camped in tents and dreamed about what it would be like to someday own a place in the mountains. Then Pearl Harbor came and swept everybody away. Pete suddenly found himself in the army corps of engineers and heading for the South Pacific. On the Hawaiian island of Maui, on what is now some of the most expensive real estate in the country, he practiced blowing up caves. Then, when their training was completed, his battalion was attached to a marine division and shipped out to use its newly learned skills in strange sounding places like Saipan. The army engineers were supposed to go in after the marines, but the world does not always work the way it is supposed to, and Pete often found himself sent in ahead of the invasion force to blast the Japanese troops out of the holes they had dug in the hills and cliffs.

Back home after the war, the gang from the Mon Valley once again began to make its way Up North where the peace of the mountains, the woods, the river and its fish helped them to forget some of the things they had seen. Eventually, Pete found a piece of property along the Allegheny River at Magee. The owner wanted to sell him most of the property from Magee downstream to the old lumber and oil town of Tidioute, about three miles of riverfront, for $7,000. But he was not a businessman, took only what he needed, and built a one-room cabin close above the river across from Fuellhart Island. The "little cabin" served its purpose well enough when it came to fishing—fifteen friends had once managed to sleep within its walls—but by the mid-1950s Pete was ready for something larger. His sister and her husband were beginning to come north with him, bringing along his nephew, Bob.

■

Like his Uncle Pete, eight-year-old Bob Burnett was interested only in fishing when his parents first took him north from their home in McKeesport. In the evenings, he would catch soft-shell crayfish in the river and then the next day, while the grownups worked on the big cabin, he would fish for bass. Since nobody in his family was a hunter, the idea of hunting never entered his mind until he got his driver's license, about the time John Kennedy and Richard Nixon were squaring off on television, and began driving to the cabin alone to fish. Then one day Joe Orris, a hunter from New Castle who owned the cabin next door, told him. "As much as you like to fish, it's a wonder you don't hunt," and convinced him to give it a try.

Bob's first hunting trips were for squirrels. Joe took him into State Game Lands 86 above the cabin and taught him about squirrels and how to hunt them. He told him it was too hard to get into shotgun range by walking after squirrels and made him sit and wait for them to come to him early in the morning and late in the afternoon. He showed him how to get a squirrel hiding behind a tree to come around toward him by throwing his hat on the other side of the tree. Then, after Bob shot a couple of squirrels, Joe helped him turn them into what everybody said was a fine dinner.

Those squirrel hunts up the ridge were a real surprise for Bob. Before then all of his time Up North had been spent close to the river. He had never known there was so much wild country just across the road from the cabin. He began to develop an interest in the land. The lay of the mountains. The trees growing on them. The headwaters of streams. The wildlife that lived everywhere. Soon he was buying maps and a compass and teaching himself to use them so he might get deeper into this exciting new world.

During his first season as a hunter, Bob stuck with squirrels. Joe saw how much he liked the sport, however, and told him, "You oughta hunt big game." So the following year, he borrowed an old .30–.30 lever-action rifle from another uncle and, on the first Monday after Thanksgiving started a long hike into Game Lands 86. He didn't get much beyond the cabin, though, when a large herd of deer appeared. He froze in his steps and they walked up to him. His eyes darted from head to head in search of one with antlers. He knew he was supposed to find a deer with "horns." But he was so green, he had no idea how to look for them.

He had never heard that bucks sometimes walk with their heads held low when they are following a doe's trail or going through heavy cover in which their antlers might tangle. His eyes saw only doe.

As the day wore on, Bob worked his way farther up McGee Run to a hemlock-covered plateau known as Forty Acres. There another large herd of deer appeared, drifting across the ridge in a line about seventy yards away from him. Again, his eyes started searching heads for antlers, until a shot came from a hunter behind him and the deer scattered. The hunter who shot came over and told him the second deer had been a buck. A spike. He had seen it through his scope, he said. Bob did not have a scope. He did not know anything about scopes. He began to think he needed one. But not that year. He did not get another chance at a buck the rest of the season.

Camelot was gone, the marines had landed in Vietnam and "Sergeant Pepper's Lonely Hearts Club Band" filled the air waves by the time Bob took his first buck. It was a three-point. Then he hit a streak that lasted almost ten years. When we met early in the Reagan Revolution, I was a reporter working the police beat in McKeesport and he was a part-time constable who had just helped police head off a fleeing bank robber. That fall he took a "triple crown"—a buck, a bear, and a turkey—and, since I also wrote an outdoors column for the local paper, mentioned it to me one day when we were together in the district magistrate's office. We talked about hunting several times after that day, and then one morning he suggested going out together sometime.

III

Of Mountains, Deer, and Lenape

The oldest part of Pennsylvania is the region geologists call the Piedmont Province. It runs in a rough diagonal across the southeast corner of the state from the Maryland line just west of Gettysburg through York, Dauphin, Lebanon, Berks, Montgomery, and northern Bucks counties to the Delaware River, and includes Lancaster and Chester counties. Comprised chiefly of land formed about 600 million years ago, it was originally part of a lofty mountain chain stretching to the north, but was worn down to lowlands by time and the never ceasing force of running water.

To the west of this mass of old rock there stretched, until roughly 230 million years ago, a vast bay. The Piedmont Province formed the eastern shore of this bay, which had its western shore in Ohio and its northern boundary in Canada. Like California today, Pennsylvania during this period was subject to a series of earthquakes. At varying intervals, the bottom of the bay rose and subsided, until a general upheaval occurred, buckling and folding the bay bed along a line running from the southwest to the northeast corner of the state until it reached the Piedmont Province. There the old rock formations held fast against the tremendous pressure of the upheaval and the Allegheny Mountains were pushed into existence, approximately 160 million years before the subcontinent of India slammed into the Plains of Bengal and created the Himalayas.

In northern Pennsylvania, the great upheaval forced a section of land to rise and form a plateau that reached roughly from northern Venango County, south almost to State College, east into Wyoming County and, along a series of fingers, north through Sullivan and Tioga counties beyond the New York state line. Labeled the Allegheny High Plateau, this land was at first nearly flat, marked only by gentle hills spread five to ten miles apart. Then approximately 70 million years ago, or about the time Mt. Everest was born, the action of running water began to make its mark. "All these waters descend through the heart of the mountain plateau in gorges which are veritable canons," wrote Andrew Sherwood and Franklin Platt in an 1880 Geological Survey report, "exceedingly tortuous and narrow, with bottoms scarcely wider than the meanderings of the streams, and with cliffs of sandstone and conglomerate, forming cornices about a thousand feet above the water-bed. Innumerable ravines descend from the tablelands between the streams and their branches, cutting sharply down to the water-beds."[1]

Sherwood and Platt were describing a portion of the plateau in Sullivan and Lycoming counties, but their description holds true throughout the region. For while there are higher spots in the state than the 2,550 feet above sea level the plateau reaches near Kapel Hill in Summit Township, Potter County, there is no area more rugged. The total relief of the plateau is some 1,600 feet from the valley floors to the plateau tops, and the paths cut by the streams are steep, with gradients of up to 65 percent. The only level ground is on the remnant plateau top, what hunters call the "flats," and on the narrow valley floors.

Aside from the continuous cutting of canyons and hollows by running water, the last major change in the landscape of the Allegheny High Plateau took place about twenty thousand years ago. Glaciers moving south from Canada, some of them a half-mile thick, scoured the landscape, pushing everything before them. The Allegheny River was once three separate streams draining into the Great Lakes. An earlier glacier joined them and turned the river south, refined its course, and sent its waters to Pittsburgh and the Gulf of Mexico.

In addition to altering the landscape, the advance of the

18

glaciers brought an ice age to northern Pennsylvania. The lush forests died, and the region became a desolate, frigid world of open ground and scrub vegetation, a tundra. It remained that way for a thousand years after the glaciers retreated. Then, approximately ten thousand five hundred years ago, the forests began to return. Pine, hemlock, beech, oak, maple, birch, chestnut, ash, and laurel claimed the terrain, growing wild and dark and grand. For more than ten thousand four hundred years it would remain that way, until the arrival of progress.

■

Almost a dozen millenniums before the last glaciers touched the Allegheny River, the white-tailed deer was roaming the land the king of England would give William Penn to pay off his debt. Ancestors of the whitetail appeared approximately a million years ago. But the animal's origins go back almost 60 million years to *Diacodexis*, a small, rabbit-size creature with a long tail, heavy hindquarters, small chest, and no antlers or horns. Antlers did not begin to develop in the deer's ancestors until about 25 million years ago in the *Aletomeryx*, a small, round-faced animal that also owned a set of fangs. Those first antlers were quite different: they looked more like the skin-covered outgrowths on the skulls of giraffes, or a modern spike buck in velvet, than the hard, boney racks so prized by hunters today.

Why the whitetail's ancestors developed disposable antlers, instead of permanent horns, is something of an evolutionary puzzle. Creatures who successully survive nature's endless trials usually do so by taking the path of least resistance. Where head adornments are concerned, that means permanent horns. Growing antlers each year requires a tremendous expenditure of nutrients, much more than horns. The requirements are almost too great for an animal to endure and continue to survive the rigors of life in the wild. Yet the white-tailed buck does it across four continents and North Africa. It has been said that if there were ever a nuclear war, the whitetail would be one of only three creatures to survive.

The other two would be the cockroach and the coyote (and the rat should probably be added).

∎

Researchers have evidence that the white-tailed deer was present in North America thirty thousand years ago, and probably long before that. During more than half of those thirty thousand years, evidence also exists showing that the white-tail was hunted by man in the Upper Ohio Valley. James Adovasio is an anthropologist at the University of Pittsburgh whose dig at Meadowcroft Rock Shelter in Washington County turned up the oldest datable evidence of man's presence in North America south of the glacial ice. He says deer have been hunted in Pennsylvania since 14,000 B.C.

"The suspected routes of migration into the New World," according to Adovasio, "involved either going down the Pacific Coast, or, more likely, coming down the drainage of the MacKenzie River in Canada, emerging on the east slopes of the Rockies, and following the ice front to the east. As soon as they got south of the ice front in the western United States, they would run into antelope, blacktail, mule deer and, in the East, white-tailed deer. Apparently, almost as soon as they saw them, they began systematically to hunt them—and anything else that was around. No other animal that I can think of has such a well documented archeological record for hunting. When you find a site that dates from 9,000 B.C., there are deer bones in it, if there are bones preserved at all. Ten thousand, eleven, twelve, fourteen thousand B.C. and anytime after that, we normally find deer bones. It was the principal medium-sized large game animal that was available in abundance just as today. Prior to European contact, deer were probably as abundant and widely distributed in Pennsylvania as any other kind of critter around."

Following the extinction of the mammoth and mastodon, the retreat of the glaciers (and with them the caribou which once roamed the ice-age tundras of northern Pennsylvania), the white-tailed deer became the main food source for the native inhabitants and was eagerly sought year-round. Penn-

sylvania's earliest hunters, which means the earliest documented hunters in North America, hunted with an *atlatl*,
a stick with a cupped end in which the base of a spear was
held for throwing. It increased both the striking distance and
power of the spear by, in effect, lengthening the thrower's
arm. "It's the equivalent of having an arm twice as long as
your own," said Adovasio. Experiments conducted by modern
scientists have shown that a properly used atlatl could drive a
spear all the way through an adult buffalo or transfix a deer
from end to end. Tipped with very large points made of flint,
calcite, or jasper, they caused massive hemorrhaging upon
impact. Spears thrown with the atlatl became "high caliber"
weapons, at close range every bit as deadly as a modern high-
powered rifle.

■

Though the brave who could successfully stalk and kill a
whitetail was always respected by his tribe, deer hunting for
early Indians was generally a communal affair. The continued
existence of the tribe depended too much on the whitetail to
allow for much individual hunting except in hard times such
as in the winter, when deep snows prevented group hunting.

The tribe employed various methods of group hunting to
best utilize the terrain, the season, and the abundance of deer.
Among the most widely used was the drive, which was practiced in several different forms. At its simplest, a selected
number of hunters would position themselves along a line in
the forest while others walked toward them from a distance,
forcing whatever game was in front of them to the hunters.
Sometimes a crude fence, built in the shape of a funnel, would
be used to concentrate the deer in a small area where more of
them could be killed faster. Minus the fence, which is now
illegal, such drives remain popular with groups of hunters
today.

Water drives, in which deer were driven into rivers or lakes
and then killed when they could not quickly flee, and fire
drives were also practiced extensively by the Indians. A fire
drive may sound destructive, but it was really quite beneficial

to both the forests and the deer, for it helped open up the old forest canopy and provide light for new trees to grow. That, in turn, produced more browse for the whitetail and so enabled the deer population to increase. In *Geographia Americae, with an Account of the Delaware Indians,* Swedish explorer Peter Lindestrom describes an Indian fire drive he once witnessed in Pennsylvania: "When now the sachem wants to arrange his hunt then he commands his people close together in a circle of ½, 1 or 2 miles, according to the number of people at his command. In the first place each one roots up the grass in the position in the circumference, to the width of about 3 or 4 ells, so that the fire will not be able to run back, each one then beginning to set fire to the grass, which is mightily ignited, so that the fire travels away, in towards the center of the circle, which the Indians follow with great noise, and all the animals which are found within the circle, flee from the fire and the cries of the Indians, traveling away, whereby the circle through its decreasing is more and more contracted towards the center. When now the Indians have surrounded the center with a small circle, so that they mutually cannot do each other harm, then they break loose with guns and bows on the animals which they then have been blessed with, that not one can escape and thus they get a great multitude of all kinds of animals which are found there."[2]

The Indians also kept their larders full of venison by hunting over lures or baits, trapping, still hunting from blinds, and running with dogs. Outside of stalking, still hunting, and the simple drive, their hunts involved nothing of what is considered sport. They were designed to harvest large number of whitetails, which they did quite well. One Moravian missionary, David Zeisberger, estimated that Delaware hunters from the Goschgosching (West Hickory–Tionesta) area of northwestern Pennsylvania killed in excess of two thousand deer in 1768. He believed each hunter took between 50 and 150 whitetails each year during the autumn. Samuel de Champlain, the founder of French Canada, watched twenty-five Huron men capture 120 whitetails in thirty-eight days by means of drives in 1615. And in November, 1794, Iroquis

Indians attending the Canandaigua Treaty negotiations in New York State brought in 100 deer in a single day.[3]

While food was the chief reason deer were sought by the Lenni-Lenape, or "Real People," as the Indians of Pennsylvania called themselves, little of the whitetail, like the bison on the Great Plains, was discarded as waste. Hides were commonly made into clothing, blankets, storage bags, tobacco and pipe pouches, wrist guards, shield covers, quivers, straps, harnesses, drumheads, bowstrings, tepee covers, thongs, and snowshoe netting. Sinew and bone were used to make awls, hoes, digging sticks, hide fleshers, fishhooks, arrowheads, clubs, corn scrapers, cutting tools, arrow straighteners, needles, gouges, daggers, and pendants. Antlers were utilized for many of those same items, as well as combs, knife handles, clothespins, whistles, glue, beads, rattles, and drumsticks. As with hunters today, large racks were a sign of prestige among some Indians, too. "Because antlers are the marks of identity for chiefs, a rack is installed with his office," writes W. N. Fenton in *Northern Iroquoian Culture Patterns*, "But as deer shed their racks, they are removed from the chief in illness or at death, or for malfeasance in office. Just as the deer rub antlers on brush during the rutting season, so the great social dance after the installation of a new chief is called 'rubbing antlers,' when they socialize and diffuse their power."[4]

One use the Indians of the northeast made of the whitetail's stomach contents, though, should astonish any modern hunter who has "gut shot" a deer, or accidentally cut into its digestive system when field dressing it, and had to face the resulting odor. According to Robert Beverley, in his work, *The History and Present State of Virginia"* (1705), the partially digested contents of the stomach and intestines were sometimes cooked into a thick broth and served to people who were starving. Reportedly, it was the only food that would not make them ill.

Despite the heavy pressure the Indians exerted on the deer, they managed to live in perfect balance with the whitetail for a good portion of the sixteen thousand documented years in which the creature has been hunted in North America. Or until the *Mayflower* dropped anchor.

IV

Pumpkin Army

It is a few minutes after ten when we finally climb into the Bronco and Dad asks the question that always signals the start of a trip up North.

"You got everything?"

I look over my shoulder at the pile of groceries, boots, duffle bags, and day packs rising about the back seat, until I spot my rifle case, and then my red and black checked hunting coat with my license pinned to the back. Once, when I was a boy, my mother had asked Dad the same question and he had answered by telling her all he needed was his rifle, shells, and license. For more than thirty years, his words have stayed in my mind, reminding me of the only pieces of equipment truly essential to a hunting trip. Everything else can be bought, borrowed, or done without. Such a philosophy, coupled with a certain amount of procrastination when it comes to packing, has sent me off to camp on occasion without towels or wool socks and only the underwear I was wearing. But never without my rifle, shells, and license.

"Yeah, I'm okay," I answer.

"Well, let's go," Dad says, and then adds, as he always does, "You don't know what the roads are like up that way."

Being Sunday morning, the roads around my home in Irwin are empty except for a few late churchgoers and people on their way to convenience stores for newspapers and maybe milk. As we shoot across Route 30 and head for downtown Irwin, Dad tells me about a story he read in the paper involving a hunter who shot a five-point buck during the recent bear season. Supposedly, he mistook the deer for a bear.

"How stupid can you get?" he demands, as if I could answer that question. "Can't tell the difference between a deer and a bear!"

I shake my head. Dad has never shown any understanding of such "mistakes" in the woods. When my brother and I were learning to hunt, he was forever drilling us on gun safety and being sure of our target. "If you're not sure, don't shoot." It was that plain and simple. In the days before hunter education courses, it was frustrating to be saddled with so many rules while most of our friends were simply given guns and allowed to hunt. Confronted with the threat of not hunting, however, we paid attention and learned our lessons well. Neither one of us has ever come close to an accident or shot something by "mistake." Yet still Dad continues to teach. Fathers never stop teaching sons. The story about the hunter who claimed to have shot the deer for a bear is meant to keep me alert to the dangers facing hunting. Such incidents circulate quickly. And, though real hunters greet them with even more scorn and ridicule than the general public, each one provides ammunition for those who oppose hunting. They blacken the sport the way linemen on steroids cheapen football, insider traders make it look as if Wall Street is full of crooks, and television preachers turn religion into a con game.

■

At Harrison City, Dad's talk shifts to deer that recently appeared in his yard. He tells me of a neighbor who was awakened by his dogs at three in the morning and saw a five-point buck and another deer standing under one of Dad's apple trees. My mother had seen a deer under the same tree one morning during the summer. A couple of other times, the neighbor had caught them running through his yard between his house and swimming pool. Dad guesses they have been coming either from a farm near Mt. Pleasant High School or from "behind the dump," an abandoned mine site that separates my parent's home from the town of Mt. Pleasant.

Such stories are always exciting because when I was growing up in the same house it was unheard of to see deer anywhere nearby. When the last mine closed in the mid-1950s, it left behind a wasteland of slag piles, raw clay, and crumbling coke ovens in which the only game that could be found were rabbits and, once in a while, a ring-necked pheasant. Through the years, blackberry, elderberry, and various grasses, then sumac, crab apple, and choke cherry reclaimed large portions of the property. Finally, in the mid-1980s the state began to process the mountain of slag towering above it all. During a childhood spent playing "army" and "cowboys" in those fields, five years of after school hunts, and several more years of sporadic outings, I can remember jumping deer on only two occasions. The first was when I was about twelve years old, two years before I started hunting; the second a couple of years after I had graduated from college.

Dad's stories remind me of the changes that have been taking place in Pennsylvania's deer herd—changes reflected not only by the five-point under Dad's apple tree, but by other recent news items. Like that of a homeowner in the wealthy Pittsburgh suburb of Fox Chapel complaining to the Game Commission about deer eating $5,000 worth of shrubbery. And over a hundred deer a year being struck by cars on the streets of Philadelphia. The morning papers tell the story in their headlines: "If you're hunting for bucks, Washington County is best bet," say the Pittsburgh *Press*. "Deer hunters may seek new trails as season opens," reports the Philadelphia *Inquirer*. "Buck picture bright in area," notes the Greensburg *Tribune-Review*.

For most of this century, Pennsylvania's deer herd has been concentrated on the Allegheny High Plateau. Plenty of cover and browse made the region ideal whitetail habitat. Deer reproduced at a phenomenal rate. Aided by the buck law, which made only male deer legal game, the state's deer herd rose from the edge of extinction in 1900 to over 1 million in 1940. Hunters from the 1930s and 1940s still tell stories of herds with a hundred or more deer in the northern counties. "You got tired holding your gun up looking for a buck," Dad has often said. But then the forest began to grow and become less hospitable to deer.

"The life of a deer in the wild is a few years at best," Ted Godshall, chief of the Game Commission's Information Division, explained to me, "but the forest on which it depends for its food has a life of a hundred years from the time a seedling is planted until that tree matures and is harvested.

"Now, that forest goes through three distinct stages of development. You've got your seedling-sapling stage, which lasts for about the first twenty years of a forest's life. The trees are under five inches in diameter, the real thick brush. That's maximum deer food. Then, it passes into the pole stage, when the trees are five to eleven inches in diameter. At that time, the lowest branches are too high for the deer to reach. The leaves at the top of the trees form a solid canopy through which sunlight cannot penetrate to the forest floor. Without sunlight, vegetation won't grow. It's a virtual wildlife desert. There's nothing there for sixty years of the forest's hundred-year life.

"But then, when you get into your final twenty years, the saw-timber stage, you got your mast production. Those trees are more susceptible to lightning. When a tree gets hit, falls over and dies, a hole is created in the leaf canopy. Now the sunlight can get down to the forest floor and some more vegetation can spring up. There's a little more deer food available in the saw-timber stage, than in the pole-timber stage. Our research—now being confirmed by the people up in the Allegheny National Forest, at Penn State, and other places— shows that we can comfortably over-winter about forty deer per square mile in the seedling-sapling stage. But that drops to ten in the pole-timber stage and then goes up to twenty in the saw-timber stage.

"Those people who used to see forty deer in a night in one place ten years ago were looking at deer in the seedling-sapling stage. Now it's ten years later and it's pole timber. They aren't going to see more than ten deer. That's all there's food for in those places. They will never again in their lifetimes see that forty deer per square mile. That only happens once every hundred years. And if you've seen it already, you're not going to see it again. You won't live that long.

"I am talking over-wintering," he added. "This is what you have to tailor your deer herds to. There's enough food for most deer in the summer. But it's that winter time. That's the critical bottleneck."

As early as 1917 a few biologists warned that the deer population of the Allegheny High Plateau was becoming too large. Five years later, deer were causing serious damage to agricultural crops and the regenerating forest. Deer hunting became a feast or famine situation. One year hunters might take 200,000 deer, the next only 40,000 or 50,000. Without a regular doe season to control the population, thousands of deer began dying of starvation during the region's harsh winters as the forest grew into the pole-timber stage. An estimated 40,000 starved to death in the winter of 1935–36 alone. Harvest records show 23,802 bucks and 46,668 does taken during the 1935 season, the first doe season since 1931. The following season, 1936, only 18,084 bucks were harvested. The deer herd had been so decimated by the weather, overpopulation, and a shortage of food that the Game Commission cancelled doe season in both 1936 and 1937 in hopes of rebuilding the herd. When it re-opened the doe season in 1938, and closed the buck season for only the second time since 1915, it was a feast once more. Hunters took 171,662 does, but that led to the 1939 famine when 49,106 bucks and only 14,581 antlerless deer were harvested.

How did a forest that should have been in the sterile pole-timber stage in the 1930s and 1940s support herds of a hundred and more deer? The answer revolves around the immense size of the territory involved, 6 million acres, and the manner in which the forests were cut.

Lumbering began in northern Pennsylvania in the early years of the nineteenth century, but difficulties in transporting the logs to market restricted cutting to areas around larger streams and rivers on which the timber could be floated to saw mills during the spring high water period. While the areas that could be reached were routinely clearcut, the absence of large streams in most locations left the majority of the region's ancient forests untouched. Then, in the 1880s, powerful locomotives were developed that were capable of climbing steep grades and bringing timber out of previously unreachable locations. Freed of logistical problems, fueled by greed, and without the slightest concern for conservation, lumber barons in the 1880s began building railroads deep into the forests of the Allegheny High Plateau and clearcutting everything in their path.

Although timber continued to be harvested everywhere over the plateau, clearcutting, like the settlement of Pennsylvania two hundred years earlier, generally progressed from east to west into the 1920s. Areas in the east were thus entering the relatively sterile pole-timber stage when those in the west were still in the seedling-sapling or brush stage, the most suitable for deer.

Further complicating the situation, lumber companies were able to go back and cut many areas that had been cut seventy-five to one hundred years earlier, in the early nineteenth century, and had grown to harvestable size again. As a result, there were large areas of brush to support deer even within the pole-timber forests.

Along with the variations in cutting, fires were quite common, too. In 1922 alone, 3,635 fires occurred in Pennsylvania, burning over 332,327 acres.[1] These fires pushed back the forest growth cycle, both in the seedling-sapling and pole-timber stages, again and again, so that in the 1930s, and even the 1940s, hundreds of thousands of acres of northern Pennsylvania's forest were in the seedling-sapling stage that supports the most deer. Hunters saw herds of a hundred and more.

"We can do the same thing again," said Paul Brohn of the U.S. Forest Service in Warren. "We can clearcut 6 million acres. Would you like to see that? If you really want to create a deer population in this country, then we'll clearcut 6 million acres and we'll have deer running all over the place. The people who want good cherry and oak will have to wait ninety years again. This country had nothing from 1900 to just about after World War II as far as timber production is concerned. So, you want to tell a logger that? Or a furniture maker? Or a pulp producer? That there is a feast or famine. Cut it all down at one time and then wait another hundred years for the next crop. In the meantime, we'll have deer running out of our ears. All kinds of deer. That's the choice."

At the same time northern Pennsylvania was being overrun with whitetails, the southern half of the state had virtually no deer. Heavily populated, industrialized, and cultivated, with only a minimum of forested land, it had very little to attract deer. That situation slowly started to change after World War II, however, when returning GIs began moving closer to the cities from their farms and small towns. The migration they started has occasionally slowed but never ceased. In fact, it gained strength during both the economic recession of the late 1970s and the boom years of the 1980s. In those two decades, people first left the country in search of work and then later in search of the "good life."

Such a population shift from rural to urban meant thousands of acres of farmland were abandoned throughout southern Pennsylvania, land that quickly reverted back to nature. The new seedling-sapling forests have drawn deer like magnets. Berks County, on the edge of Philadelphia, now has the most bucks per square mile of forest of any county in Pennsylvania (11.3) and Washington County, next door to Pittsburgh, is second (10.8). The northern counties average only half as many. Potter County, Pennsylvania's most famous deer-hunting mecca, gives up only 5.3 bucks per square mile of forested land. That does not mean more bucks are taken from Berks County than Potter County, only that more bucks are taken per square mile of forested land. Since there is a lot more forest Up North, the totals are still higher in the counties of the Allegheny Plateau. They are also home to the mystique of deer hunting. "It's just different world," one urban hunter told me. "It's so peaceful out in the woods. The quiet is deafening. And the people are different. Simpler. They're country people. They don't play all those games you have to put up with in the city. They're friendly. Glad to see you. I love it."

■

On Route 66 north of Delmont, we catch our first glimpse of blaze orange. It comes as a pair of coveralls hanging on a clothesline and blown full by the breeze. I am a bit surprised the color has not shown itself sooner. But the roads north have not yet begun to funnel down to a few main arteries. Still, we are far enough out of the suburbs that a few miles later a fire hall appears with a sign advertising "Hunter's Breakfast, 4 A.M. Monday." Then in Apollo a man carrying a bag of groceries crosses the street ahead of us dressed in a new camouflage design orange jacket. Its brightness stands out sharply in contrast to the dull, old Jeep Waggoner he enters. When we see a husband and wife posting a piece of property along the road, Dad begins to tell me about a friend of ours in Mt. Pleasant whose brother-in-law has posted his property for the first time.

"That's where that guy shot that albino doe for him," he says, as if I know what he is talking about. "They told him, 'Go ahead and hunt, just don't shoot that albino.' And that's what he did."

Now he is having it mounted and the property is closed to everybody else. It is another troublesome story. But one I do not feel like thinking about at the moment. The sight of blaze orange has started to excite me and make me think about what is ahead. I am glad when the conversation shifts to Standard Shaft Citizens' Club and how it has been empty the past two days. Everybody headed for camp on Friday and Saturday, Dad tells me, and then he brings up Jack, a friend of his who for years has been teasing him about driving all the way to Warren County to hunt. But during the recent bear season Jack accepted an invitation to hunt out of a friend's camp near Marienville in Forest County. He came back a convert, full of plans for spending the first week of buck season Up North next year. I have to smile.

In the cardboard container factory where he works, Jack

31

has enough seniority to "get the first week of buck season" next year. But few younger hunters could do so. Buck season is jealously guarded, prime vacation time in the factories, machine shops, garages, stores, and offices where deer hunters work. A news story I recently came across estimated that two-thirds of Pennsylvania's male workforce is in the woods on the first day of buck season. Since so few of Pennsylvania's million plus hunters—often the highest total of any state in the nation—can schedule time off for the first day, absenteeism is rampant. The same is true in rural high schools where classes of twenty-five or thirty students suddenly hold ten or twelve or even less. Many businesses and school districts long ago gave up the fight and simply made the first Monday after Thanksgiving, the traditional start of deer season in Pennsylvania, a holiday. Unions have even had it written into contracts.

Though their numbers have remained consistent over the years, the behavior of hunters, like the demographics of the deer herd, has changed tremendously from the 1930s and 1940s, and even the 1950s. Traveling Up North was once a real chore. Trains provided the first access to northern Pennsylvania and its deer, but soon gave way to the car. Aside from a few old army Jeeps, however, nobody had ever heard of four-wheel drive, and the roads were beyond description. "There were two ruts going up over the mountain," Dad has often said. "You got in them and stayed there. You didn't even have to steer." Faced with such obstacles, hunters traveled to camp with the idea of staying a week or even the full two-week season.

Then in the mid-1950s, President Dwight Eisenhower signed legislation creating the interstate highway system. The interstates were built with the aim of transporting troops when the Cold War finally heated up. But what they also did was make travel to northern Pennsylvania a lot easier. Gradually, the Allegheny High Plateau was boxed in by Interstate 80 to the south, Interstate 79 to the west, Interstate 81 and the Northeast Extension of the Pennsylvania Turnpike to the east, and New York's Southern Tier Expressway to the north.

Off those major arteries ran new or improved state roads. Trips that had once taken a full day were cut to two or three hours and, instead of week-long stays, hunters were driving to the region for only a day or two. Interstate 90 and Interstate 80, coming out of Cleveland and Youngstown, actually make the plateau region more accessible to hunters from Ohio than to those from parts of southern Pennsylvania, which is one reason for the large number of Ohio hunters it attracts.

Before the interstates were built, towns like Kittanning were bottlenecks in the great northward march of hunters. Route 28 was the main road leading north out of Pittsburgh. At Kittanning it was joined by Route 66 and US 422 carrying traffic from east and west of the city. The Sunday before opening day it could take an hour to get through the town, more if it was snowing. Though a new bridge and by-passes now keep the traffic moving, Kittanning still sits at the center of a giant pincer. Practically every other car, truck and van, Blazer, Bronco, and Jeep passing through the town shows blaze orange. It appears mostly on the heads of drivers and passengers, but also as jackets and pants hanging in the side windows of cars or lying pressed against the rear windows of truck caps high atop piles of other equipment. The "Pumpkin Army" is how some journalists have described the sight.

■

North of Kittanning, we soon find ourselves number twelve in a line of traffic that includes another ten vehicles behind us. The disc jockey on the country music station the radio has faded onto announces Willie Nelson's "On the Road Again," and I smile and tap my foot when the music starts. It fits the scene so perfectly. As if caught by a strobe, images of camp flash in my mind. The living room over-heated by a wood fire. Giant snowflakes falling through the light around the thermometer outside the kitchen windows. Fuellhart Island jutting dark and forbidding up the center of the Allegheny River. The smell of bacon and coffee cooking in the early morning silence. Heavy leather boots treading on bare wood floors. A table spilling over with shells, knives, flashlights, binoculars, compasses, maps, boot dressing, and ropes.

Seeing so many hunters also makes me certain once more of what I am doing. Since the Tet Offensive and the senselessness of Vietnam enrolled me in college, and then the process of earning a living drove me into the suburbs, I have lived mostly among people who have never hunted. And, though I cannot recall anybody ever directly challenging me about being a hunter, the presence of so many nonhunters and regular attacks against the sport in the newspapers has led me to wonder at times exactly why I hunt. I have looked at arguments both for and against the sport. Hunters are needed to control deer numbers. A quick bullet is a better death than the slow starvation brought by overpopulation. A hunter is a man who has never grown up. His gun is an extension of his penis, a substitute for his sexual inadequacies. Hunters pay for the protection of wildlife and habitat with their license fees. Hunters have pushed many species of wildlife to the brink of extinction. The hunter is a natural man in an America where the only daily contact most people have with nature is walking from their cars to the controlled atmosphere of their work place. The hunter is an emotional cripple wallowing in blood lust. Hunting gave rise to civilization. The need to organize for the hunt led to the development of language, and the extra food obtained from hunting meant a tribe no longer had to abandon its older members. Out of the memories of those people grew traditions and then cultures. Hunters will destroy civilization. If allowed to continue, the predatory instincts of the hunter will someday press the button that launches a nuclear holocaust. On and on the arguments go, making it impossible for me to say in any clearcut way why I hunt. But the further out into the country we get the better it feels and the less it all seems to matter.

■

Broad Street through New Bethlehem is jammed with vehicles almost from the bridge over Red Bank Creek at South Bethlehem to the red light in the center of town. The traffic that collected at Kittanning has been caught and slowed. Men in orange caps and wool shirts, or nondescript work jackets, are everywhere on the sidewalks, moving in and out of hardware stores and gas stations, standing in line at restaurants.

As in the big woods country of the Allegheny Plateau, towns lying along the routes north try hard to capitalize on the heavy influx of people to their region during buck season. Exact figures are difficult to come by, and soon would be out-dated anyway, but studies undertaken by the Game Commission in the late 1950s and early 1960s showed that 25 to 40 percent of Potter County's economy was dependent on the first week of buck season. Ted Godshall believes those figures remain valid and can be applied to most of the northern counties. Another Game Commission survey found approximately eight thousand hunting camps in Forest County, or about three thousand more camps than permanent residents. If only six thousand of those camps are used by an average of four hunters each during the deer season, that means businesses in Tionesta suddenly find themselves with twenty-four thousand new customers. The U.S. Fish and Wildlife Service, in its *1985 National Survey of Fishing, Hunting, and Wildlife Associated Recreation*, the latest available, says that hunters spent more than $3.7 billion nationwide on hunting trips in 1985.

"I know down here at the little A-Plus Market where you cross the bridge and come in, their business on the weekend before the opening of buck season is almost triple of what it is on any other weekend," says Dan Shaffer, a local insurance agent and member of the New Bethlehem Chamber of Commerce. "And I wouldn't say that's unique for them. People coming through stop on a regular basis. Darl Bish has a restaurant up here—the Dinner Bell. He's only been open two years and he said it is just unbelievable the traffic he gets starting that Thursday. His business goes up like ten times. He said he never has people waiting in line to eat breakfast except that weekend—all the hunters stop for breakfast. The Newbie Restaurant, it's no bigger than a couple of average rooms, but during hunting season you can't get in that place. His volume of business is just astronomically high.

"And, of course, the sporting goods places up here do real good," he continued. "Rich Lincolnfelder's sporting goods used to handle just fishing equipment and boat sales. But with so much traffic coming up through here and stopping in he has started carrying hunting items. He says now it's become approximately 20 percent of his total volume of business."

Along with individual businesses, the town of New Bethlehem as a whole has sought to take advantage of the customer windfall deer season brings by sponsoring an annual "Big Buck Contest."

Buck pools are probably as old as deer hunting and are common in social clubs, bars, factories, and offices. In its most basic form, a group of hunters throw a specific amount of money—two dollars, five dollars, ten dollars, or whatever is agreed upon—into a pot which at the end of the season goes to the hunter who bags the biggest buck, usually meaning the one with the largest antlers. Since the early 1960s, New Bethlehem has institutionalized and expanded the practice to include cash prizes not only for the buck with the most points, but the heaviest deer, the smallest deer, and the first deer. In addition, the entry fee gives hunters who register for the contest several chances to win such prizes as guns, knives, bows, and gun cases. The popularity of the contest can be seen by the fact, that it annually draws between twelve hundred and two thousand entries, and has produced winners as far away as Florida. The heaviest deer ever to win the contest weighed in at 247 pounds; the largest rack was a sixteen-point with a twenty-four-inch spread separating the front two tines. Both deer were taken back in the early 1970s.

■

As we approach Clarion, Dad points out places where we saw deer standing in fields and along the edges of woods last year or the year before or five years ago. While seeing a whitetail in the wild anywhere, and at anytime, is a thrill, on the way north the Sunday before opening day the sight takes on a special excitement as it stirs thoughts of success. But this time, we see only a few cows and horses, and then the buffalo at the Diamond M Ranch. I wonder if the absence of deer along the roads might be a bad omen, but decide not, since whitetails seldom appear in the open at midday. Then we are in the traffic on Clarion's main street and passing the "Hunter's Breakfast" sign in front of the Immaculate Conception Church. Like every other town along the way, Clarion's stores and sidewalks hold their share of blaze orange, but college students dominate the scene more than hunters. Clarion is focused in another direction.

In silence, we follow US 322 through town and across the Clarion River to Route 208 on the edge of Shippenville where the first sign for Tionesta stands. The spot has always been a landmark for me. It narrows the perspective and adds a certain tangibleness to the journey. Twenty-four miles to Tionesta and then another fourteen to Tidioute and three more to camp. I think Bob, Mike, and Garth probably will be out scouting when we arrive. Mike and Garth were supposed to head for camp Saturday morning. Bob was leaving straight from his job as a mechanic for USAir as soon as his shift ended on Saturday night. I had put off leaving until Sunday in order to finish a story I had been working on.

As we move down the road another difference between hunting before World War II and now suddenly shows itself with a loud pop. A half-dozen hunters have gathered behind a white cottage perched on the edge of the road to sight-in their rifles. In the old days on the farm, such work would have been done long before the eve of opening day. Practice back then was mostly a matter of walking out the door. There was no need to find a gun club with a range or wait until reaching the mountains as in today's urbanized world.

Seeing the hunters behind the cottage reawakens the ache in my shoulder. Work had kept me from practicing with my own rifle until just two days ago. Then I had fired so many rounds it felt as if my shoulder was separated when I left the range, and the next day it turned blue. But my conscience was eased. I was not going to aim at the chest and hit the head like last year.

■

The nearer we get to Tionesta, the more intense grow the feelings and images of deer country. A boy of maybe twelve riding his bike wearing a blaze orange hooded sweatshirt. Leaves blowing across the road make me hope the woods will not be windy tomorrow and deprive me of my hearing. Men in orange caps unloading boxes of groceries from the backs of pickup trucks. A bearded man in jeans carrying a rifle and target toward the woods. Hunting clothes airing on porches. Hopes for snow that will make it easier to see in the woods. The parking lot of a crossroads gas station and general store jammed with trucks and four-wheel drives. Then we pass two deer lying dead along the side of the road, no more than ten yards apart.

"Whoever did it must have hit both of them," Dad says.

The deer are two of over thirty-five thousand whitetails killed by vehicles on Pennsylvania's highways every year. Estimating the average repair bill for each collision at about $1,000, the state's insurance companies exerted heavy pressure on the General Assembly in the 1960s to pass a law requiring the Game Commission to reduce the deer herd. Fortunately for Pennsylvania's hunters, the bill failed. But the Game Commission was convinced that something had to be done to reduce deer numbers, and it increased antlerless deer permits. "The companies have not complained lately," Ted Godshall told me. "They just pass the cost on. That's one of the reasons why your insurance premiums are so high. We're paying for it one way or another."

■

A few miles outside Tionesta the strip of bottom land on which Route 62 continues north narrows to barely more than the width of the roadbed. On one side of the pavement, the Allegheny River bends tight under the guard rail, its waters held in check by a few feet of height and countless truckloads of rock. On the other side, a stone-faced mountain, arrayed in ribbony waterfalls, lush ferns, and dark hemlock, denies any relief by plummeting sheer to the shoulder of the road. By any standard, the passage is a close one, tight enough to quicken the heart a beat or two in the fog, rain, and snow that can roll off Lake Erie and down the river at any time in November.

But it is not the precarious lie of the highway, nor the fickleness of the weather, that makes the spot special. Route 62 touches the river and mountains almost as closely at a half-dozen or more locations on its way to Warren. And suffers through the same weather in all of them. What makes this particular piece of road below West Hickory different is the illusion of wilderness it creates. Allegheny National Forest may be a "civilized forest," full of roads and trails, but for a few moments along Route 62, when the only sights outside the windshield are of river, mountains, woods, and sky, it is once again the land Captain Céloron de Blainville knew when he traveled down Conewango Creek to the Allegheny River in 1749. Gone are the parking problems and rusting factories of the city, the phoney glitz and nebulosity of the suburbs, and even the gentle beauty of the farmland through which most travelers to the region must pass. All that remains are the river, mountains, and sky.

The sight thrills me now. But I can remember being a bit disappointed when I first saw it as a child. Raised on a Saturday morning diet of Roy Rogers, Sky King, Rama of the Jungle and assorted 1930s adventure movies, I had half hoped to see rocky, snow-covered peaks like the ones in those films. The thought makes me remember the majestic alps Robert De-Niro and his friends hunted in *The Deer Hunter* after a single night's drive from the Monongahela Valley. Their trip left everybody who knows anything about Pennsylvania's topography sitting open-mouthed, and every deer hunter laughing at the appearance of a red stag at the end. Not to mention the insistence of DeNiro's character on carrying only one shell, without any concern for what he might do if he wounded a deer.

I am still lost in my daydreams as we cross the bridge over

the Allegheny River to Tidioute and pull into the small gas station on the other side. As Dad gets out to talk to the attendant, I look at the Marina Bank, the VFW, and the Landmark Hotel. Their Victorian architecture makes me think of Jesse James and then John Denver. It seems a stupid combination, but I cannot help thinking of Denver's song "Country Road." The line, "Life is old there, older than the hills. . . . " Then Dad climbs back into the Bronco as two hunters pull into the station on a last minute search for propane, and we head down main street and upriver, past a growing number of camps with names like "Honey Do," "Rain-EE," "Tapawingo," and "It Will Do," until a familiar faded orange wall comes into sight.

"There it is," I say.

V

To Sell the Sky

Prior to the arrival of Europeans in the New World, the Indian and the white-tailed deer co-existed in "benign symbiosis."[1] Survival of the Indian in large part depended on the venison and other products the whitetail supplied, while the deer benefited from Indian land use practices that opened up the dense forests and provided them with a more abundant food supply. But beyond his material dependence on the whitetail, the Indian viewed him as a brother in those days before the white man. To the Native American, the deer was an embodied force of nature who surrendered willingly to needy hunters and was therefore regarded with awe and reverence. Nature to the Indian was a life-force of spiritual vitality. If it were interrupted by irreverence or disrespect, catastrophes such as famine, flood, madness, or disease could result. A prayer to the spirit of a slain whitetail was not an apology; it was a confirmation of the bond between man and animal, and of man's place in nature.

Because of his deeply religious attitude toward nature, many people today consider the Indian to be an ecological hero. That view does contain a good deal of truth, but as soon as Europeans and their trade goods arrived in North America everything started to change. The benign symbiosis between Indian and whitetail collapsed, and the Indian became an enthusiastic accomplice in the bloody fur trade, a commerce that was far more important to the Europeans than the search for gold and silver. The whitetail was slaughtered, its numbers reduced by half, in exchange for some second-rate pots, blankets, beads, rifles, and whiskey.

Why did the Indians so readily abandon their ecological principles and spiritual values? Numerous theories have been advanced; for instance, that the Indians' primitive reasoning powers may have prevented them from seeing the consequences of altering their successful lifestyle. Or they were indifferent to them. Another maintains that the Indians joined the fur trade because the goods they received from the white man increased their leisure, prestige, and power. A third says the only reason the Indians did not overexploit wildlife earlier was because they lacked the technology to kill on a mass scale and, more importantly, the ability to market the harvest. Still another theory holds that when the Indians began suffering from Europeans diseases—smallpox, cholera, diphtheria, and the rest—even though they had not violated any hunting taboos, they believed their compact with nature had been broken, and they retaliated.

Each theory has its supporters and detractors. But most likely the change in the relationship between the Indian and the whitetail had many causes. The results, however, are beyond dispute. In pre-Columbian times, some 23 to 32 million deer roamed North America; by 1800 the Indians, aided only by the white man's rifles and markets (European hunters played a very small part in the early trade), had cut that number to roughly 11 million.

■

Following the Indians' "selling of the sky," for they believed the deer, like the sky, belonged to everybody, North America's whitetail population actually increased, rebounding to almost 14 million by 1865. The total was small in comparison to the pre-Columbian herd, but it was still an increase. This upward trend had more to do with transportation problems and the westward push of settlers than any change in the public's thinking.

By 1800 deer hides had lost their prominence in the fur trade, due mainly to drastically reduced deer numbers in settled areas where they could be easily obtained. In many sections of the Northeast and Southeast, the whitetail had become nothing more than a curiosity. Then, in response to the American Revolution, the vast English market closed, halting the immense profits that might have continued the slaughter. The push of population to the West improved and expanded the whitetail's habitat, too, as settlers opened up forests and abandoned their farms in the East, land that reverted back to nature and become ideal habitat for the whitetail. So its numbers climbed.

Although the trade in whitetail hides declined during the first half of the nineteenth century, pressure on the animal did not cease altogether. The whites of the period had almost as many uses for deer as the Indians. They used the hide for clothing, wall covers, rugs, upholstery fabric, saddles, handbags, harnesses, book bindings, even windowpanes and splicing for broken telegraph lines. Antlers were made into umbrella stands, coat racks, hat racks, chandeliers, knife handles, bootjacks, forks, buttons, ornaments, and were used in the production of ammonia. Deer hair became stuffing for carriage blankets, saddles, and furniture, while, on the frontier, venison fed settlers, lumbermen, and miners. But for the poor state of transportation linking the wilderness regions where large numbers of deer still existed to the major tanning centers in New York, Philadelphia, and Boston, the killing never would have slowed down. As it happened, however, the whitetail was given a fifty-year respite before the railroads began their great expansion and launched the most intense slaughter of wildlife the world has ever known.

■

Driven by an unfailing belief in free enterprise, the railroad system in the United States grew from a mere 23 miles of track in 1830 to more than 220,000 miles by 1900. During the single decade of 1890 to 1900, some 70,000 miles of track were laid across the country. It was a record that was considered "a marvelous achievement unparalleled in the economic history of any other country in the world."[2]

Riding the railroads into the interior of the country were millions of immigrants from Asia and Europe in search of fresh farmlands. Behind them came the businessmen who represented the lumber and mining companies, eager to feed the Industrial Revolution occurring in cities like Pittsburgh, Bethlehem, and Philadelphia. Supporting all this growth and change was the "market hunter," the man who, with his new repeating rifle, hunted solely to provide game for an increasingly insatiable market. Hence the slaughter began.

While the Indians killed a larger total number of deer in the previous three hundred years, the intensity of the slaughter from 1865 to 1900 had greater impact because the whitetail population was less than half what it had been before the European invasion. Moreover, there were millions of people involved, with an insatiable demand for deer and other game. "You can eat grouse three times a day if you please, and the finest flavored trout and venison are a drug on the market," noted a Philadelphian of meals available in St. Paul, Minnesota, in 1870.[3] "Some of the latter-day market hunters were so set on whopping takes afield that their mood occasionally spilled over to influence restaurant and hotel owners. Whenever this happened, menus would very often feature extravagant game feasts. Some of the immoderate adventures in gluttony are on record, and one inordinate affair, lavishly referred to as a 'Procession of Game,' included venison, multigame broth, ham of bear, buffalo tongue, five different kinds of ducks, woodcock, quail, wild turkey, wild goose, rabbit, raccoon, sandhill crane, opossum, elk, squirrel and other edible wildlife. Remarked one paying guest: 'Partaking of variety, heedless of waste, seemed from the outset to mark the diner's primary resolution.'"[4]

Prices from the Exploitation Era show venison selling for anywhere from 4¢ a pound for the less desirable cuts to 35¢ for the choicest steak. Prices for whole deer ranged from $4 in rural areas to $15 and $20 in the cities. Other game, and nongame, species were equally cheap. Quail could be had for $1.37 a dozen in eastern cities in 1873; grouse were 50¢ each; jacksnipe, $1.25 a dozen; mallards, $3 a dozen; and teal, $2 per dozen. Not even robins, orioles, blackbirds, blue jays, thrushes, meadowlarks, and flickers were safe from the pot, and generally sold for about 5¢ each.

Pennsylvania witnessed considerable activity by "game peddlers," especially near the end of the era. One farmer showed up on the streets of Philadelphia huckstering 96 woodcock he claimed were taken in a single day. Another market hunter bragged of shooting 34 black squirrels without moving from his tracks, while a third reported taking 12,085 head of game by the time he reached age twenty-six. A father and son in Minnesota claimed to have killed 6,000 whitetails in a single season, or more than 8 each during every day of the year![5]

Dr. William T. Hornaday, director of the New York Zoological Society, tells of a raid by the newly established Pennsylvania Game Commission on a game-dealing ring in Pittsburgh in *Our Vanishing Wildlife* (1913). His story concerns quail and ruffed grouse, but similar incidents unquestionably involved the whitetail, since venison was in such demand. The incident he describes also occurred after laws were passed forbidding the sale of game in the marketplace. One can imagine how much worse the slaughter must have been before laws were enacted.

"In the winter and spring of 1912," he writes, "the State Game Commission of Pennsylvania found that quail and ruffed grouse were being sold in Pittsburgh, in large quantities. The state laws were well enforced, and it was believed that the birds were not being killed in Pennsylvania. Some other state was being robbed!

"The Game Commission went to work, and in a very short time certain game-dealers of Pittsburgh were arrested. At first they tried to bluff their way out of their difficulty, and even went as far as to bring charges against the game-warden whom the Commission had instructed to buy some of their illegal game, and pay for it. But the net of the law tightened upon them so quickly and so tightly that they threw up their hands and begged for mercy.

"It was found that those Pittsburgh game-dealers were

selling quail and grouse that had been stolen in the thousands, from the state of Kentucky! Between the state game laws, working in lovely harmony with the Lacey federal law that prohibits the shipment of game illegally killed or sold, the whole bad business was laid bare, and signed confessions were promptly obtained from the shippers in Kentucky.

"At that very time, a good bill for the better protection of her game was before the Kentucky legislature; and a certain member was vigorously opposing it, as he had successfully done in previous years. He was told that the state was being robbed, but refused to believe it. Then a signed confession was laid before him, bearing the name of the man who was instigating his opposition—his friend—who confessed that he had illegally bought and shipped to Pittsburgh over 5,000 birds. The objector literally threw up his hands, and said, 'I have been wrong! Let the bill go through!' And it went."[6]

So ferocious was the competition among market hunters, price wars even erupted. Squirrels that normally sold for 40¢ each would sell for a quarter. Seventy-five-cent rabbits would go for 50¢. Mallards $1.50 a dozen. Wild geese $4.50 a dozen. "Nearly everything from woodcock to deer," were available in markets within the state," one observer reported, "the latter being hunted with dogs the year round . . . and finally becoming so scarce that by 1888 whole winters would go by in many Pennsylvania counties without anyone seeing a single deer track."[7]

■

At the start of the exploitation period much of the Allegheny High Plateau was still covered by forests dating back to the glaciers. Hemlocks of ten and twelve feet in diameter were surrounded by almost as majestic beech, white pine, maple, and chestnut. The only openings in the forests were a few natural meadows and rough mountain tops, or places where the Indians and early settlers had built villages and planted crops, or set fires to aid their hunting and traveling through the primeval landscape. Although a sawmill was established in Warren County as early as 1780, and some timber was cut for market from then on, lumbering activities were limited, centering mainly on white pine and then hemlock, the bark of which was needed by the hundreds of tanneries that had sprung up on the plateau to process the countless deer and buffalo hides being brought in by the market hunters. "Up until about 1880," writes David A. Marquis in *The Allegheny Hardwood Forests of Pennsylvania,* "forest cutting on the Allegheny Plateau was characterized by patchiness— small stands of pine here and there were harvested, scattered groups of pine throughout the remainder of the area, and some small proportion of the hemlock along the major drainages. But the major portion of the virgin forest was still intact, although some cutting had occurred throughout. Most of the heavy cutting had been restricted to the stream valleys by the necessity of water transport for the logs."[8]

In 1801, on probably the first lumber raft to float down the Allegheny River, approximately thirty thousand board feet of pine was shipped to Pittsburgh. Within the next nine years that total grew to an annual average of 3 million feet, and by the start of the War of 1812 was up to 7 million feet. As the Civil War approached, rafts 60 to 70 feet wide and 250 to 300 feet long were carrying 20 to 30 million feet of timber. One record raft actually held 1.5 million feet of lumber and covered over two acres of water surface. These totals are all before clearcutting era, and involve only logs floated down one river. Williamsport, near the other end of the plateau, reported 190 million feet of pine and 20 million feet of hemlock passing through its boom on the West Branch of the Susquehanna River in 1875, and 187 million feet of hemlock and 33 million feet of pine in 1893. Ten years after the start of the Civil War, Williamsport's thirty sawmills were producing more than 300 million feet of sawed lumber a year.

About 1880, the development of locomotives capable of climbing the region's steep grades, along with cranes and other logging equipment, provided the means to transport timber from even the most rugged valleys, at any time of year. No longer was it necessary for loggers to work near a stream or to wait for the high water in spring to ship logs to market.

At the same time, giant band mills made possible large lumbering operations capable of financing the construction of railroads into the timber. The growth of the chemical industry provided a market for virtually every size and specie of tree growing on the plateau. Loggers could cut hardwoods as well as pine and hemlock. From logs for construction and bark for tanning, the market expanded to include railroad ties, barrel staves, furniture, tool handles, clothespins, mine supports, wood alcohol, acetic acid, and charcoal. Even a heating and power market was found for slabs, edgings, and sawdust, which until then were waste products. Between 1880 and 1920, the virgin and partially cut forests of the plateau were almost completely clearcut. Six million acres. It was the greatest lumber boom and the highest degree of forest utilization the world has ever witnessed.

Such intense cutting, accompanied by fires that frequently took root and burned for weeks in the debris left by the loggers, turned the Allegheny High Plateau into a wasteland. Photographs from the period show a landscape as broken and desolate as the battlefields of World War I. This loss of habitat, coupled with the market hunting then underway, appeared to spell the end for the whitetail in Pennsylvania. *Where to Hunt American Game,* a guidebook published by the United States Cartridge Company in 1898, tells the story in a single paragraph: "The records of Dr. B. H. Warren, state geologist, show the number of deer killed during the season of 1895–'96 as follows: Potter County, 1895–'96, twenty-five deer; Schuylkill, 1896, two; Snyder, 1895–'96, from five to ten; Venango, 1895–'96, probably fifty—later returns say five or six were killed in 1896; Warren, 1895–'96, at least twenty-five; Wyoming, a few killed in the western part; Luzerne, 1895–'96, eight; Monroe, about fifteen; Adams, about fifty in 1895 and about thirty in 1896; Mifflin, 1896, twelve to fifteen; Franklin, 1896, probably twenty-five; Wayne, 1896, about twenty-five; Centre, not many—deer were scarce; Forest, 1896, probably thirty or forty; Clearfield, twenty-five; in Lebanon deer were formerly quite abundant, but they are scarce now, five or six only being killed each year; in Fulton a few deer are killed annually; Tioga has a special law protecting deer for three years; the last deer reported killed in York county was in 1873; in Diamond Valley, Huntingdon County, eleven were killed in 1896—eight years ago about seventy were taken in this valley."[9]

How many white-tailed deer were left in Pennsylvania by the start of the twentieth century is impossible to say. But their numbers were few enough that whenever one was spotted, it rated a front-page story in the local newspaper. T. S. Palmer of the U.S. Bureau of Biological Survey, forerunner of the U.S. Fish and Wildlife Service, estimated that approximately three hundred thousand whitetails remained in the entire United States in 1890. Ernest Thompson Seton, a well-known conservationist and one of the founders of the Boy Scout movement, suggests that the deer count for all of North America was five hundred thousand, but other researchers believe that figure may be a maximum estimate, and the total for the entire continent could have been a mere three hundred fifty thousand animals.[10]

"To look at it objectively," noted Paul Brohn of the U.S. Forest Service, "had it not been a way of life with the plain citizen, it would never have happened. So you can't blame one individual—the gas mogul or the barons of this or that. It was a way of life. There was always more upon the horizon. The Horn of Plenty. Brazil, with the rain forest, is doing exactly what we did a hundred years ago. They won't learn from us, and we didn't learn from Europe. We had to go and do it our own way. And it's just the way of people, I guess."

VI

Big Bucks, Falling Pants, and Carbohydrates

Echoes of hunters sighting-in their rifles reverberate in the mountains above the river as I unlock the door and we step into the cabin to be greeted by piles of hunting equipment and bags. The stuff is everywhere—on the bed against the front wall, the table, the chairs, the old sofa at the far end of the room, the floor. Even the door of the unlit wood stove is draped with a pair of wool socks, and the fireproof flooring around it is packed with boots. Most of the gear seems to belong to Bob, dropped as he walked through the door after his race from work the night before, and then left there in his hurry to get out into the woods.

"Nobody here?" Dad asks.

"No," I answer, and automatically switch on the television to feed my football habit.

While I am busy with the channel selector, Dad takes a quick look around to see if anybody might be asleep in one of the bunks or if a note has been left behind. When he finds nothing, he walks back out to the Bronco, drops the tailgate and carries in a bag of groceries. I try a couple more stations without finding the Steelers, and then move outside to help. We unload the Bronco in a headlong rush, adding our share to the clutter in the living room and piles of food in the kitchen.

Food is one commodity always in abundance at a hunting camp. Hunters today may not stay at camp as long as those in the 1920s and 1930s did, but it is doubtful they have cut back much on the food they bring along. Not even the tremendous appetites stirred by the mountain air and twelve hours in the field are enough to deplete a good camp's larder. The menu, though, may take a dietitian squirm. By the time we finish squeezing our contributions onto its already packed shelves, the refrigerator holds six dozen eggs, five pounds of bacon, three or four pounds of hamburger, five pounds of chicken wings, at least two pounds each of salami, "jumbo," baked ham, chipped ham, and pepperoni, a couple of different cheeses, three quarts of homemade spaghetti sauce, and a half-dozen different beers. On the long table in the dining area are bags of potato chips, pretzels, oatmeal cookies, molasses cookies, crackers, nut rolls, poppyseed rolls, candy bars, and a pumpkin pie left over from Thanksgiving three days earlier. But for the six heads of lettuce, green peppers, tasteless hothouse tomatoes, olives, and radishes jammed into the two crisper drawers at the bottom of the refrigerator, and the apples and bananas scattered over the table, the menu would be pure carbohydrates, cholesterol, and animal fat.

However, a certain amount of tradition and reason lies behind these choices. Like ease of preparation. No small consideration when a day spent scrambling up and down mountains leaves every joint and muscle aching with exhaustion. Turn up the heat under the chili pot, toss a salad, and dinner is on. Boil water, throw in a box of spaghetti, heat up the sauce, and another meal is ready. Food like spaghetti also is a good energy source. "What do you think those runners all eat," Bob points out every year.

The cold cuts, cookies, and fruit, of course, are for lunches in the field. The candy, with its "sugar rush," also is for the woods and a quick energy boost, though thinking on that has been changing and there seems to be less in camp every year. Bacon and eggs are required simply because they taste wonderful and the smell of them frying is the essence of the mountains and deer camp before dawn.

"Well, I am going to have a sandwich," Dad announces, just as I finish squeezing the last package of cold cuts into the meat drawer. I look at him, thinking he could have said something sooner, and then check my watch to find it is one-thirty.

51

I reach back into the drawer and hand him the baked ham, then take out a beer for myself. Life is getting better all the time.

■

As we eat our sandwiches, I fiddle with the television until the Steelers finally appear. We watch for about fifteen minutes, commenting on problems the team is having, until the boring rhythm of the contest becomes apparent, and then switch to a Buffalo station. But the Bills offer no more excitement than the Steelers, so my thoughts drift to Bob, Garth, and Mike. I wish they were at the cabin. I am anxious to hear hunting talk—whether they have seen anything and where they are going to hunt tomorrow. A conversation I had with Bob a couple of weeks earlier slips into my mind. "I think the biggest part of successful buck hunting," he said, "is to get up there before the season opens and spend at least four or five days, probably more, checking different areas. Sometimes you can hit two areas in a day. But not more, because it's going to take you at least four or five hours of just walking around to see what's there. Because things change. The deer might be in one location one year but not the next. Bucks will congregate at different times in different areas. It's proven. And you've got to determine where you're going to hunt, where the most bucks are. That's just basic. A good hunter will find out where the deer are running, above all where the buck rubs are. Because that's where the bucks are loafing."

Bob's advice is solid. The way things should be done. But for most hunters, it also is something of an ideal, impossible to achieve because of distance and work. It takes almost three hours to reach Tidioute from our homes outside Pittsburgh. When families could live on a single income, there seemed to be more time for trips Up North. Now, though, when two incomes are needed simply to keep from losing ground, it is tougher to find time. So scouting has dwindled to maybe a weekend during turkey season in early November, or just the day or two before the season opens.

Still, I have to wonder about priorities. Taking more time off to hunt may be tough, but what memories will be most precious when we are too old to leave our homes? Those days spent bent over a lathe or behind a desk? Maybe in a few cases. Or those days spent leaning against a tree listening to a woodpecker and watching a herd of deer pick its way closer?

In any event, Dad and I already know where we will be tomorrow. The same place we go every year on opening day. That may not be the smartest move from a hunting perspective, but we love the area and the memories it holds, and that can be just as important as a new place with a lot of buck signs.

■

By four o'clock, the scattered shooting has turned into a barrage. I cannot recall ever hearing so much shooting the afternoon before opening day. I wonder how many shots might be aimed at bucks that have wandered too close to a camp in the failing night. It happens every year. A New York State study found that as much as 53 percent of the deer taken by hunters in camps are taken illegally.[1] Of course, that includes many other violations besides preseason poaching. But the large number is very disturbing. Especially since the same study found that local people are even more likely to violate game laws. The thought makes me remember an old mountain man in Potter County telling a friend of mine how he could never understand why anybody would want to live in a city. He had a whole lot of reasons why the mountains were better, but one of them was "if you're hungry, go out and shoot a deer."

"It's going to be warm tomorrow," Dad says, as he steps through the door from another walk around the yard. "It's over sixty degrees out there still."

Without answering, I get up and run through the television channels again. I would like to catch the end of the Steelers' game, but the search is also something to do since it is too late in the day to drive back to our hunting area and do some scouting. I am getting more anxious to see the others. I won't feel as if I am truly at camp until everybody is together.

When I cannot find the game, I plop back down in the cushioned chair next to the table and pick up the sports pages of the Pittsburgh *Press*. "Deer tick can give a sorry aftermath to hunting season," I read. The story under it is about a tiny tick sometimes carried by deer and capable of infecting hunters with Lyme disease. Suddenly, I understand the call from my Aunt Kate three days earlier warning me about picking up a disease in the woods. I had had no idea what she was talking about, and, since she had been a nurse and always overly concerned about my health, wrote off her worry with a shrug.

"To guard against Lyme disease," I read, "the following precautions were recommended. . . . Tuck pant legs under socks; wear long-sleeved shirts. Use tick repellant. Check for the pin-head-sized 'deer ticks' after returning from the field." Within two to three days, the article goes on, people with the disease experience fever, headache, malaise, and muscle aches, much like a flu. Two days to two weeks after the infection, most of the victims develop a circular rash. Even without treatment the rash will soon fade, but months later "Lyme arthritis" could strike. In one out of five untreated cases, this means pain and swelling in one joint and then another. Dizziness, weakness, and irregular heartbeat, intermittent headaches, difficulty concentrating or sleeping, irritability, neck stiffness, and poor motor coordination are other symptoms. The name comes from a mysterious outbreak of arthritis in Lyme, Connecticut, in 1975.

According to the story, about two hundred cases have been reported in Pennsylvania during the year, most in the southeast corner of the state. It adds that the deer tick is most often carried by small, burrowing rodents and is most prevalent from May through October. I picture some fussy hunters I know fretting about coming down with the disease now that it is in the papers. I suppose it is good to know about it, but I cannot help thinking how we try so hard to sanitize life in America. We're always making people more afraid than need be.

■

Dad is poised in the doorway when the Blazer finally arrives. He calls to me, waking me out of the doze into which I have drifted, and then hurries out onto the porch. By the time I reach the door, he already knows that they hiked three miles and saw three bucks, "one a good one."

"I know where I am going tomorrow," Mike announces, as I shake hands with Garth, and Bob rushes past to find the tools he needs to fix a problem with the battered Blazer.

Being at camp may always be enjoyable, but the first moment everybody is together is electric with excitement and anticipation. Often it has been months, or even an entire year, since some of the hunters have seen each other. Yet conversations are picked up, stories and jokes exchanged as if only a single day has passed.

"Hey, big bucks," Dad calls to Garth.

"Big bucks," Garth laughs. "We saw 'em today."

The remark reaches back to last year when two giant bucks walked out of the woods about forty yards in front of Garth. The sight of them so surprised and awed him, he only stood and stared as the deer crossed the tram road he was on and disappeared back into the woods. A short time later, an old hunter happened along who also had seen the deer. "Big bucks," he kept repeating, holding his hands up, fingers spread wide, to the sides of his head. "Big bucks. Man, they was big bucks."

Garth Indyk lives in White Oak, Pennsylvania, between Bob's home in McKeesport and mine in Irwin. A self-described "little guy," with twinkling, mischievous eyes and a quick laugh, he and his brothers are partners in Indyk Construction, a company specializing in demolition work, tearing down vacant buildings in the depressed steel towns of the Monongahela Valley. He has been a friend of Bob's for a dozen years, during which time Bob continuously urged him to "become a hunter." He managed to beg off, claiming too much work,

until four years ago, when, at age thirty-one, he finally suc-
cumbed to the lure.

Although he became a hunter later in life than anybody
else in camp, Garth already has developed a real love for the
sport. Before he started deer hunting, he was like many other
self-employed people and rarely took time off from his business. Work was an obsession with him. It left him drained and
tense, and took much of the joy out of living. Then he came to
the mountains and experienced the simultaneous relaxation
and excitement of deer hunting, the calming sounds of the big
woods and heart-pounding rush of the approaching quarry,
and announced himself a "natural born hunter."

Garth also has a natural talent with a rifle. Practically as
soon as he was handed one, he began shredding the bull's-eye
and then dropped two does in his first three seasons. But his
lack of experience as a hunter—he is the only member of his
family who has ever hunted—often shows in humorous ways.
Last year, for instance, during the two-day antlerless deer season that follows the buck season, he shot at a doe and she ran
off. But he never bothered to check the spot where she had
been standing. When Bob and Mike reached him a few moments later, Mike walked down to the spot and found a large
blood spoor. They started following it and found the deer lying
only sixty yards away. "I didn't know," Garth laughs. "I
thought whenever you shoot them they're supposed to fall
right there. That's the stories I heard. Boom—this guy got him
in the neck. Boom—he fell right there. I figured that where I
shot him, he should have fell."

Garth's belief that deer always fall where they are shot was
reinforced during the buck season last year. It happened when
a buck was walking toward him. At the very moment he
picked up the deer in his scope, a shot rang out and it dropped
out of sight. "I said, 'Here comes the buck. There he is waiting
for me.'" he recalls. "Then I heard this rifle and saw him fall
right in my scope. I said, 'sonofabitch.'"

But Garth's best story, so far at least, has to do with field
dressing his first deer. To farm boys who have grown up seeing

cattle and pigs butchered for market or their own table, field dressing is a natural part of life. But very few urban hunters ever see the insides of large animals before they start deer hunting. To them, meat always has come on a tray, wrapped in cellophane. Many old timers enjoy teasing rookie hunters about the procedure, making it sound far more gruesome than it really is.

"I cut its belly open, the first one," Garth recalls. "I didn't want to stick my hands down in that stuff. I'm breaking branches off trees. I am trying to dig this stuff out. But it ain't workin'. So, I upset it. Pick it up by its front legs and I am shaking the hell out of it, tryin' to dump this stuff out. But nothin' is coming. So, I say, 'Oh, hell,' and get down there and start whacking away a little bit. Then I reach into my pocket but hell, I ain't got no deer drag. So, I pull my belt off. My pants are too big. I wrap my belt around his neck. I'm dragging him, my pants are falling off as I am going up the hill. I am thinking, 'This is a real rookie deer hunter.' All that was needed was a video camera. I was laughin' at myself. I was just glad there was nobody around watchin' me."

■

Dusk is settling by the time Bob finishes with the Blazer and hurries into the kitchen. He wants to start a pot of chili and another of spaghetti sauce. The fact that we already have three quarts of sauce in the refrigerator does not cause him to hesitate for a second. By nature Bob is a serious person, and in camp he is all business. But his enthusiasm sometimes pushes him into situations that do not always turn out the way he expected. Still, his excitement is contagious and we often follow him without thinking.

So, as he browns hamburger in a skillet and empties cans of tomato sauce into a pot on a back burner, I begin chopping onions, garlic, and green peppers. Then we go through the collection of herbs on the shelf above the stove, dumping oregano, basil, black pepper, bay leaves, garlic powder, and parsley flakes into the pot. But no salt. The health risks of too much salt have even penetrated deer camp.

No sooner is the spaghetti sauce mixed and simmering, than Bob is browning more ground beef for chili and calling for Garth to recite his wife's recipe. I continue to chop onions, peppers, and garlic, thinking even the Frugal Gourmet would be proud of our massive garlic consumption. In a good deer camp, everybody volunteers to do their share without being asked. But few kitchen stoves are made to handle three adults at the same time, and we are soon bumping into each other. Garth and I look at each other and then Bob, and smile.

■

With the spaghetti sauce and chili underway, we drift into the dining area adjacent to the tiny kitchen where the talk naturally flows toward deer and hunting. Stories lead to opinions, opinions back to stories. The range is wide and loose.

"Lyme disease," Bob says after scanning the newspaper article. "All these years we've been hunting deer and now they come out with that."

"Yeah, I read it before," I say.

He flips the paper onto the table and a concerned Garth grabs it.

"They're saying some people have caught Lyme disease," Bob tells him. "You know, that's probably been going on for years." Then he adds, "That's them do-gooders, don't want you out in the woods hunting deer."

The talk of Lyme disease makes Dad remember a hunter who shot a diseased doe last year. For the obvious reason that nobody wants to eat spoiled meat, hunters are always interested in such stories. But they also hold a certain fascination as a glimpse of the way life used to be when men had to rely upon their knowledge of nature to feed themselves and their families. A deep streak of romanticism runs through hunting.

"It was probably spoiled," Bob remarks about the deer. "They probably didn't bring it back in time."

"No, they killed it that day and the same day took it down to the slaughter house," Dad says.

"What if you don't gut a deer out in two hours?" Bob asks then. "Maybe they didn't find it right away. You might as well throw that deer away if you didn't gut it out within two hours. I don't care what they say."

Garth mentions a deer he saw two days ago lying dead along a road near his home. Then Bob tells of another one he saw in the same area, and of a spike he spotted on the west end of the Fort Pitt Tunnels, less than a mile across the Monongahela River from downtown Pittsburgh. When Dad hears of those deer, he brings up the ones in his yard. But everybody agrees a hunter has to be lucky to get a deer in southern Pennsylvania.

"Up here, you're out in the woods," Bob says. "You're gonna see deer. Even if you don't get a shot at one, you're gonna see them."

Seeing deer is an extremely important part of hunting. The goal may be to kill a deer, but the actual shooting comprises the tiniest part of the experience. If a hunter sees game, feels his blood quicken at the sight, senses his body tense and his mind focus so completely that the world beyond vanishes with the approaching deer, it is possible to go home satisfied, with a sense of having hunted. The satisfaction may not be as complete as when he actually shoots a deer, but the person who sees game knows he has hunted.

■

"Legs hurting yet?" Mike asks, as he wanders blurry-eyes into the kitchen.

"My legs are fine. I got no problem," Garth answers.

"Mike got a half-hour's sleep over there," Dad teases. "He was snoring."

Mike denies the snoring, but admits to his legs tightening up from the afternoon's scouting trip. Garth tells him he should try walking over rubble all day, adding: "I feel good, but I am not as old as you yet."

At twenty, Bob's son, Mike, is the youngest hunter at camp.

But this is already his seventh deer season and tenth year Up North. At first he was a reluctant visitor to the cabin. He would have preferred to stay home with his friends and play "football" or "army," or whatever other games a ten-year-old might dream up. But at that age a person does not have much say in what he is going to do when the rest of his family is headed Up North. So he got to know the mountains early and has since grown to love them, scheduling his vacation from the auto parts store in McKeesport where he works to spend a week in camp during buck season.

In *Walden,* in the chapter "Higher Laws," Thoreau writes: "Yet notwithstanding the objection on the score of humanity, I am compelled to doubt if equally valuable sports are ever substituted for these [hunting and fishing]; and when some of my friends have asked me anxiously about their boys, whether they should let them hunt, I have answered, yes,—remembering that it was one of the best parts of my education—make them hunters, though sportsmen only at first, if possible mighty hunters at last, so they shall not find game large enough for them in this or any vegetable wilderness—hunters as well as fishers of men."[2]

To look at Mike's fresh face with its scraggly mustache is to see Thoreau's observation come to life. For there is a clear distinction between Mike and his friends who were not raised as hunters. Being a young man, he naturally wants to fit in with his friends, share the usual adolescent adventures with drinking and girls and cars, act with a toughness and talk with a knowledge not really earned. But where his friends seem to be drifting, he shows flashes of a stability that will be with him throughout his life. In his case it is directly related to hunting, though others have found it in music, art, cars, even computers. I can see it in Mike because Dad had given me the same thing. When I was Mike's age, college was ending, Vietnam was breathing down my neck, friends were shooting up drugs, and generally nothing was the way we were taught it was supposed to be. I often took my rifle or shotgun into the woods and the world turned right again. At the time, I did not understand what I had been given, and I am sure Mike does not now, but someday it will become clear.

■

Long before the flavors in the spaghetti sauce have had a chance to blend, Bob decides it is time to eat. He loads a pot with spaghetti and heats up the sauce I brought from home. Then we settle around the table, staring out the windows at the big, round thermometer glistening in the rain under the dusk-to-dawn light. It reads sixty degrees. We wonder how we will dress in the morning, whether it will stay warm and continue to rain. Or be cold and snowy on top of the mountains where we are going.

"Now, think of this," Bob starts. "Say you hunted three, four, five hours already, and you're walking. You're still far back in the woods. You see those deer standing up there where we did this afternoon. I'd say about a hundred-forty yards away. Not a bad shot for a good hunter. But the thing about it is, you're buck hunting. You can't take a wild shot and hit a doe. You got to wait them out under those conditions. You wait them out because they weren't spooky. But they still knew something was wrong."

"Did you see the buck when you first walked up on them?" Garth asks.

Bob tells him he saw the small buck in the herd and he thinks another, bigger buck was following along behind. That was why the herd was waiting. But the second buck saw them first, snorted, and was gone. Everybody laughs at the wiliness of the whitetail.

"That's part of learning how to really be a good hunter," Bob says. "Not this luck crap, you wait in the woods all day and something runs into you. There is such a thing as a hunter making his own luck.

"You don't know what way those deer are going to go," he continues. "They're up there and within shooting range. All right, the wind was blowing in our faces. They couldn't pick up our smell. That was in our favor. But you can't get closer to them because the leaves are crunchy. If there was snow on the ground, maybe you could sneak a little bit. But now, all you could do is wait them out for about a half hour. When you don't see them no more, maybe you can take a couple of steps to the first tree. Then you can get your gun resting so you can let your scope do the work. You know the general area where you saw those deer. You'll be surprised what you can pick out with a scope that you don't see with the naked eye. You might see an antler sticking out from a tree."

"I'll tell you something you want to watch," Dad breaks in then. "You see doe coming. You don't see no buck. You wait about fifteen minutes or so and you'll see a buck."

"Sometimes, yeah," Bob agrees.

"I'll tell you another thing," Dad says. "You see about ten in a herd and there's always one standing up. He's watching. And that's the one you gotta find first."

"That ain't always true either," Bob disagrees. "Let me tell you what happened to me up in McGee here. I hunted my way from this camp clean up back there where we drive the Jeep in. It was like eleven, quarter after eleven in the morning. I hunted my way back there to get away from hunters. I walked around, didn't see any hunters. So, I sat down by a tree to eat my sandwich, drink my pop. Soon as I started eating that sandwich, a big herd of deer came trotting up. About a hundred and twenty yards, a hundred yards away.

"But it's too thick. It's new growth. You can't shoot a deer through there. But there is one opening. So, I am scoping them out through the opening. By the time they got to it, they were walking. I got a good scope on every one of them. Every one was a doe. They didn't even know I was there. They were feeding, walking. They didn't have a lookout. I am eating my sandwich, I am not moving. In comes another deer trotting on the same plane. The same path. The eleventh deer. I almost tasted it was a buck. I got the gun up to that same opening and I shot him on a run."

"I said," Dad argues back, "if one of them is just standing there eating, the rest of them are bedded down, there's always one standing up watching."

"I don't know," Bob says. "I walked on three deer here. It was in turkey season. I was coming back to the cabin, walking down over the hill and I saw a deer ear sticking up. And I knew it was a deer ear. I stopped. I looked. That was all I saw. I started sneak walking. A little closer, closer. I wanted to see how close I could get to those deer. I got within twenty-five yards of them. They were all lying down. Finally, one got up, walked, looked at me, then started walking up over the hill, and the other two got up and started walking. There's a case where they didn't have a lookout."

"You wait until tomorrow, though," Dad laughs. "After tomorrow you'll see. As soon as they see a little movement tomorrow, they're gone."

"No matter how you try to out think those deer, you'll always learn something new everytime you go into the woods," Bob says. "They don't always do the same thing. You never know. I've had deer jump up out of their beds, fifteen, twenty yards from you, and if you were ready you could have got a shot, but since you weren't ready the deer got away. They just needed that one split second, because a good hunter will not squeeze the trigger unless he knows he got the sights on brown. That's it."

"You know what I saw up past Hearts Content years back? " Dad starts. "I saw these guys following these deer tracks. There was this big rock. The deer just walked behind the rock and these guys went past."

"Because they didn't see any movement," Bob says. "Deer don't want to see movement. When they got on the other side of that rock, they didn't see any hunters, they were happy."

"Yeah," Dad laughs.

"That is what shakes a deer up quicker than anything," Bob adds. "Movement over smell. The first day of hunting, the smell is all through the woods."

Enthralled by the talk of the two most experienced hunters in camp, we sit mostly quiet. The image of deer hiding behind a rock while two hunters walk by goes through my mind and makes me think of a cartoon. I would laugh, but none of us knows how many times the same thing might have happened to us.

■

Television and telephone may seem out of place in a hunting camp, but Bob's Uncle Pete spends a good deal of time at the cabin during the year and likes the amenities of modern life. Bob has said if he ever takes over the camp completely, the first thing he is going to do is have the phone removed. He has never said anything about the television, except when Mike has MTV on, because he likes it for keeping track of local weather and an occasional movie in the evening.

A movie is what is on when we filter into the living room after dinner. Sally Fields and Michael Caine are tied together. They are supposed to be nude, but glimpses of Sally's body stocking keep appearing on camera. Nobody knows the title of the movie or what is happening. But Garth instantly loves Sally Fields. He cannot believe how good she looks for fifty. I tell him I don't think she's fifty, but he does not believe me. All he knows is she looks good, he tells me, and cracks open a Budweiser.

The drunken, bloodthirsty hunter is an image often conjured up by people who oppose hunting. And, in all honesty, such creatures do exist. But no more than the drunken golfer or drunken boater or drunken skier. Possibly even less. Peer pressure, brought by the fact the person drinking is armed with a lethal weapon, usually works to keep most hunters in line. At least that has been my experience. A few camps I have heard of do not even allow alcohol. But those seem to be the exception. Generally, beer can be found in deer camps and usually some old bottles of hard liquor, dusty from their years on the shelf. Bars in deer country may do a brisk business during buck season, but the men who frequent them are on a par with the aprés-ski crowd and not real hunters. Others are often successful hunters who already have their deer but are not ready to head home.

"Last night I didn't get drunk," said Garth, whose love of

beer is second to none. "Tonight I didn't get drunk. Maybe tomorrow, after we get them buckies, I'll be drunk."

"You know what that means," I tell him. "You're serious this year, buddy."

He laughs.

"I wouldn't be surprised if you get a buck," I tell him. "Attitude has a lot to do with it. The first buck I ever got, I knew before we even left I was going to get one that year."

"Last year, I didn't have a feeling," Mike adds. "This year, I don't know. I have a good feel about over there where we were today."

"So do I," says Garth. "I like it there. I like it there a lot."

"That plays a part in it," I say. "I don't know if it just makes you more aware—you pay more attention and are thinking more about what's going on—but I know it plays a part."

The talk drifts to the weather, and then the best gunpowder for reloading, and stories of hunters lost in the mountains. It is nine o'clock and still fifty-eight degrees. Slowly, everybody becomes busy sharpening knives, making sure they have their drag ropes, and working another coat of Bear Grease into their boots. The atmosphere grows quietly serious. By ten o'clock, people begin disappearing into their bunks.

VII

Recoil

Although market hunting continued largely unchecked into the twentieth century, by the end of the Civil War most states had enacted laws protecting the whitetail. The first such law was enacted in 1646 by the town of Portsmouth, Rhode Island, whose residents already had noticed a decline in deer along their section of the eastern seaboard. It stated "that there shall be noe shooting of deere from the first of May till the first of November; and if any shall shoot a deere within that time he shall forfeit five pounds."[1] The fine is a stiff one for a time when barter was the main form of exchange and most people did not see twenty pounds in the course of a year. But the law covered only a single town, outside of which practically all of the killing was taking place and, more importantly, nobody was appointed to enforce it for more than fifty years.

Still, the Portsmouth law was eventually adopted by Rhode Island and established a precedent. In 1679, New Jersey prohibited the export of dressed skins killed by Indians. Then, in 1689, Massachusetts and Connecticut became the first colonies to set a whitetail harvest season. The preamble of the Connecticut law even reflects official concern for the whitetails' future, primarily because of the economic problems the disappearance of deer might cause the colony. "The killing of deer at unseasonable times of the year hath been found very much to the preiudice of the Colonie, great numbers of them have been hunted and destroyed in deep snowes when they are very poor and big with young, the flesh and skins of very little value, and the increase greatly hindered."[2] Nobody was appointed to enforce the Massachusetts law until 1739, however, when the first game wardens in North America were hired on a commission basis. The Connecticut law was not enforced until 1866.

Pennsylvania's first law protecting deer was enacted by Governor Sir William Keith on August 26, 1721. It closed the season on whitetails from January 1 to July 1 and set the fine at twenty shillings, but no one was hired to enforce the law for nearly two centuries.

Aside from a lack of hired enforcement, early game laws were ineffective because they were more concerned with profits than with protecting and maintaining whitetail numbers. The Rhode Island General Assembly showed this in 1705 when it noted that members "hath been informed that great quantities of deer hath been destroyed out of season, either for skins of flesh, which is great destruction of the creatures, without profit, and may prove much to the damage of this Colony for the future and to the whole country, if not prevented."[3] Seasons were closed during rut or winter yarding periods (when the deer were confined to small areas by deep snow) only to make more deer available for slaugther at other times of the year, when their meat was better and their hides were more valuable. No bag limits were set and hunting methods were prohibited only when they endangered citizens or livestock. Fire drives were outlawed when they threatened villages and pasture lands. The practice of skinning deer and leaving the carcass in the woods was stopped because it attracted wolves. Hunting close to settled areas was banned mainly to protect people within towns and villages from stray gunshots. And devices such as pits, snares, and traps were outlawed after they began to catch livestock.

Another major problem with early game laws was that adjacent states often had very different hunting regulations, making it almost impossible to restrict the traffic in game and wildlife products. A hunter could always claim that the deer he had in his possession, or was offering for sale, had come from a neighboring state where local officials had no authority. Not until Congress passed the Lacey Act of 1900, which prohibited interstate traffic in wild game taken in violation of state law, was market hunting and the decimation of wildlife for commercial gain effectively ended. By that time the white-tail was already so close to extinction it was rarely hunted, but public opinion, spurred by twenty years of agitation by hunters seeking to imitate the British model of sportsmanship and individuals like George Bird Grinnell, editor of *Forest and Stream* magazine, had begun to change in favor of wildlife, making its protection politically safe.

■

Exactly how much truth lies in the story about John M. Phillips and his fear of having killed the last whitetail in Pennsylvania is difficult to say. There is nothing to support it in the handful of fragile, yellow newspaper clippings about Phillips in the Carnegie Library of Pittsburgh. Nor is there a word in the half dozen local histories on the library shelves in which Phillips's name appears. Ted Godshall at the Game Commission can only vaguely recall hearing the tale. But what a wonderful piece of folklore.

The wealthy industrialist, inventor of the Phillips Automatic Cross-Over Dump, a machine used everywhere coal was mined, travels to the mountains of Pennsylvania to hunt deer. Although it is only the dawn of the Gay Nineties, much of the state's ancient forests already have been clearcut and the land left a raw scar of rocks, mud, and wood debris.

Within this scene of utter devastation hardly a songbird survives. But somehow, the young man, still in his twenties, stumbles across a deer. And, being a product of his time, believing game is to be hunted until it is gone, kills it. Afterward though, for reasons not even he may understand, he comes to believe he has shot the last whitetail in Pennsylvania. The thought horrifies him. Hunting has always given him so much pleasure. Now he has destroyed the very thing he loves the most.

He confesses his feelings to friends. Like him, they are

mostly well-to-do and educated. They agree that something must be done or soon there will be no wildlife left for their sons and grandsons to hunt. They gather as the Pennsylvania State Sportsmen's Association in the Erie County town of Corry to discuss the waste and destruction they see everywhere. Out of their work the Pennsylvania Game Commission is established on June 25, 1895, to try to stem the tide of slaughter.

If the truth behind the story is untraceable, clouded by time and by fires in the State Capitol in 1897 and 1915 that destroyed early Game Commission records, available information leaves little doubt that Phillips was capable of being overcome by feelings of remorse for a wild creature and of responding with action. Nor is there any question that he played a major role in early efforts to end the slaughter of wildlife in Pennsylvania. At his death at age ninety-two on September 8, 1953, the Pittsburgh *Sun-Telegraph* called him the "Grand Old Man of Conservation," and a 1937 story in the Pittsburgh *Post-Gazette* touts him as the "father of conservation in Pennsylvania." Though he lies forgotten today, his name evident only on a few trophies in the Hall of Mammals at the Carnegie Museum of Natural History, at Phillips Park in the Pittsburgh suburb of Carrick, and on a bronze plaque on State Game Lands 25 in Elk County, in many ways his story exemplifies the type of person who stepped forth to save the whitetail at the end of the nineteenth century. Many were quite prominent in their own time, although today they are overshadowed by such giants as Teddy Roosevelt and former Pennsylvania Governor Gifford Pinchot.

John MacFarlane Phillips was born in Pittsburgh on February 15, 1861.[4] He was the son of James Phillips, one of the founders of the Oliver Iron & Steel Company, whose own father had come to western Pennsylvania from Northern Ireland in 1795 to work as a blacksmith. Phillips attended local public schools and then studied engineering and was made superintendent of the bolt works and foraging plants of the Lewis, Oliver & Phillips Company. Later he became manager of the company's mining equipment department and, in 1889, with his Uncle John, purchased the company's mine supply division and established the Phillips Mine & Mill Supply Company.

In addition to business, Phillips always took an active interest in civic affairs—he served as a Pittsburgh city councilman, a member of the Pittsburgh-Allegheny County Planning Commission, and as a director of the South Side Hospital—but it was the outdoors that he loved above all else and where he has left his most lasting legacy.

Believing that conservation education was the only way to make certain the nation's natural resources would never again be needlessly wasted, Phillips organized the first Boy Scout troop in Pennsylvania, the second in the nation, around 1910. He frequently supplied the scouts with seedlings for planting on public lands and encouraged them to feed wild birds in the winter. He is believed to have been one of the first people in the country to advocate feeding wild birds. In Crawford County he campaigned for the construction of Pymatuning Reservoir, and in Clarion County he sued, using his own attorneys, to stop cutting by lumber companies in Cook Forest. Outside the United States, he convinced the Canadian government to establish a game preserve on 500,000 acres of wilderness between the Elk River and Bull River in British Columbia, a region he first explored at the turn of the century, and where a mountain now bears his name.

Several sources mention Phillips as the author of the basic game code for Pennsylvania. Although he did not serve on the first Board of Game Commissioners, he was a member of the commission from 1905 to 1924, including several years as president, when some of the most far-reaching game laws were enacted and the first deer were stocked in Pennsylvania. For his conservation work, he was awarded the gold medal of the Permanent Wild Life Protection Fund and the Outdoor Prize Award in 1924. That same year, he was appointed chairman of the Committee on Conservation of Fur-Bearing Animals by President Calvin Coolidge. In 1950, 1951, and 1952, the Pennsylvania Senate named him one of the state's most outstanding citizens and its "greatest conservationist."

Why Phillips has virtually disappeared from the annals of conservation history is impossible to say. The fact that he never held high elective office certainly played a part, but also significant is his unassuming personality. Hardly any news story quotes him directly. The only one that gives a hint of the inner man is an impressionistic article in the Pittsburgh *Post-Gazette* (October 28, 1932) entitled "Minute Biographies:" "a slight, quiet man with grayish mustache . . . sleeps with the bedroom windows open . . . even in mid-winter . . . has a fondness for limburger cheese . . . and usually has hard-boiled eggs and cocoa for breakfast . . . never eats any dinner . . . only apples and nuts . . . while reading one of his favorite Western or detective story magazines . . . has two big hunting dogs . . . 'Joe' and 'Jesse' . . . named after two prominent Pittsburgh coal men . . . never wears gloves . . . and has to be coaxed into putting on an overcoat . . . once had a zoo containing 14 animals in rear of his home . . . always wears a red bandana handkerchief around his neck at home on Sundays . . . the symbol of the Campfire Club . . . hikes in the woods almost every Saturday afternoon with his dogs . . . has five pet crows."

Other telling glimpses of the man are offered by William T. Hornaday in *Camp-Fires in the Canadian Rockies*, written after a 1905 hunting trip he and Phillips took to British Columbia, and *Camp-Fires on Desert and Lava*, about a 1907 expedition in the mountains of northern Mexico. Phillips took most of the photographs for both books and wrote, in a totally unassuming style, small sections.

On the Canadian trip, Phillips managed to photograph a wild Rocky Mountain goat from a distance of six feet while hugging a sheer rock wall. Hornaday said the shot represents "what I believe to be the most daring, and also the most successful feat in big game photography ever accomplished" (p. ii). The American Museum of Natural History agreed when it awarded the photograph first prize, over almost seventeen hundred entries, in its 1922 worldwide photo contest. Phillips downplayed the deed when he returned to camp, but that night could not hide the fright he had felt hanging onto the cliff and awoke sweating and screaming from a nightmare in which he was falling.

Neither could Phillips control his feelings about what Hornaday calls the "only serious accident of the whole trip." It involved a ground squirrel that Phillips and one of the guides spent over two hours trying to capture for Hornaday to take back to the New York Zoo for study. When they finally caught it, they had nothing to put it in but Phillips's binocular case. So they removed the binoculars and drilled a small air hole with a knife in the lid of the case.

"When I saw the smallness of the air-hole that had been drilled for the animal through the thick leather," writes Hornaday, "my mind was filled with dread and I hardly could muster up courage to open the lid. But no time was lost on that account. When I looked in, poor 'Little Mike,' as Mr. Phillips called him, was curled up in the bottom, stone dead.

"For several days Mr. Phillips was fairly racked by regret and remorse. That small creature's death haunted him nearly to Minneapolis, and he continually wondered whether 'poor Little Mike' smothered because they did not give him enough air. I think the animal was hurt internally when captured, or else died of a 'broken heart,' as even bear and deer sometimes do when caught and crated" (pp. 221–22).

■

Despite the efforts of men such as Phillips, William M. Kennedy, the former mayor of Allegheny City (now Pittsburgh's North Side), who served as president of the first Board of Game Commissioners, and Dr. Joseph Kalbfus, a Williamsport native who spent his youth hunting on the Great Plains and became the Game Commission's second executive director, the fight to turn the tide of killing and save what little remained of Pennsylvania's wildlife was a long and difficult one. Leading politicians of the period, fearful of having their power curbed, and supported by market hunters and other groups with an interest in continuing the slaughter, bitterly fought the creation of an independent Game Commission. For five years after it was first proposed by the Pennsylvania State

Sportsmen's Association in 1890, no progress was made. So strong was the opposition that even after Richard F. Baldwin, a legislator from Delaware County, managed to force an act establishing the Game Commission through the General Assembly and have it signed by the governor, it was more than another year before the first board members were appointed and over two years before the first game protectors were picked by the commission on October 9, 1897.

Even with the first Board of Game Commissioners named (Kennedy, Charles Heebner of Philadelphia, Irving A. Streans of Wilkes-Barre, James H. Warden of Harrisburg, E. B. Westfall of Williamsport, and Coleman K. Sober of Lewisburg) and the first game protectors hired, the political battle did not end. To keep the commission, all of whose members served without pay, from causing too much trouble, the legislature appropriated only $800 for its budget—the money was used for postage. It was fortunate the members were mostly men of means, since they frequently had to dip into their own pockets to keep the fledgling agency operating.

Old attitudes occasionally led to fights among commission members. In 1901, for example, while the commission was attempting to get the legislature to pass a tougher law against market hunting, Commissioner Sober objected publicly to efforts by Director Kalbfus to muster support from organized sportsmen. In an open letter to sport hunters around the state, Kalbfus had called attention to one market hunter who supposedly killed seventy grouse in a single week and another who hauled more than fourteen hundred to market during a recent season. Sober, an exceptional shot who loved to hunt birds, said he saw nothing wrong with market hunting. The pronouncement led an angry President Kennedy to call a special meeting during which the issue was hotly debated. Sober was accused of circulating petitions in his district opposing legislation that would prohibit market hunting, shorten seasons, set bag limits on game birds, and forbid the sale of game. He denied those accusations, but admitted forwarding petitions to the governor from people who opposed such laws, Dr. C. B. Penrose, who replaced Heebner on the board, stated the feelings of the other commissioners when he told Sober: "I do not feel that I represent any constituency. I am a Game Commissioner to do what the law directs for the best interests of game and bird protection."[5]

■

As tough as was the political fight to save Pennsylvania's wildlife, it was nothing compared to the dangers the new game protectors faced in the field. In 1906 alone fourteen game protectors were shot at by people violating the new game laws the legislature was beginning to pass. Three were killed, three seriously wounded and one slightly injured. One of the murders led directly to the enactment of an alien gun law, forbidding unnaturalized, foreign-born residents of the state from owning guns.

Through the first decade of the twentieth century, the most common game law violations were hunting out of season; running and killing deer with dogs; selling game; taking game by traps, pits, and other forbidden methods; hunting on Sunday; killing song and insectivorous birds; and hunting by nonresidents without a license. Arrest records show that over half of all violations were committed by unnaturalized, foreign-born residents. In *Our Vanishing Wildlife*, Hornaday devotes an entire chapter to the role of immigrants in depleting wildlife at the turn of the century. Freed from the restrictions of Europe, where only wealthy landowners enjoyed the sport, they eagerly turned to hunting, not for pleasure, but to add to the dinner table. The meager wages paid by such mine and mill owners, as Andrew Carnegie and Henry Clay Frick, who are now praised for their philanthropy, seldom allowed workers the luxury of meat for dinner. Hunting was one way to fill the pot. They did it year-round, without regard for seasons or species. Songbirds that could be used in potpies or to add flavor to sauces were as eagerly sought as the whitetail. In Lancaster County, an entire work camp became ill after eating turkey vultures, a carrion eater that is one of the most disease-carrying creatures on earth.[6]

Into this hard and volatile world stepped Seely Houk, a

brash young game protector who worked the western part of the state. His strict enforcement of game laws quickly earned him scorn and threats from the foreign-born population. The New Castle area was particularly dangerous, and Commissioner Phillips warned him not to work the area alone. Houk assured him that he had a revolver and could take care of himself, a belief that held true until March 2, 1906, when he disappeared while working in Lawrence County.

Silence immediately followed Houk's disappearance and then rumors started to circulate that he had "skipped out" to avoid being arrested for his own wrongdoings. Phillips, who knew Houk well, did not believe the stories, and on April 26 his suspicions were confirmed when the warden's shot-riddled body, the back of his head blown away, was found in the Mahoning River. The raincoat he had been wearing was pulled up over his head, loaded with rock and tightly belted.

Although both state and local police investigated the murder, they could turn up no leads in the close-mouthed foreign community. Finally, Phillips went to Governor Samuel Pennypacker and obtained permission to hire a Pinkerton agent with private funds. The detective moved into the New Castle area and found work in a limestone quarry. By keeping his ears open and talking to people he met, within a few months he was able to obtain enough evidence to arrest Rocco Racca, a man who had been arrested and convicted on various charges thirteen times in his native Italy. Testimony during the trial revealed that Houk had shot one of Racca's unlicensed dogs for running deer and that Racca had vowed "just as my dog died in the woods, so shall this man die." Along with a friend, he ambushed Houk while the game protector was walking a railroad grade. They fired in the air and when Houk went to investigate, they hit him with a load of buckshot. Racca then ran up, placed the muzzle of his shotgun in the officer's mouth, and pulled the trigger. Houk lay on the tracks until after dark when the two men returned, filled his raincoat with rock, and pushed the body into the river. Racca was convicted and hanged for the murder in 1907, but the other man fled the country and all efforts to extradite him failed.[7]

Despite political and public resistance, the young Game Commission slowly began to make a difference. In 1897 alone, it made the first extradition from another state for a game law violation, banned the killing of deer over salt licks, made it illegal to sell game birds killed in Pennsylvania, and prohibited the spring shooting of wild ducks. Then, through the first two decades of the twentieth century, it passed the first game refuge law, the buck law (which made only antlered deer legal game), and the alien gun law, established licenses for residents and nonresidents; purchased the first State Game Lands; and banned buckshot and automatic rifles for deer hunting. It also protected the black bear (the first state to do so) and the beaver; stocked beaver and ringneck pheasants; and banned night hunting of all game birds. Gun manufacturers and market hunters, who were reaping tremendous profits from the sale and use of automatic rifles, fought the ban on automatic weapons all the way to the Pennsylvania Supreme Court, which ruled the ban constitutional on the grounds that the state has the right to say how its game may or may not be taken.

The passage of new laws protecting the whitetail and other game animals was only a small part of the battle. Since, for all practical purposes, Pennsylvania no longer had a deer herd by the 1890s, the commission purchased fifty white-tailed deer from Michigan in 1906 and began a restocking effort that continued to 1925. By the time it was finished, 1,192 deer were stocked, mostly in the northern part of the state, purchased from private reserves in the state (524), from Michigan (417), or from other states (251). Due to those stockings, and the buck law, state hunters were able to harvest 1,287 whitetails by 1913, a number that has climbed to over 300,000 a season today.

■

Shortly after Pennsylvania began passing new game laws and restocking its mountains with whitetail, Congress came to the conclusion that possibly the only way to save something of the East's once great forests might be through public ownership. Private ownership, with its "rape and run" phi-losophy, had long ago shown it cared nothing about preserving even a single tree of cutting size if a dollar could be made.

The Weeks Act (1911) authorized the federal government to create national forests on lands within watersheds of navi-gable streams or rivers. These new public lands would be used to regulate stream flow and revitalize the forests. They would be under the control of the U.S. Forest Service, but the loca-tion had to be agreed upon by federal, state, and local govern-ing bodies. They could not be taken by condemnation, but had to come from a willing seller.

In Pennsylvania, one piece of land that met the criteria of the Weeks Act lay on the western edge of the Allegheny High Plateau. The land had been clearcut by the lumber interests, drilled by the oil companies, and extensively burned by forest fires. In 1908 alone over a million acres of forested land, or the debris left by the lumbermen, burned in this area and in other parts of northern Pennsylvania. Some of the fires were so in-tense they consumed all the humus, exposing the clay and rocks beneath. Runoff from these hundreds of thousands of acres of bare land regularly sent flood waters raging down the Allegheny to Pittsburgh. Millions of dollars worth of property was destroyed and dozens of lives lost in the floods, which at times left portions of the city under forty feet of water.

The federal government made its first purchase of land in the region, some sixteen hundred acres, at the headwaters of Morrison Run in Warren County in early 1923. The cost was $2.50 an acre, but it did not include mineral rights. Oil had been king in northwestern Pennsylvania since Colonel Edwin Drake sank his famous well in Titusville in 1859, and people in the region were accustomed to keeping the mineral rights when they sold a piece of property. Nobody knew what might be under all those rotting stumps and brush. Since the land would have cost a great deal more with mineral rights, the government did not mind owning only the surface. The only oil wells in the area were widely scattered and not considered a problem worth the expenditure of tax money.

Nine months after that first land purchase, on September

24, 1923, President Calvin Coolidge signed a proclamation creating Allegheny National Forest. This new piece of public land was to cover approximately seven hundred forty thousand gross acres in Warren, McKean, Elk, and Forest counties. Inside this area—bounded on the west by the Allegheny River, the south by the Clairon River, the north by the New York state line, and the east by a line running south from near Bradford, past Kane to Ridgway—the federal government would consider purchasing whatever land was available. Within three years roughly two hundred forty-five thousand acres of brush land was added to the public domain, land that made ideal habitat for the whitetail. When coupled with the new game laws and stocking efforts of the Game Commission, it soon produced an explosion of deer.

VIII

Buck Fever

Picking and searching, the herd drifts closer. At its head is a big doe, followed by two smaller ones and then three more, too far away to identify. In and out of the gray-green boulders and open timber they move, disappearing behind a hummock on the mountain's side, reemerging to chew on a fern or sniff at a twig. The lead doe looks in my direction. Something seems wrong, ever so slightly askew. But I am hidden in the tight fork of two trees growing close together and she cannot place the problem. She nips at a dormant bud, takes a few steps, and stares again. The others glance at her and then toward me, but never stop feeding. Through my binoculars, I see the third and fourth deer are does, too. The fifth holds behind a boulder. I wait. It takes another two steps and its head shows. A buck! I drop my binoculars and go for my rifle. I have him all the way. Then the alarm clock buzzes, driving the image that has been replaying in my head for the past half hour into consciousness. It is finally time. I throw off my sleeping bag, slip on my wool socks, hunting pants, and lined flannel shirt, then climb down the ladder to the bedroom below.

When I reach the still humming clock in the living room, though, I see it is only twenty after four. I had not paid close enough attention to the dial when Bob asked me to set the alarm. We had agreed that a quarter to five was early enough. Bob, who is sleeping on the bed next to the door, now awakes

79

long enough to ask the time. When I tell him, he rolls back toward the wall. Nobody else stirs.

Since I never have been able to sleep much on opening day, and enjoy being alone in the quiet of the early morning, I light-foot it into the kitchen to make a pot of coffee. Remembering the density of Uncle Pete's brew, I hope it is strong enough, and then sit down at the corner of the table to stare out at the dark river. The positive feelings of last night are still with me. A good sign. But I do not want to dwell on them to the point of harming my concentration. I look at the thermometer on the tree. Forty degrees. It will be colder on top of the mountains, in the woods, but almost unbelievably warm for the end of November in northern Pennsylvania.

As the smell of brewing coffee begins to fill the kitchen, Dad steps out of the middle bedroom wearing his orange hunting pants and scratching his head. He asks if anybody else is up, and I tell him I set the clock too early. Then he walks over to the kitchen window and checks the thermometer. He, too, cannot believe the temperature. Weather takes on a whole new importance during the hunting season. Men who live most of their lives under climate controlled conditions must, like their ancient ancestors, adapt to the weather during deer season. On a late fall day in the mountains, it can rain, snow, turn foggy, sunny, windy, and then eerily calm all within a single hour.

■

By the time the first skillet of bacon is popping, Bob and Garth drift into the kitchen. Their laughter and easiness of the night before, however, has given way to a serious quiet. We pour coffee and make small talk about the weather, lunch, and equipment. When somebody asks about Mike, Bob says:

"He better get up, 'cause I'll leave him. I've done it before, I panicked. It was a little after six. I left them."

"The whole camp? " I ask.

"Yeah," he smiles. "They had to get another car. I mean there were vehicles there and they knew where we were hunting. But I took off."

The story makes Garth chuckle. But only for a moment. Everyone is too far into his own thoughts to joke. Then a dazed Mike appears in the doorway with his hands stuffed deep into the pockets of his jeans.

"Your Dad was gonna leave you," Dad tells him.

Mike shrugs as if he has heard the warning a thousand times before, and then walks over to the refrigerator and takes out the orange juice.

With everybody awake, breakfast moves quickly. Garth works on the toast and then, after the Thermos bottles are filled, another pot of coffee. Bob starts the eggs while I continue with the bacon. When everyone has eaten, there is a colliding rush to make sandwiches and a last minute check of equipment. Finally, Dad's Bronco and Bob's Blazer are loaded, "good lucks" exchanged, and we are out the door.

■

Normally, the road in front of the cabin would be silent and empty of traffic in the predawn hours. But nothing is normal on the first day of buck season. Even before we pull out, three vehicles pass. As we turn around at the end of the road, three more appear heading up the mountain. On the way to Tidioute the lights of at least a half dozen others cut through the dark.

Though all of the stores and bars are closed, Tidioute itself is so alive with traffic and people it could be eight o'clock in the evening. I glance at the signs in the store windows— "Welcome Hunters, Come In and Browse," "Good Luck Hunters"—then automatically check the vehicles parked in front of the Landmark Hotel. I am searching for my Uncle Joe's Bronco but do not really expect to find it. Now in his mid-seventies, he can no longer walk without a cane. But one of my cousins might have borrowed it to come north from Cincinnati or Pittsburgh. For years we stayed at the Landmark, making our reservations for the next year the day we left for home. Its crooked floors, ancient gas heaters, sagging beds, and doorless bathrooms will always symbolize for me a real mountain hotel. A good time. Chili in the bar. Deer hanging from the second floor balcony. Lining up at the phone booth out front to call home. Counting the antlers on the bar walls. I wonder if the rooms look the same or have been remodeled. Last year I stopped in the bar for beer, but it has been fifteen years since I was upstairs. For a moment, I think it might be fun to stay there again sometime. I can see my brother and Dad, Uncle Joe, and my cousin, Timmy, twenty years ago marching down the dark halls in the same silent anticipation that filled the cabin this morning.

As soon as we cross the bridge over the Allegheny, we find ourselves in a line of traffic moving up the mountain. We are the third vehicle in a line of five. In front of us is a truck with New York plates and ahead of it one from Ohio. For as long as I can remember, I have heard Pennsylvania hunters complaining about "those guys from Ohio." I don't know if resident hunters in other states have a similar attitude toward nonresidents, but in Pennsylvania the out-of-state hunter seems to be blamed for practically every game law violation or lack of etiquette that occurs during a season. Believing that every group contains a certain number of slobs, I have tried to avoid placing any undue blame on "those guys from Ohio." But I also have never given them credit for what they do for hunting in Pennsylvania. And probably I still would not except for talks I've had with people from the Game Commission and Forest Service who pointed out that most of Pennsylvania's nonresident hunters are people who used to live in the state, but had to move for jobs or other reasons.

"That nonresident hunter who's paying eighty dollars for his hunting license is paying a disproportionate share of the cost of wildlife management in Pennsylvania," Ted Godshall told me. "Absolutely. If you're selling a million resident licenses at twelve dollars apiece, that's twelve million dollars. But if you're selling seventy thousand nonresident licenses at eighty dollars a piece, thats six million dollars. The nonresidents make up only 10 percent of the hunters, but they're paying a third of the bill. We used to have over one hundred thousand, but when they jacked up the price to eighty dollars that cut back the total to seventy thousand."

■

Hunters and daylight appear in fits and flashes in the mountains. At one moment we are in a line of vehicles, the next we are alone in space. Then we are running a guantlet of cars, trucks, four-wheel-drives, vans and RVs. Thirteen in one indistinguishable spot. Twenty-six on a bend. Fifteen in a Game Lands parking lot. Blaze orange moves around the vehicles, highlighted in the dull streams of flashlights, the glow of trunk and dome lights, and an occasional lantern. On the edges of the road, our headlights turn the hemlocks to silver.

"Holy smokes!" Dad shouts when a hunter absently wanders out of the pack onto the road in front of us. "Come on, buddy! Wait 'til I get through here."

Foot traffic on the back roads of the mountains on the first day can be as stupid as in any city. Whether it is the anticipation of the hour, a sense of being in another time, or simply the absence of concrete and glass, I don't know. But every year men who should know better step in front of our Bronco. They have done it even on days when the roads were so icy a person could barely stand on them and vehicles were sliding from side to side like billard balls.

Rounding another bend, the sky lightens so suddenly it is startling. It is a phenomenon I have noticed many times before in the mountains, but never so strongly, it seems. I wonder if the surge has something to do with the angle of the clouds or the height of the mountains, and then if dawn comes the same way in Irwin. Probably it does, but I have never paid attention to it. Or maybe it's just lost in the street lights, traffic, and electric signs. The idea makes me realize how far earning a living has taken me from the natural world. My grandfather was always talking about the light or the feel of the air or the look of the clouds when I was a boy in the country. Now, practically the only contact I have with nature are planned outings. Other times I live in the world of a person who works at a desk. How nice it would be to have a cabin in the mountains where at the end of the day I could step outside to watch deer and downy woodpeckers or listen to a distant stream and see the sun settle behind a stand of pine instead of a Gulf sign.

■

In the dark, in the mountains, even a familiar road can confuse. Several times we think we are coming to the Forest Service road we want only to spot a landmark that proves us wrong. We do it so many times, I have to wonder if our confusion might have something to do with the sharpness I feel growing. Very soon now we will be in the woods, waiting and watching for a snatch of movement, straining our eyes in hope of antlers and our ears for the sound of dead leaves rustling under hoofs.

When we finally reach the road a slight disappointment strikes. Eight vehicles are parked around the gate. Though it is nearly impossible to find a backcountry access road without vehicles parked adjacent to it on opening day in Allegheny National Forest, the sight of so many makes me think I may have made a mistake in urging Dad to try this new way back to Baldy. Not half as many vehicles would be parked at the trailhead we used to use on the other side of the mountain, because the walk in is tougher. Down one mountain and up another. Around deadfalls and over rocks. Through marshy springs and across creeks. The road, on the other hand, is completely level. I like that for Dad. I would never say anything, but he is the reason I searched out the road. "These mountains are tough on those old-timers," Bob told me last year. I noticed then that Dad no longer moves as fast as he once did. He is in good shape for a sixty-five-year-old, but his best is long past. With the aid of the road, I hope to add a few more years to our time together on Old Baldy.

As we ready our equipment, I keep reminding myself that Baldy is immense and few hunters are likely to go all the way back to where we hunt. Chances are good we will be able to avoid a crowd. I think of the time my Uncle Ernie came Up North with Dad and got caught in a crowd. Every time he heard a shot, he ran to the opposite side of the tree where he was posted to hide. Dad still teases him that he spent the entire day running in circles. A lot of nonhunters worry about getting shot. With all of the rocks, trees, and hollows in the mountains to catch a bullet, though, I have never really worried about it. Most hunting accidents involve turkey hunters dressed in camouflage clothing, not deer hunters in blaze orange. During deer season, more people seem to die from heart attacks caused by climbing up and down the mountains when they are out of shape.

■

The sky is already light enough to walk without a flashlight by the time we step around the ends of the gate. It is later than we would like. Nearing seven o'clock. But I am not worried. Larry Benoit, a Vermont hunter famous for taking big bucks, says the only hunters who need to be in the woods before daylight are those whose sole chance of success lies in waiting for a buck to walk up to them. Then the hours before nine o'clock are critical. Hunters who make their own luck, or are expert trackers, such as Benoit, can enter the woods later and find success. Though I will never be in Benoit's class as a hunter, I have accepted his statement about time. I've only shot one buck before nine in the morning. All the others were late in the morning or in the afternoon. Or the week. A paralyzing icy storm on the first Saturday about five years back kept us from getting into the woods until after nine. Twenty minutes later I had my first eight-point. Of course, there was a lot of luck that drove the buck toward me and made him stop broadside twenty yards away. But it started me believing the best time to be in the woods hunting deer is whenever a hunter can make it. Especially if he is willing to work hard—sneak, and watch, and listen, and go into the tough places the others avoid.

It is almost two miles back to where we hunt. As we walk, the day brightens in quick snatches. I turn my head or lower my eyes and when I look up again the sky has gained another watt. Suddenly a shot booms in the distance. I check my watch. It is two minutes before seven.

"How in hell can they see to shoot?" Dad asks.

When I was a boy, I often hoped for a quick, predawn shot to get me out of the cold and rain and snow, but I never got it. Now, I would regret it, feel robbed. Besides, I don't understand how anybody can tell a buck from a doe in such darkness. The only explanation I've heard came from a retired Pittsburgh police detective who said he shot a buck early one season when it stepped out onto a logging road and light reflected off its antlers. I suppose it happens. But what a waste. A whole season gone within an hour.

A second shot explodes then. Much closer. I check my watch again. It is two minutes after seven.

"Are you loaded? " I ask Dad.

"No," he answers.

We scan the dark woods in the direction of the shot, unsling our rifles, and quickly load, our eyes focused on the darkness from where the shot came.

■

In the clearing at the end of the road we split up. I post on a sandstone ledge running along the top of the ridge. Dad starts down into the laurel where he lost a buck last year. He had had one shot, taken it, and hit the buck. But not hard enough. The deer ducked behind a rock and, while Dad was waiting for him to come out, another hunter finished him off.

The rock I have chosen is in big timber with little brush in the way. I can see a couple of hundred yards in every direction except to my right, where the laurel starts about twenty-five yards away and quickly fills the landscape. The view is fine but the area too open. There is nothing to attract deer—no food, no cover. Still, anything can happen on the first day with so many hunters in the woods. I tell myself to wait a half hour and lean back against a tree.

A few minutes later, threatening gray clouds gather and a light hail starts to fall, rolling off the collar of my Woolrich down my neck. I button the collar of my shirt to stop the flow and stare ahead at a cairn erected by eons of freeze and thaw. All faith in the spot begins to slip away. I am beginning to feel edgy. Though barely fifteen minutes have passed, I decide to leave the shelf and drift down the mountain to a spot where we have taken several bucks. I pick my way slowly, pausing at the corner of a boulder to survey the terrain ahead. Then two beech trees sharing the same root system. Then a small hemlock. The hail picks up, and picks up some more, bringing with it a haze that quickly obscures most of the mountain. Once I missed a buck in a similar mess. He ran straight up to me. Stopped no more than twenty yards away. But it was so hazy and snowing so heavily I could not make out if it was a buck or a doe. By the time I found his antlers he had spotted me, too. For a brief moment everything froze. Then he gave what might be described as a shrug and tore off in a quick bound down the mountain. I missed him four times. Across the creek at the foot of the mountain he ran into another hunter who was ready, though, and brought him down. A four-point.

■

By eight o'clock, the mountains thunder with the sound of high-powered rifles. The noise rolls off distant ridges and echoes up the stream valleys on either side of Baldy. Surrounded by so much shooting, I feel the woods must be full of bucks and wonder when my chance will come. The edge builds. Every speck of movement brought by the breeze that has started to blow catches my eye. A flapping shread of bark on a downed tree could be a deer's ear. Branches rubbing against each other turn into a deer's snort. A dead leaf still clinging to a tree becomes a twitching tail. Even after I identify the movement, it still catches my eye again and again.

Sneaking always nearer to Ricky's Rock, I stop on a small mound where three trees grow together. Such spots make good stands because they provide cover in almost every direction and allow a hunter to brace his rifle against something solid. From my new position, I scan the mountain as far as possible through the hail and fog, searching for anything horizontal. Individuals who do not hunt think the way to see a whitetail in the woods is to look for the entire deer. But that normally leads to nothing. A good hunter looks for something that does not belong, for pieces of the animal. An ear or pair of legs. Rump or brownish back. Most objects in the woods are vertical, so anything horizontal should instantly draw a hunter's attention. Looking for an entire deer is the way to go home without seeing a thing.

Hearing, too, is very important when it comes to finding deer in the woods. At times a whitetail can move as silently as a shadow. But just as often they make as much noise as the clumsiest hunter. Or at least enough so they can be heard coming before they are seen. Dried leaves and buried twigs crinkle and snap almost as easily under a hoof as a boot.

■

As eight-thirty comes and goes, I begin to feel a bit anxious over my failure to see deer. Carefully, my eyes search through the woods. A mistake many hunters make is to leave a spot before giving the territory around it one last hard look. On a stand, the mind can wander and become careless, and a hunter neglects to watch a section of woods. Then he stands or steps into the open, and a deer, or even an entire herd, bolts from fifty yards away, maybe taking with them his only opportunity for a buck.

When nothing shows around me I step out from between the trees and start up the mountain to a collection of boulders at the top. I think maybe with all of the shooting a buck has sought refuge among the many paths winding through the rocks. We have jumped deer from the spot in the past. Then, as soon as I enter the rocks, a turkey flushes. A big turkey. Crashing through overhead branches, he goes up no more than fifteen yards in front of me. A perfect shot. I smile.

■

A half hour later I am back down the mountain near Ricky's Rock. The hail and fog have given way to light snow flurries. A shot sounds just over the ridge, and then another off toward the face of Baldy. For a second, I wish I had stayed in the rocks. The first shot sounded so close to them. I stare up the mountain and think that if the shot was a miss the buck might come my way. Three of my bucks have come in that manner.

As I watch, the snow picks up, further reducing visibility. Then, at ten after nine, I see my first deer of the season. Moving at a fair clip, but without excitement, they come up a shallow crease in the mountain maybe fifty yards to my right. I inspect each one through my binoculars, but I cannot raise antlers. Eight does. Still, the sight renews my edge.

The does' winter grey coats allow them to fade quickly into the haze of the background. When they are gone, I better arrange myself to watch the route for a buck. Then the snow changes back to hail, cutting visibility to the point where I feel as if I am hunting in a cloud. The hail striking the crisp, dead leaves and trees takes away most of my hearing. Waves of sound flood over everything. I glance up at the sky and try to remind myself that the deer are deafened too. That makes me feel only a little better. I squint down the mountain at the place where the does had emerged, but see nothing. I wait.

■

After forty minutes of seeing and hearing nothing but a woodpecker tapping at dead tree, I abandon the stand and slowly weave my way to the rock with the small hemlock atop it where Dad often sits. As I move, the hail and haze turn back to snow which begins to cover the ground. Three shots sound in rapid succession from below Ricky's Rock. I curse myself for not having gone down that way. Then a fourth blast echoes up at me. I think it is probably to finish off the deer, and I relax a little.

A moment later, however, another rifle goes off. This one is so close it makes me flinch. I step behind a tree. Maybe this time a buck will be pushed toward me. And then, maybe 150 yards away, a deer trots through the woods. I wrestle my binoculars from my coat and hurry to focus in on it. Another doe. She looks back over her shoulder and then nibbles on something growing at her feet, takes a few steps, and repeats the procedure. Perhaps there's a buck running with her. I lower my binoculars to take in the wider view, but see nothing. When I look back the doe is staring straight at me. I feel confident she cannot see me behind the tree, but I wait until her head is turned before I bring the binoculars up. A hunter can be standing in the middle of a clearing, without any cover whatsoever, and not spook a deer if he remains motionless. The deer will see him, have an idea something is not right, but if he does not move they will seldom spook. Biologists say the whitetail lives in a black-and-white world in which even blaze orange is not an assault on the senses.

Through my binoculars, I watch the doe slowly browse her way in a line just above the lip of the mountain and disappear in and out of the trees. No matter how many times I have seen it, I am still amazed at how a deer can vanish behind a single tree and then, the next time I see it, be looking directly at me. I think the doe in front of me now would be an awfully long shot with my open sights. I study her face. It has the clear, open look of a young pup. Probably a yearling. I lower my binoculars and then, almost immediately, spot another deer moving up behind her. Quickly, I press the glasses back to my eyes and search the trees for the second deer. When I finally pick it up, I see it, too, is a doe. Together they move off past Ricky's Rock and toward the creek below. My brother's old stand must still be in a high traffic area.

Looking at the rock, I find it impossible to believe twelve years have passed since he last sat on it. For three or four years in a row he had taken bucks off it, all of them with the same shell, or rather the same casing, that he reloaded at the start of every season. After the accident, it had been terribly painful to go back to Baldy and see the rock. So painful that Dad wanted to give up deer hunting altogether. But now the mountains bring mainly happy thoughts of him. Memories of the morning we both took bucks within an hour of each other, and then when we got home had our Uncle Ernie pose between them with a skillet because he was always teasing us about never bringing anything home for the skillet. Then there was the season he reloaded his shell with the maximum amount of powder and hit a spike so hard he knocked it against a tree and scattered fur for twenty yards around. And the time he shot his big six-point. We helped him drag it to within a half mile of the truck, then told him we were going back to hunt for a couple of hours. When quitting time came, we found him only about a hundred yards from where we had left him. That was as far as he'd gone because every hunter who passed had stopped to admire the deer and talk to him. "He spent the whole time, bullshittin'," Dad would tell everybody later, but his eyes were sparkling with pride. Deer season always makes him live again for a few moments.

■

As the morning wears on, the day settles into a rhythm. The sky brightens and the snow on the ground melts. Then the clouds return and fog fills the air between the trees and it begins to hail. The hail changes to snow and the fog lifts. The ground turns white and then the clouds part and sunshine floods the woods.

Sneaking from stand to stand, waiting and watching the rocks and big timber and the cut area back toward the road, I am surprised at how many deer I see. They seem to be everywhere—the most I've seen in a single place since I started hunting. A herd moves along the lip of the mountain where I can barely make them out with binoculars. From behind me three does quick-foot it past to the right. An old doe focuses in on me, stomping and snorting to find out what is in back of that tree, while the young one with her nips at a shrub. The herd of eight appears again heading over the top and then later trotting back down. Four suddenly run by, spooked by somebody above. Between two boulders three pause. The third one does not show for a long time and makes me imagine a buck, but when it finally steps clear it comes without antlers.

At noon I stop to eat my two ham sandwiches. Midday is usually the worst time to hunt because deer are bedded down, but not on opening day when so many hunters are in the mountains. I finish my sandwiches and wash them down with water from a tiny spring. When I drink the water, I think of my high school chemistry teacher twenty years ago saying he always carries a Thermos of water into the woods with him when he is hunting because "you don't know if there is a dead deer lying a hundred yards up that creek you're drinking out of." I remember an article I read warning against drinking untreated water from streams because giardia cyst have been found even in the backcountry of the Rockies. I think Pennsylvania is nowhere near as clean as the Rockies. My mind tells me I am being stupid, but I have been drinking from the streams around Baldy for so long I feel I am immune to any nastiness. "Mountain dew," Dad used to call the water when we were kids and he brought it home.

When my sandwiches are gone, I wonder what has happened to Dad. Normally, we run into each other a couple of times during the course of a morning in the woods and often have lunch together. But I have not seen him since we left the road. I hope one of those shots from the laurel was his and he is dragging a deer out. Then I push myself up and drift to the top of the mountain in search of dragging signs. If he has a deer I want to help get it out.

Finding no drag trail, I head back into the woods and further down Baldy. Most of the deer I've seen have been low on the mountain. The only ones near the top have been those crossing over. Then the hail and fog come back with a vengeance, carving visibility down to only fifty yards. A cartoon from an old issue of *Pennsylvania Game News* flashes in my mind. The first frame, labeled "1944," shows a miserable GI marching through a snowstorm and swearing that when he gets out of the army he will never go out in such weather again. The second frame, labeled "1964," shows the same man dressed in hunting clothes walking through a similar storm. He has a wide smile on his face, and the caption reads "Every deer season since."

■

As my watch pushes past one o'clock, I begin to think it is time to start working my way back to the Bronco. Something tells me I have seen all the deer Baldy has to offer. If I hunt slowly, I should reach the Bronco right about quitting time.

But I don't have much faith in seeing deer along the way. Too many hunters had been strung out along the road when we were walking in. The deer on the way back will probably be spookier than on Baldy. I slowly rise from the log I am sitting on and head for the fence at the end of the road. I lift the overhead gate and step through, then pause to survey the scene. In front of me is what looks like twenty-five acres of cut timber, brush, and saplings. The Forest Service has rimmed it with a six-foot fence to try to keep the deer out and give the young plants a chance to grow. It is ideal habitat, full of browse and cover, but it doesn't inspire me. I see plenty of tracks running along the outside of the fence, but none inside the wire. I think not many deer have been jumping the fence. Then I look across to the next ridge and a hunter on the rock. The area is so open that if deer were in it he would have to be blind to miss him. I sling my rifle over my shoulder and start down the road.

On the other side of the clearing, I enter big woods that run to the bend in the road where there is another, smaller timbered area with a thick stand of saplings next to it. Having seen plenty of rubs on trees along the edge of the stand during turkey season, I think a buck might be hiding in the heavy cover and pick my way to a spot in the center of the cut area where I settle down to watch the saplings.

Without trees to block the wind and snow, a chill soon penetrates my Woolrich. I raise my collar to block what I can and wish I had worn a hooded sweatshirt under my coat. My shivers remind me of the igloos my friends and I used to build when we were kids. I have not thought about those days for years. That is another part of the allure of deer hunting. Time alone on a stand brings back so many things. Some people might call it escape, but I don't believe that is the right word. And if it is escape, so what? There are worse ways for a person to flee the world. I like remembering igloos and my brother and mountain dew and the Landmark Hotel and the thousand other things attached to deer hunting in my mind.

I am still lost in my thoughts when a shot blasts on the other side of the saplings, snapping me awake and confirming

my thoughts about a buck hiding nearby. The cold disappears
from my back and my mind clears. The edge returns. I wait,
trying to burn a hole through the saplings with my eyes, but
once more nothing shows.

■

It it two-fifteen when I have my first contact with another
human being since leaving Dad. A father and son. I meet them
walking along the tram road on the far side of the saplings.
The son, who is not carrying a rifle, tells me he dropped a
spike in the morning. They dragged it out together and now
want to see if they can scare up another one. The son is going
to drive the saplings for his dad. Considering the size of the
stand, I don't see much chance for success with one hunter
driving, but I wish them luck anyway before moving on.

The sound of voices, even the whispered voices we were
using to avoid alerting any deer in the area, is disturbing after
being enveloped in the flow of the woods all day. The world of
man has returned. Though in reality that world has never
truly left. Airplanes have been passing overhead all day, and a
few times I thought I heard a chain saw. But those were distant and detached. The father and son were in front of me. A
news story I saw a few weeks ago comes to mind. It was about
a man in Oregon or Washington who took two years off to
record the sounds of nature. It took him a year and a half to
find one spot where planes were not lining the skies overhead,
trains rumbling down a track in the next valley, or trailer
trucks humming on a highway a couple of mountains over.
Being so accustomed to those sounds, we usually do not hear
them. But the voices of the hunters could not be overlooked.
They demanded a response, and, in the process, a spell was
broken.

■

Deafening as a freight train riding the eighth notch, a wind
roars through the trees as I find myself a spot under three
small hemlocks and settle in to watch a gully of rocks and
more hemlocks. It continues to blow hard until almost a quar-

ter after three. Then, as suddenly as if someone has thrown a switch, it stops. A silence so heavy it verges on spooky descends upon the woods. I close my eyes and lean my head back against the trunk of one of the hemlocks. The mistakenly early morning and tough hunting up and down Baldy are exacting their toll. My head nods.

■

When my chin hits my chest, I snap awake and, blinking automatically scan the woods. Nothing. I can feel myself giving up. I check my watch. Only a few minutes have passed, but even that small amount of sleep has refreshed me. I glance over the gully again to make sure a deer has not wandered near while my eyes were closed. Then I push myself up and slowly begin to move in the direction of the Bronco.

Morning in the mountains may come in snatches, but darkness seems to fall evenly. In the fading light, I think more about returning to the cabin and finding out how everybody else has done than spotting a buck. Out of habit, though, I stay in the woods about a hundred yards off the tram road and pause to look every few minutes. During turkey season, we saw deer several places along the road and nobody knows where or when a buck might show.

Moving at such a slow pace, I find myself still a good half mile away from the Bronco at four-thirty when practically all of the light is gone. I decide it is time to give up completely and head for the road where I pick up my step. I know Dad will be worried about me. No matter what their age, parents never stop being concerned for their children, and to Dad, Allegheny National Forest remains the unmarked wilderness he was lost in forty years ago. The crisscrossing presence of dozens of hiking trails and roads cut by the oil crisis of the 1970s mean little to him. One of the first things he taught my brother and me when he brought us to the forest was that if we got lost we should follow a creek downstream. Sooner or later it would lead to a road and a way out. That remains the way he looks at the forest.

In the disappearing light, I pick up several signs of dragging in the mud and snow-covered parts of the road. A hope builds that the marks were left by Dad. It has been five or six years since his last deer, I think, and then I am hit with a sudden fear that something might have happened to him. I remember what a friend of mine said a few years back about how our parents are getting older and we have to start assuming some responsibility for them. I have not seen Dad all day. That has never happened before. Not in all the years we've hunted together. Even though he is in good health, I cannot keep from imagining him lying hurt or sick in the winter woods. I see him with a leg broken in a fall, and with a heart attack brought on by dragging a deer without my help. I tell myself I'll never leave him alone in the woods so long again. I think if anything has happened I will be to blame. Faster and faster I start to walk, straining to catch some sign of the main road. A truck's headlights. The street lamp above the trailer across the road. The sound of a passing car. But nothing comes. I wish I knew the tram road better so I would have an idea of how much further I have to go. Then I glimpse the light above the trailer and, finally, the Bronco. It looks as if he is inside, but I am still too far away to be certain there is an orange hat in the window. Then I see the windshield wipers move and breath easier.

"Did you get a deer?" I ask as soon as he unlocks the passenger's door.

He purses his lips and shakes his head.

"Everybody else is already gone," is all he says, and I can see he is upset with my lateness.

IX

Leatherstockings

Pennsylvania produced one of the best-known hunters in history on November 2, 1734, when Squire Boone and the former Sarah Morgan, Quakers who came to Pennsylvania to escape religious persecution in their native England, became the parents of a son they named Daniel in Oley Township, Berks County. As the model for Natty Bumppo, the hero of James Fenimore Cooper's classic Leather-Stocking Tales; mentioned in Lord Byron's epic poem *Don Juan*—"Of the great names which in our faces stare / Is Daniel Boone, backwoodsman of Kentucky"; the namesake of eight counties, twenty-two towns, countless rivers, mountains, and roads; a character in a dozen movies and hero of a long-running television series, the name Daniel Boone is known to practically every American from childhood.

But such notoriety also long ago metamorphized Boone from flesh and blood into a national myth. Even when nuggets of truth can be gleaned, Boone does not teach us much about hunting in Pennsylvania during the pioneer period. Daniel was only fifteen years old when his family moved to North Carolina. Though he returned to Pennsylvania as a wagon driver for both General Edward Braddock, in his disastrous expedition against Fort Duquesne in 1755, and General John Forbes, in his successful capture of the fort at the forks of the Ohio three years later, he never lived in his home state again. Today, he is much more closely associated with Kentucky than his birthplace. Many people do not even realize he was a Pennsylvanian.

Fortunately, however, another frontiersman, a contemporary of the elderly Boone, did choose to remain and hunt in Pennsylvania. And, a year before his death in 1855, he produced a book entitled, *Pioneer Life; or, Thirty Years a Hunter.*[1] Though published only in a very small edition, never widely circulated, and almost lost (a state history buff managed to borrow a copy and bring out a second edition of five hundred copies in 1928), it must rank as one of the greatest hunting books ever written by an American. "The late Theodore Roosevelt once said that no matter how thrilling a hunting narrative might be it had no appeal to him if it was not good literature," Henry W. Shoemaker, then chairman of the Pennsylvania Historical Commission, writes in the preface to the 1928 edition. "To such an exacting standard *Pioneer Life, or Thirty Years a Hunter* would meet the erudite 'faunal naturalist's' views exactly. As a work of literature, as well as of absorbing interest this book by Philip Tome can be unhesitatingly recommended as the great, outstanding contemporary narrative of the Pennsylvania big game fields" (p. vi). The *Saturday Review of Literature*, in an article on a second, small reprint of the work published in 1971, called it "a source book for the mores of the fringe of the first American frontier."[2]

■

Philip Tome was born March 22, 1782, in Dauphin County on the edge of Harrisburg. He thought his parents were of German extraction, but historians have determined them to be French Huguenots. When he was four years old, his family moved up the Susquehannah River by keelboat to what they called Farris Creek, now known as Larrys Creek in Lycoming County. They stayed only about four months before an Iroquois uprising drove them back south to Cumberland County and a small house five miles outside of Harrisburg. There they remained for three years, until the troubles with the Indians subsided, and then headed north once more, this time to Warry Run, described as about two miles above the junction of the North and West Branches of the Susquehanna River, or near the present town of Northumberland.

In 1791, Tome's father, Jacob, purchased four hundred acres of land near the Slate Run tributary of Pine Creek in Lycoming County and paid a group of men, in advance, to build a house where he planned to move his family. The men raised the walls and roof, but left the house without chinking, a chimney, door, windows, or floor, and with bushes ten feet high growing in the center. The family—father, mother, three sons, and two daughters—survived its first night on the frontier only with the aid of a large fire and the placating effect of Philip's mother on his father. Two days later, they had the walls of the cabin chinked, a chimney built and the floor cleared and laid. A month later the nine-year-old Philip had his first experience with the hunt.

"At that time game, such as bears, elk, deer and wild turkeys were very plenty in that section of the country. I had two brothers old enough to hunt, but they had no gun except an old musket which my father had used while training. In the morning we would frequently find the deer feeding within twenty rods of the house. Sometimes we would see a drove of elk, fifteen or twenty in number, crossing the river. At other times we saw bears traveling back and forward. But we had no hunters among the six men [Jacob, his three sons, and two hired hands], and no gun but the old musket, and that was out of order. On the 5th of December two of our nearest neighbors, (who lived twelve miles distant) came to see us, bringing two guns and two dogs, but no ammunition. There was no powder or lead in that part of the country except what my father had, and he supplied them what they needed. They then hunted about two days for my father to procure him a supply of wild meat. Notwithstanding they were little skilled in hunting, and the weather was unfavorable, they killed four deer, and two large fat bears" (pp. 2–3).

Five days after the family's arrival on Pine Creek, Jacob Tome began work on a mill. He had to cut, hew, and split all the logs, build a dam, and dig a race for the waterwheel, but still managed to finish it all in a little over three months, giving the Tomes the only gristmill within thirty miles.

Though Jacob was not a hunter when the Tomes moved to Pine Creek, the need to provide for his family in the northern Pennsylvania wilderness eventually forced him to become one. And, by the time he was thirteen years old, Philip was accompanying his father on extended hunting expeditions for elk and deer. Then, at the age of seventeen, he signed on to replace a sick member of a survey crew that had been sent out from Philadelphia to map the country around Pine Creek. They came traveling in "a keel boat loaded with flour, pork, sugar, chocolate, tea, and all kinds of clothing for the men" (p. 20). His reverential tone shows how startling was such abundance to a family used to living on wild plants, game, fish, and the odd patch of wheat they managed to grow in the deep forest. Tome left home with a warning from his father not to get lost and returned with an intimate knowledge of the region.

Not long after Tome returned from his surveying job, he received his first formal lessons in hunting from an old hunter named John Mills who lived nearby. Mills wanted to move to Canada and offered to sell Tome his dog and teach him everything he knew about hunting for $15. "The following autumn," he writes, "I went out on a hunting expedition, taking with me the dog I had bought of Mills and another one which I had previously owned. I followed the directions I had received, and with a success which showed their value. From the early part of October until the first of February I killed twenty-eight bears and a large number of deer. Mills also taught me, among other things, how to train dogs for hunting, as well as the kind of animals to select" (p. 106).

■

Many of the deer hunting methods employed by the frontiersmen—salt licks, hounding, and fire hunting—are illegal today and have been illegal since the late nineteenth century. But they remain fascinating examples of how the pioneers

adapted and survived with little more than their own inge-
nuity to depend upon.

"During all my hunts I kept a constant lookout for deer
licks, and if I found none in a place favorable for deer, I made
one near an unfailing spring. The manner in which I made the
lick was to bore several holes in a black oak log with an augur
which I always carried with me for the purpose, and into them
put about three pints of salt, with a small quantity of salt-
peter, and insert a plug in each hole. The wood soon becoming
saturated with the salt, the deer would gnaw it. If I found a
lick to which the deer at the proper season resorted, I proceeded at once to build a scaffold, in order that the deer might
become accustomed to the sight of it before I made use of it. If
a tree stood within three or four rods of the lick I built my
scaffold upon that. If there was no tree in a favorable place, I
set four crotches in the earth, lay poles across, and make a
screen of bushes or bark to conceal myself from the deer. . . .
In hunting at these licks, I mounted the scaffold by a ladder
which I drew up after me, and patiently awaited the approach
of the deer. If none came during the day, I prepared a torch of
pitch pine, sometimes adding lard or bear's grease, which I
swung upon a pole reaching from the scaffold to the ground.
The torch was attached to a crane of withes and bark, made to
slide upon the pole, and slipped down by a cord to within
three feet of the ground. As the deer came along, they would
stop and stare at the light, forming an easy mark for me"
(pp. 104–05).

Fire hunting, another method that depended upon the
whitetail's fascination with the unnatural light from a torch,
was done along rivers and streams from a canoe and with
a crew of hunters. Tome would occasionally do it with his
brothers while out spearing eels by torch light.

"Sometimes as we were out fishing, deer would come to
the river to eat moss, within sight of us. When we saw them,
we would all get into the canoe—one held the light, another
sat in the forward part of the canoe, generally with two guns,
and the third one sitting in the stern, would push the canoe

along the stream as carefully as possible. Sometimes we could approach so near as to shoot them as they raised their heads erect to look at the light. Sometimes they would stand still long enough for the hunter to bring down a second one with the other gun. At other times they would start away, when we would wave the light, and as they ascended the bank they would become frightened at their shadows, thinking it was a wolf or panther, and run directly to the light, where they remained looking at it, till we could get another and perhaps two more shots at them. In this manner we would proceed up the stream from five to six miles, and in that distance we could often kill from two to four deer, and if the night was favorable we could catch from sixty to a hundred eels, besides a quantity of salmon, pike, and rock-fish. We would generally fish while passing up the stream, and hunt in passing down" (p. 26).

Early hunters also took advantage of the whitetail's fondness for open spaces and the easy browsing they afforded in the midst of heavy forests. On occasion, the method was even refined to include the use of a fence to hold the deer in the open as long as possible.

"In 1805 a colony consisting of about forty families of English people, made a settlement between the first and second forks of Pine Creek. They cleared about two hundred and fifty acres of land, and built several good houses, but being unaccustomed to the hardships and dangers of pioneer life, they abandoned the settlement after struggling along for five years. As soon as the coast was clear, the deer from all the country around came to feed in the cultivated fields and sunny pastures of the deserted settlement. This afforded a capital opportunity for hunters, and the place became a favorite resort for them. We would lodge in the upper story of some deserted house, and in the morning looking out of a window, could see perhaps forty deer. I have often shot a couple of deer from the window before leaving the house in the morning" (pp. 106–07).

Good dogs were extremely important to the pioneer hunter. Tome preferred the larger variety of dog, "half bloodhound, a quarter cur and the other quarter grayhound." Two dogs of such a mixed breed were better than four smaller ones, he maintains, claiming his own would not lose one out of ten deer once they picked up a trail. "Those wishing to hunt successfully should always procure at any cost, the largest and best dogs to be found," he counsels. So famous were his own dogs in the mountains of northern Pennsylvania that when "neighbors saw them running, they would exclaim, 'There are Tome's dogs; the deer cannot be far off'" (pp. 107–08).

As strange as it might seem in view of the animal's evil reputation—undeserved though it may be—wolves were another predator used by the frontier hunter to take deer. Tome actually sought to have wolves accompany him on hunts. Sometimes they even worked with his dogs to corral and bring down a deer. Usually, however, one would chase the other off.

"During the first few years of our residence here, we would often look up the [Pine] creek in the morning, and see a deer, coming at the top of its speed, followed by three or four wolves—sometimes two on each side of the creek. We would immediately prepare and go out to meet them. Sometimes we captured the deer with very little trouble, but often the wolves would catch and spoil it before we came up. In this manner the wolves ran the deer from the first of July until the last of January. During the winter, when the river was covered with ice, the deer would fall into the air holes and become an easy prey. We took off the skin and if the deer did not prove to be very good, we would leave half of it to the wolves, but if it was good, we left the refuse parts to encourage them in pursuing the deer. . . . we considered them of great assistance to us in hunting. As there was no bounty on wolves at that time, and we had no sheep for them to kill, we never destroyed them. They often aided us to three or four deer in a week. When we were fire-hunting, and had killed a deer, we often stopped to dress it, and left the wolves their portion, and if we had not the fortune to catch one, we would catch fish and leave them, to keep them in our vicinity. The howling of the wolves upon our track was generally mingled with the scream of wildcats, and often they would fight over the food we left them. Frequently when our dogs were chasing a deer the wolves would take it from them, and the dogs would sometime take one from the wolves in the same manner. The wolves and the dogs would often be in pursuit of the same deer, but when we were near enough, we could generally take it from them" (p. 29).

Although the pioneer hunter would resort to any method or trick to keep his larder full, as well as obtain game for barter and sale, his feel for nature, the harmony Cooper writes about, is evident throughout *Pioneer Life.* In "Hunting Deer at Different Seasons," Tome relates changes in whitetail behavior and movement during the usual hunting season of June to late January, revealing a knowledge of the animal and its movements possessed by very few outdoorsmen today. "In June they frequent beech and maple woods, or feed in the marshes bordering on the streams. About the last of July they take to the highlands, among the chestnut and white oak woods, feeding on pea-vines and other herbage. In the hot weather of August they lie in the thickest shades upon high hills, and at this time the manner of hunting them is to watch by a spring, as near the summit of a hill as may be found. . . . The last of September the deer begin to leave the thickets and move from one place to another, and for several months they are constantly in motion. The hunter has only to station himself near one of their paths, and shoot them as they pass. When the first snows come they can be tracked to the places where herds of them lie at night, and the hunter can keep near a herd and pick them off with his rifle. . . . Every seventh year in April, they move west in herds of from three to fifteen, generally going about thirty miles from their usual haunts, and remaining, if undisturbed until some time in July. If they are molested, they return at once to their old haunts. . . . From the last of June until September, deer are light and in good condition for running, and at this season they are not easily run down. . . . By the last of October they are very fat, taking immediately to the water when pursued, and do not cross it, but run either up or down a mile or two, so that the dogs lose their scent" (pp. 106–09).

Tome's hunting expeditions have been described as Homeric odysseys that ran for a month or more at a time.[3] Deer and elk hunts were viewed as arduous affairs, almost military campaigns, terminating only when the snow melted and the tracks of deer and elk could no longer be followed. Like the modern hunter, Tome also started his hunts well stocked with all the essentials and more. Venison or elk, of course, was the meat dish during a hunt. But plenty of flour, potatoes, sugar, chocolate, and corn also were hauled into the woods, the same staples people in the towns were living on at the time. When Tome and his companions reached a town or farm, they also traded venison for bread, vegetables, and whatever other food items were available.

Among the equipment carried by the typical four-hunter group that Tome favored were a canoe, six empty barrels for meat, a large iron pot, a kettle, four axes, one broad axe, a chalk line, a canoe howel for bailing, a drawing knife, two augurs for making salt licks, six tomahawks, three to four pounds each of black powder and lead. Personal gear included a rifle and musket for each man, two knives, a quart cup, four shirts, two blankets and, somewhat surprising for the period when personal cleanliness left a lot to be desired, an ample stock of soap. Accompanying the hunters, too, would be four good, large dogs. Two hunters would generally paddle the canoe, while two others would hunt the banks (p. 63).

Despite the fact that he was hunting to survive and would use any trick to take a deer, Tome also shows a great respect for the whitetail and a certain ethic to be followed when hunting. "I never wantonly killed an animal, when I could gain nothing by its destruction," he writes. "With a true hunter it is not the destruction of life which affords the pleasure of the chase; it is the excitement attendant upon the very uncertainty of it which induces men even to leave luxurious homes and expose themselves to the hardships and perils of the wilderness" (p. 100).

■

Pioneer Life is an important, exciting, and literate account of life on the state's northern edge before the lumber companies destroyed the primeval forests and the market hunters slaughtered the deer. Frequently the author pauses in mid-narrative to describe the settings of his hunts in great detail, though his sense of distance and size sometimes is off the mark, as when he estimates the height of the mountains above Pine Creek at a mile.

Within Tome's descriptions of the wild land also can be seen the seeds of future destruction. They appear in the form of the first sawmills, the disappearance of wildlife in certain areas, the discovery of coal, the spread of farming, the selling of game in the marketplace and, even at that early period, the clogging of the Allegheny River with timber rafts on their way to Pittsburgh. "When the business was driven to its extent in 1836–38," he writes of local lumber baron Guy C. Irvin's operation, "he frequently sent to market twenty million feet of lumber in a single season, and both shores for a mile above Pittsburgh are sometimes lined with rafts, waiting a rise of the water" (p. 119).

Elsewhere, he foreshadows the days of market hunting and the decline of game: "Fish and venison being so abundant in the vicinity where we lived, and very scarce at the mouth of Pine Creek, twenty-six miles distant, we used them as articles of traffic, and by exchanging them with inhabitants there, for wheat, rye, corn, buckwheat, salt, leather, and other necessaries, we obtained a supply of those articles" (p. 26).

■

While he does not discuss his schooling in *Pioneer Life,* the quality of the writing and range of observation shows Tome to have been an educated man and no backwoods illiterate. Probably he was taught by his mother, Jane, and his father, who has been described as "an active and enterprising man" (p. 146). And hunting was not Tome's only pursuit. At one time, he served as interpreter for the famous Indian chiefs Cornplanter and Governor Blacksnake. The final chapter of his book is a reminiscence of Cornplanter. He relates several incidents about the chief's childhood and dealings with the whites, including attempts by the Warren County Commissioners in the early 1820s to collect property taxes on Indian lands. "The old chief resisted, conceiving it not only unlawful, but a personal indignity. The sheriff again appeared with a small posse of armed men. Cornplanter took the deputation to a room around which were ranged about a hundred rifles, and with the sentious brevity of an Indian, intimated that for each rifle a warrior would appear at his call. The sheriff and his men withdrew, determined to call out the militia." A group of local citizens intervened, however, and convinced the old chief to pay $43.79 in taxes. Cornplanter did it, but then complained to the governor, who returned his money and exempted him from paying property taxes in the future (p. 126). It may be one of the few times the Indians ever won in their dealings with whites.

■

Glimpses of Tome's character are evident throughout his book. He seems to have been a generous man, always ready to share his hunting success and help a friend in need. Though quite sure of himself, he was not cocky or abrasive. Neither did he take himself too seriously, as can be seen from a fire hunt he and two friends conducted in July 1805. "When we had gone a short distance farther, two of us saw a deer in the stream, and both fired at the same time, but neither appeared to hit it. We re-loaded and directed the man who was steering to run the canoe to the shore. We then stood on the shore, about thirty rods from the deer, and each fired eight shots at it, as rapidly as we could load, when our guns became so hot that we were compelled to stop. The steersman had been holding up the torch for us to see by, yet the position of the animal was the same as when we first observed. At each shot it had seemed to spring up, each time higher and higher, and dropping into the same spot. We now threw sticks at it, to drive it away, when it gave two or three leaps, and suddenly disappeared. This affair may appear somewhat strange to the reader, as it did to me, but the facts are as I have stated, and always appeared to me unaccountable" (p. 81).

Perhaps Tome, the man, is best revealed in this account

of a hunt down the Allegheny River from Kinzua Creek to Franklin in 1823 with "a Mr. Whitmore," Marshall Whitcomb, and John Campbell. "That evening I was at Oil Creek, three miles below, and there I heard that two men named Carns, had threatened, if we hunted any farther down the river, to shoot our dogs, tar and feather me, and then, if the others did not leave the vicinity, to treat them to a coat of the same. I told my informant that I should come down there and hunt, and give the Carns an opportunity of executing their threat, if they could; but I thought it was a game at which two could play. I considered their interference entirely uncalled for, unless I killed a deer on their own land. Mrs. Holiday, who kept a tavern for raftsmen, said they were ugly men, and advised me to keep away, as she was unwilling to have an old customer injured. The next day the Carns went down to Franklin, five miles below their residence, and said that a man named Tome, and two others, were hunting down the river, killing all the deer, and that they would tar and feather him, kill his dogs and send him home, if he came any further down. They asked a man named Thomas Hewling, who kept a tavern there, what sort of man Tome was. Hewling said he was a good-natured sort of man, but if they attempted any violence they would find trouble, as he was a stout, active man, and not easily frightened. Campbell was rather timid, and thought we had better leave the vicinity. I told him that I should hunt there one day, at least, to see what they would do. Whitmore went off with the dogs in search of deer, and I told them if they would hunt down the river to Franklin I would join them there at night. Whitmore proceeded to hunt on one side of the river, and I on the other, within fifty rods of the house of one of the Carns. Before I had been there a long time, Carns came out and asked if I was hunting in their vicinity. I replied that I was, as game was more abundant there than where I lived. He said that he would join me a short time, and I told him that I had no objection to his taking an equal chance with me. Whitmore killed a deer in the water, and drove another into the river which Carns shot, and we divided it equally with him. On our arrival at Franklin we found Campbell there, with a large buck which he had killed. The next day we killed in that vicinity three deer, the following another, and the next day two more, when we started homeward. While going home, the water was so high that we did not try to fish, except in one place, where we obtained over one hundred fine salmon. We killed, during the hunt, sixty-seven deer. This was my last hunting expedition" (p. 96).

Philip Tome died on April 30, 1855. The site of his home, like the village of Kinzua, near which it once stood, is now under the waters of the Allegheny Reservoir. His grave lies near that of his friend, Chief Cornplanter, in the Riverview-Corydon Cemetery on a hill above the reservoir just below the New York state line.

X

Counting Coup

Twisting to catch the glow from the light above the trailer, I unload my rifle and slip the shells into a pants pocket. Dad watches, pointing out again that we are the last hunters leaving the woods, and then, for good measure, adds he has been waiting for almost an hour. I say nothing, experience having long ago taught me it is better to keep quiet when his voice takes on the sharpness it has now, and crawl into the Bronco.

"There's a big one running around," he tells me, as he shifts into drive. "Four guys missed him."

"In a row?" I asked, surprised.

"He run right past them," he says, his voice full of contempt at their marksmanship. "The one guy missed him, couldn't have been fifty yards away. In the open. He went right over top the mountain, right past where you was standin'."

The disappointment I was beginning to feel at having hunted so hard without seeing a buck suddenly turns to chagrin. A big one had passed my first stand, the rock shelf I left because it did not feel right. Lack of patience had cost me a chance at a trophy.

"Two years he told me it's been runnin' around," Dad continues. "He was the first guy to miss it."

Staring ahead at the dark, I imagine a buck as large as Dad's ten-point trotting up to me and stopping, head held high, for a perfect broadside shot. I am disgusted with myself but try not to think about what happened. As far as we know, nobody got the buck. Maybe I'll get another chance at him, I think. But I know trophy bucks do not make the same mistake twice or they would not have grown to be trophies.

"They were all running along the fence," Dad says.

"That was where I kept seeing them, too," I answer quietly. "All does, though."

He mentions then how all the deer he saw were on the bottom of the mountain. I tell him I noticed the same thing. Nothing was holding on top. Even the deer I saw on top were just crossing over heading for the bottom.

"I saw a lot of deer around Ricky's Rock," I tell him.

"That's where all the shootin' was," he says, and then falls silent. Although a dozen years have passed since my brother's death in a one-car accident, Dad still finds it difficult to talk about him; but deer hunting has helped him tremendously.

Part of his immediate reaction to Ricky's death was to announce he was giving up hunting. He said he could never go back into the woods without my brother, but the family agreed he had to. Though Baldy would have been too much that first season after the accident, we persuaded him to go to State Game Lands 42 near New Florence in Westmoreland County. It turned out to be the best therapy possible. Neither of us returned with a deer, and Dad has never said anything about what might have gone through his mind that day, but from then on, he was on the road back.

"Guy said you didn't even have to use a scope," Dad starts again, his voice softer, as we pass the sign for Hearts Content. "He was runnin' with two doe. He said the two doe come and then that buck come right after them."

"He say how big he was or anything?" I ask, though I have never quite understood how someone can take the time to count a buck's points before shooting.

"He just said he had a big rack on him."

Another twinge of disappointment hits me.

"The only hunter I talked to got a spike," I offer.

"That green truck that was parked where we was at, they just pulled two out," Dad says. "Loaded them in the back and left."

"Spikes?"

"I don't know what they were."

We both turn quiet then, watching the edges of the road for the orange glow of whitetail eyes or the shadows of hunters. But the skittish deer are staying back in the woods, and all the vehicles that were parked along the road are gone. The only hunters we see are moving in the light around cabins.

We see some deer hanging from poles and crossbeams at camps near the road, but it is too dark to make out the size of all but a few. Riding down the mountain in the dusk of opening day and pointing out cabins where bucks are hanging has always been a favorite little part of deer hunting for me. Counting coup, as the Indians used to say when they touched a worthy opponent in battle. When I get a deer, the sight of one hanging outside a camp gives me a pleasant feeling of kinship with both the deer and hunter who shot him. When I don't get a deer, the sight makes me try harder. I wish I had left the woods earlier so we could see better.

"I wonder how Bob and those guys did?" I say absently.

"I don't know," Dad answers, and we stare at the road.

■

Tidioute is the same blinding array of lights as in the morning, only now there is more activity on the streets. Men dressed in orange pants and wool seem to be everywhere, ducking in and out of the hardware store and supermarket, pumping gas, laughing their way into bars and restaurants, jumping in and out of trucks and standing, hands buried deep in their pockets, remembering on the sidewalks. After the quiet and dark of the mountains it is almost startling.

"There's one." I motion my head toward a buck hanging from the second floor balcony of the Landmark Hotel.

"Yep," Dad answers.

On the hotel's porch there's a line of hunters waiting to call home from the public telephone. Dad and Uncle Joe, their pockets bulging with change, used to do the same thing when we stayed at the hotel. I hope there is always a telephone at the spot and, for a brief moment, I long for the days when we stayed in the hotel. I see my cousin, Tim, and myself, fourteen and fifteen years old, walking Main Street, eating hamburgers in the little restaurant across the street that either burned down or was knocked down by the tornado, I cannot remember which, and then nosing around in the sporting goods store next to it. We had felt so grown up, being on our own like that in a town so far from home, though Dad and Uncle Joe were only upstairs in the hotel. I never even missed having a television in our room. We would read in the evenings—*Sports Afield, Field & Stream, Outdoor Life.* Typical fare for hunters. Sometimes Dad would bring a cheap detective magazine. One season during college I brought along a copy of Albert Camus' *The Plague.* My existential period.

Although it is just a few days after Thanksgiving, several houses in Tidioute already are decorated for Christmas. In a couple of windows there are even Christmas trees visible. The only places back home with holiday decorations are department stores and malls. I don't know anybody whose house is decorated so early. But every year at deer season a good share of Tidioute is outlined in lights. I have often wondered if people do it for the hunters. After all, buck season brings a lot more people and money into the town than Christmas.

As the last of Tidioute's old Victorian houses gives way to the first hunting camps, I feel myself getting anxious to see Bob and Garth and Mike. Hear how they did. Success has eluded us recently. Bob, Mike, and Garth have taken does, but my eight-point last year was the first buck for any of us in the past few years.

"Looks like they're there," I say, when the lighted windows of the cabin come into view.

■

Before Dad is on the steps leading to the cabin, I am at the back of Bob's Blazer. The windows are so dirty it is difficult to see inside, but I can make out a head and a pair of eyes.

"Somebody got one," I yell to Dad and then dash up the steps into the cabin. Garth is standing alone in the middle of the living room with a Budweiser in his hand. "Do I see a couple of eyes staring at me from the back of the Blazer?" I ask smiling.

Garth only laughs.

"Two?" Bob says, as he walks through the hallway between the kitchen and the living room. "You sure you don't see six eyes?"

"You get three?" I ask in disbelief.

"We coulda got five," he says.

"Are you serious?" I ask, thinking they are probably putting me on. Led by Garth, I can see them planning it since they got back, setting us up for a laugh during dinner.

"Go look," Bob tells me.

Dropping my rifle and coat on the bed against the wall, I run back outside to the Blazer, cup my hands around my eyes to shield out light from the street lamp above the cabin and dart from window to window until I am sure there are at least two deer inside, one a spike. I think they might not be needling me after all. Then a twinge of jealousy strikes. I feel the gulf that separates successful and unsuccessful hunters. I hope the season is not over and they will not want to head home tomorrow.

"I can see a spike and another one," I say, when I walk back into the cabin. "What did you guys get?"

"Two spikes and Garth got an eight-point," Bob tells me.

I look at Garth. He is still standing in the center of the living room, smiling and sipping on his Budweiser. I think he looks suspiciously calm for somebody who is quick with a story and has just taken his first buck. I wonder what happened. But then I remember how I had tried to downplay my first buck, pretending it was nothing out of the ordinary, something I had done before.

"Your first buck!" I smile and extend my hand. "Congratulations." Garth laughs and thanks me. "Didn't I tell you I had a good feeling," I add.

"You called it," he says.

"Nice deer, too," Bob says, and then tells Garth to go out and open the back of the Blazer for a better look.

Dad and I follow Garth out the door and wait to the side as

he drops the tailgate. Then we move to check his eight-point. The rack is not heavy, but the tines are long and well shaped. We both congratulate him again. He says he is going to have it mounted. Then Mike appears and we look over the spikes. His is the larger of the two and was the first deer of the day. Bob's was the last. They were finished hunting by noon.

"I coulda gotten a better one," Bob tells me, when we're back inside the cabin, "but Mike and Garth already had their bucks and I didn't want to make them wait all day for me."

"The pressure was on," Garth teases him.

Bob ignores the remark and says he wants to butcher Garth's deer after dinner. One shot hit it in the side, soiling some of the meat with digestive juices. He thinks if he butchers it now, instead of waiting to get home, and then soaks the damaged meat in salt water he will be able to save most of it. The idea exhausts me. Pumped full of the adrenaline required to stay alert, I usually don't feel tired in the woods. But back at camp, enveloped in the overheated atmosphere of a wood stove, a bone-deep fatigue can take over. Add dinner and a couple of beers and bed is not far off. I think if the deer were mine, I would let it go until morning. But the tone of Bob's voice says his mind is made up. I walk into the kitchen and take a beer from the refrigerator. The smell of chili simmering on the stove makes my stomach growl.

■

"Saw this old guy in the woods today," Bob starts, breaking the fatigued silence of a meal that up until then had been mostly the clink of stainless steel on porcelain and mumbled requests for crackers and pepper. "He hunted over there for twenty-eight years and he got his first deer. He shot five shots at it. Then he reloaded the gun and got it with the sixth shot."

"What?" I laugh.

"The deer never ran out of there."

"He was probably so confused. With all the noise he didn't know what to do," I say.

"I ask him, 'You always hunt here?'" Bob continues. "He said, 'Yeah, always under that tree.' That's his problem right there." He shakes his head and looks at Garth. "Yesterday, how far did we walk? About three miles?"

"Oh, yeah. At least," Garth answers.

"We didn't see anything. I said, 'This ain't where we're gonna hunt.' We rode up there where they're startin' to log. We looked at all them new cuts and I said, 'I don't even have to see no deer. We can hunt here.' And that's where they were at."

"Exactly, right," Garth agrees.

"You got to move around," Bob says then. "You can't hunt the same stump every year. You are not going to be successful if you do. You've got to move around."

Bob's talk of hunting the same area season after season makes me think about Baldy. It has been several years since either Dad or I have taken a deer off the mountain. I wonder if tomorrow we might not be better off hunting the tornado area where I got my buck last year. I recall Brad Nelson, a biologist with the Forest Service, telling me the tornado was a "real blessing for the deer," opening up four hundred acres of big woods to new growth. Browse that attracted deer like a magnet does iron ore. Then I picture Baldy the first time I saw it twenty-four years ago. There was definitely more brush on it. More ferns, too. I remember watching deer nibbling their way through big patches of ferns. Now the ferns are only scattered here and there. I think Baldy is probably in the pole timer stage, but that does not quite jibe with the more than forty deer I saw during the day. Even discounting the repeat appearance of that herd of eight, I still saw at least two dozen deer. I had spent many days in more accommodating areas without seeing anywhere near as many. I guess the timbered areas and saplings on the back of the mountain must be what has kept deer on Baldy. Most of the deer Dad and I saw were running to or from those areas or along their edges. I think maybe we should go back tomorrow and hunt closer to those places.

"I have a half a dozen hot spots," Bob continues. "I found them through turkey huntin'. Usually, that's how I'll find a good spot. I'll find it beforehand, during turkey huntin'. I might hunt every one of my spots in a season. Six, I prefer."

Garth, looking as if he has heard it all before, suddenly pushes his chair back, walks into the kitchen and calls out for seconds. Dad gets up from the far end of the table and follows him. Then Mike rises and leaves to find more crackers. The commotion stops Bob's dissertation, but only for a moment.

"Beaver down there," he tells me, when everybody is gone. "They're already choppin' trees down." He pauses for another mouthful of chili, and then adds, "You can hide there. Allegheny National Forest."

"It's a big place," I agree.

"That's one thing nice," he says then. "They'll never get all the deer. There's just too much area to cover. It's spotty. There are places where you can hunt—"

"And not see any," Dad breaks in as he returns.

"Hunters," Bob looks at him. "That's what I look for. I stay away from hunters. But then you'll find places there ain't enough hunters. You have to be in those areas on days when it's suitable for that kind of huntin'. If the ground's crunchy, you have dry leaves or frozen leaves, forget it. You ain't gonna hunt those places by yourself."

"While I was waitin' for him to come out," Dad says, nodding toward me, "I counted thirty guys comin' off that one road."

"How far does the road go back?" Bob asks.

"At least a couple miles," I tell him.

"All right, that ain't many guys if the road goes back three miles."

Dad tells him hunters also were coming out of the woods further up the road, across from a collection of cabins.

"That's why I don't hunt on this side of the river," Bob says. "You go up over the hill and there are too many huntin' camps. These guys think they got to hunt right beside their cabins. You see a hunter here a hundred yards, you see a hunter there a hundred yards. You try to circle around them, you try to go up in between, there is another hunter there a hundred yards. I don't like to mess hunters' stands up. I try to walk around them, but you can't. You will not find a place to hunt on this side of the river without seeing orange."

Although we saw more hunters than I can ever remember around Baldy, very few were more than a hundred yards off the tram road. The thought makes me remember another remark from the Vermonter Benoit, about all white men being afraid of the woods.

"Boy, that Allegheny National Forest," Bob says, full of admiration. "You can always find a place to hunt by yourself without other hunters. And you can still-hunt. Provided the conditions are there to still-hunt. There's snow, or the leaves are wet. Not crunchy. And what I mean by still-huntin' is not stump huntin'. What I mean is you stalk a little bit, stop, stalk. It might take you three hours to go two hundred yards. You know what I mean? "

Bob's mention of still-hunting leads me think of an article I read a couple of months earlier about Theodore Van Dyke and his book, *The Still Hunter: A Practical Treatise on Deer Stalking*. Before seeing that story, I had always thought still-hunting meant stump hunting, sitting in the woods and waiting for a buck to wander past. While I was familiar with the technique of still-hunting, and had practiced it for much of my deer hunting career, I hadn't known what it was called.

"I walked on deer today that were feedin', never spotted me," Bob starts again, as Garth and Mike gather their bowls and dump them in the sink, then disappear into the living room. They look as if they have heard enough of Bob's stories. "Let them feed away from me. When you see them feedin' a hundred and fifty, two hundred yards through the trees you can do that. People think you can't hunt deer that far away. you can do it if you look."

"Where we were today," I tell him, "you could hunt even further than that. It was really open in that big timber."

"I've let deer feed away from me," he says. "I didn't move because I didn't want them spookin' and runnin' out of the area."

I tell him of the eight does that kept circling up and down the mountain. He says if I had moved and scared them they would have taken everything out of the area. We both mention the possibility of a buck following a herd of does, using them as decoys. But I have never actually seen that happen. I know both Dad and Bob have taken bucks trailing does on several occasions, but not me. Four of my bucks were running with does when I got them, but that was not the same. I realize I have been repeating things I read or heard, without personal experience to back up my statements. I need to spend more time in the mountains.

"Did you ever watch a group of bucks in the woods? " Bob asks.

"Not a group. No," I say.

"I've seen them, three and four together. Did you ever see them go along sniffing the ground? " I tell him I have. "Maybe they're looking for a deer herd. Maybe they're eatin'. Who knows? I don't know what they're doin', but I've seen them. I've seen them walkin' along with their heads on the ground." The tone of his voice becomes incredulous. "They're not walkin' to hid their racks."

"That's what a lot of people think," I tell him, and then add, "I've seen them do that. I stood up above this little swamp and had one pass no more than ten feet from me and not know I was there."

"I've seen already three big racks walkin' together," Bob continues. "I've seen three buck and another deer, probably a small buck that lost his horns, together—and the same thing. They were sniffin' the ground. I don't know whether they're eatin' or lookin' for does."

"I'll have to check that out," I tell him.

"I've seen a buck jump on a doe too," Bob says then. "I didn't have a buck yet. I was all excited. I was ready. But when I got a good look there was no horn whatsover on that deer. It was a matin' buck without horns. And this is the truth. I know for sure it was a buck because that deer got off and he walked right up to me. He was within thirty yards when he finally looked at me. And it was a ruttin' buck because he didn't even get scared. He just walked away. And there was no bone on his head at all. Whether he lost them, maybe he was a buck who never grew horns, I don't know. But he was a nice size deer." He pauses for a second, staring out the windows at

119

the reflected darkness. "I hope it got killed in doe season, because it wouldn't be good breedin' stock. You'd end up with a lot of bucks that are maybe button bucks or a lot of small spikes forever."

■

By the time Dad has finished the dishes, everybody is comfortably sprawled in the living room staring at the television, hoping to catch tomorrow's weather and maybe a piece on the start of deer season.

Bob ignores the news and everybody's condition, though, and announces he has decided to butcher not only Garth's eight-point, but his spike, too. It will save him from doing the work at home, he says, and a moan passes through the room. Beaten down by a stomach full of chili, salad, and beer, I can barely imagine changing clothes, let alone butchering a deer. I hope nobody is offended when I don't volunteer to help. Neither of the deer belong to me, I tell myself as an excuse, and I would not expect anybody to handle my deer. "You shot it, you clean it," my mother always told us, making it plain she had no desire to act out the Great American Myth of the pioneer woman in a time of processed foods.

A movie I saw several years ago comes to mind. In it, the actor playing Franklin D. Roosevelt complained about being unable to get fresh orange juice, only "this thing in a can." Then I recall how my grandfather used to raise chickens, ducks, geese, pigs, and rabbits for the table, and grow all the family's vegetables, which my grandmother canned for use during the winter. That was self-sufficiency. Probably there are still some people like that around, but nobody I know. Now the "thing in a can" is the norm.

We gave up butchering our own deer several years ago when Dad began taking them to the butcher shop where he buys most of his meat. For twenty-five dollars and the hide, he can get a buck cut into steaks, chops, and roasts, ground into hamburger with pork added for a little fat, and then wrapped into individual packages for the freezer.

When I was younger, and money was tighter in the family,

Dad used to butcher all of our deer himself. He even bought a meat saw for the purpose. My brother and I would help him hang the buck by its hind legs from the garage rafters. Then we would watch as he skinned it and cut the carcass into quarters. We would salt the hide to preserve it for sale to a local fur dealer, cut the antlers off with a hacksaw, and collect the legs and head and other leftovers for the garbage. When we learned more about Indians and the respect with which they once treated the whitetail, we began burying the leftovers behind the garage. I know the legs and head and the rest now end up on the butcher shop's refuse pile. What happens to them after that I have no idea, probably they are sold to somebody for processing into fertilizer, but I have accepted that fact as part of my adult life, where time is more important than self-sufficiency and, sadly, respect for the natural world.

On those occasions when I regret the change, I remember icy December days standing in an unheated garage waiting while Dad quartered the deer so we could carry it into the house. I recall the kitchen full of the stink of raw meat. And the hours spent cutting and trimming and grinding and wrapping venison for the freezer. Then I don't miss it so much.

"People today, particularly those from the urban, suburban environment," Ted Godshall once pointed out in a conversation we had, "do not realize that in order for a human being to live, something must die everyday. A human being cannot live unless something dies. They don't think anything about pulling a vegetable out of the ground, ripping it up by its roots, cutting off the top, taking a knife and slicing it down the sides, scraping the skin off, and chewing it up and swallowing it. They have killed that vegetable. Something must die in order for people to live."

Godshall's example is extreme, but, nevertheless, true. All of us kill continually, either directly or indirectly. *Homo sapiens* is, generally speaking, carnivorous, and we don't think twice about the beef or chicken or pork or fish that we buy everyday in the supermarket. But blood has been spilled in every instance, and perhaps far less humanely than in hunting, where a sporting code is followed. Moreover, the person who wants to abolish hunting and let nature take its course does not understand how man has disrupted nature with cities and farms, automobiles and airplanes. The size of the deer herd in Pennsylvania right now is unnaturally high because of land use practices (opening up the forests and planting of crops), selective hunting, and the destruction of large predators, all of which have led the whitetail to reproduce beyond the normal carrying capacity of the land. The alternative to hunting is to allow thousands of deer to die of starvation each winter.

A true hunter is as concerned about the preservation of wilderness and wildlife as any member of the Sierra Club or the Wilderness Society. As John F. Reiger points out in *American Sportsmen and the Origins of Conservation,* sportsmen "have become handy scapegoats for Americans unhappy with the declining populations of many wildlife species and the deterioration of the environment generally. The real causes for this wildlife reduction, 'development,' pesticide contamination, water pollution, etc., are generalized, amorphous phenomena that seem incapable of being controlled, while the hunter is a specific group that can be focused on and attacked."[1]

■

Bob has the hide half off Garth's buck by the time guilt finally gets the best of me and I muster the will to rise from the easy chair and walk down to the small cabin Uncle Pete built when he first bought the property.

"See what happened," He says when I enter. "This meat would be wasted."

Shuffling from side to side around the deer, he slices and pulls until the whole of the deep blue and red bruise left by the gut shot is exposed. Garth moves forward to examine the wound and then nods his agreement.

"I see what you mean, Bob. That bullet did do some damage."

The room is so tiny there is barely enough space for Bob to maneuver. Mike is squeezed into the far corner, while Garth is pressed near the door. Nobody is saying much. I watch the progress of the work for a few minutes and then, my worry about helping relieved by the sight of Garth and Mike standing idle, decide to head back to the big cabin.

I am barely inside the door when Mike appears. It is his third or fourth trip up from the river since the butchering began. On his other runs, he always left immediately, carrying rope or newspapers to cover the floor or some other ordered item. Now, though, he drops into the easy chair and pulls a jacket up over his chest.

"Cold?"

"I'm freezin'," he answers, and then adds with a glazed stare, "He has to have me next to him every second."

His remark makes me smile, but I know for him the situation is not so pleasant. Though I am eighteen years older, I always have felt a certain kinship with Mike. His thin build, scraggly beard, and wiry manner not only remind me of my brother, but the way Bob treats him is almost identical to the way Dad worked Ricky and me. I would not have believed it possible when we were the ones being taught, but Bob demands as much from Mike as Dad did us. Things will get easier, but at the moment Mike is a son straining to take the first steps out of a father's shadow. I think of the day last season when I got my buck. I was sitting against a tree waiting for everybody to come out of the woods when Mike and the friend who was with him appeared on the road. As soon as they reached me, they asked if I had seen Bob. When I told them he was looking for them, they said they knew and were hiding from him, trying to make him think they were lost. "Mike should know better!" his friend imitated Bob. "Goddamnit! I told them what to do!" They asked me not to say anything and then hurried off to hide and watch Bob's reaction, coming out only after he finished complaining and was about to head back into the woods looking for them.

"Okay. What happened today?" I ask, both because I haven't heard the story of the deer yet and because I think if Bob comes in and sees us talking he'll leave Mike alone.

"It was pretty good." Mike laughs and then pauses, staring

off at the door until I ask again. "Okay," he smiles. "In the bottoms, over in Queens. We were about three hundred yards up from the creek. Garth was down to my left about seventy-five yards. My dad was down toward the creek more. I couldn't see him.

"Anyway, I was sittin' there. One deer snuck past me in the morning, just before it was gettin' light. I saw him sneakin' down through the trees, but there was no way of me tellin' what he was. I scoped him out, but he just disappeared between the trees. It was too dark.

"So, I waited. It was a little before eight. I saw Garth lookin' down toward the creek. Then he raised his gun to look. I knew something was down there because I heard something rustlin' in the leaves. The leaves were still dry then. I pulled my gun up. Turned it up to nine-power and I saw some movement. Then I saw a deer. Garth was scopin' it out. The deer was comin' up closer toward us from the bottom. He was closer to Garth. I caught a glimpse of a horn. I think, 'Why isn't Garth firin'?'

"Still, I was just waitin' it out. Waitin' it out, wonderin', 'Why isn't Garth firin' at this deer?' Then I thought, 'Huntin' has been too bad over the last few years. I can't pass him up. It's eight o'clock. I can't pass him up.'

"So, I fired and the gun went—CLICK. I said, 'What's the matter with this thing!' I looked. I got a pump and it wasn't engaged all the way. I hit it. It went CLICK again. The deer heard it. He took off. They don't like that sound. But he didn't know where it came from. So, he came closer to me. He came runnin' around in front of me and off to the right. He slowed down to a trot. I had him in the scope. He stopped right between two trees. BOOM. I shot. He went right down. That was eight o'clock in the morning. I'd have to say it was the best huntin' season I ever had."

Mike is almost glowing by the time he finishes the story. We sit silent, Mike still lost in the day and me staring blankly at the television, until we hear a Bronco pull into the driveway and the driver jump out and head down through the yard to the small cabin.

"There's Eddie," I say.

Eddie Gretz is from the Pittsburgh suburb of Millvale and has a cabin on the mountain above Tidioute. Tall and powerfully built, with a shock of reddish hair and beard, he is another intense deer hunter. He began hunting Allegheny National Forest with Bob several years ago. Through the grapevine, he had heard about Bob and John Arva, a hunter from Monongahela in Washington County, and the success they had been having around Chapman Dam State Park. Eddie's brother-in-law knew Bob from fishing trips Up North and arranged for the two to meet. A good talker, Eddie is full of stories. Two years ago, he also was the victim of a hunting accident. He was shot in the head, hit by a couple dozen pellets from a shotgun, while turkey hunting. Before the accident, he was a strong believer in the necessity of camouflage clothing for turkey hunting. Now, he is just as certain a person can hunt turkey wearing blaze orange and has proved it by successfully doing so.

I owe Eddie an assist for my last buck—he was the one who jumped it and forced it in my direction—and I also want to congratulate him for the eight-point he called to tell everybody about earlier. But I am enjoying Mike's company and don't feel like moving. With so much going on and so many people around, it is not often two hunters get a chance to sit quietly and talk in camp.

"What happened with Garth?" I ask.

"Garth," Mike laughs and then stops.

I picture Garth dragging his first doe up the mountain with his pants around his knees and think the story must be a good one.

"Yeah," I say. "He gets his first buck and doesn't even talk about it. What's the story? It must be good."

Mike smiles and shakes his head, then starts: "I took my deer up to the Blazer. I was tryin' to get him up in the tree and I was by myself and couldn't do it. Finally, I managed to do it. It took me an hour or so. Then I left my gun at the Blazer and went down and sat beside Garth. I asked him where my dad went, and he said he went up over the peak and would meet us back at the Blazer at lunch time. This was around ten o'clock.

"So, we were sitting there. A few deer went past up the hill. They were does. We just kept sitting there. Then I looked off to the left. I said, 'Hey, Garth. Here comes two.' He scoped them out. I said, 'Can you see their heads?' He said, 'No.' They were only about fifty yards away, but they were up behind the trees. The hemlock.

"Anyhow, they knew something was wrong. They knew we were there. They kept lookin' in our direction, flickin' their tails. Finally, they shot off down toward the creek bottom. We just waited. 'Just wait a while,' I said. 'My dad says sometimes buck come behind doe.'

"Well, we waited, and sure enough, about ten, fifteen minutes later we see some more legs movin' under the tree line. They're comin' in the same direction. But these deer have their heads low. One of them, or all of them, had to be bucks I thought.

"Well, they came trottin' along and they stopped. Right where the does took off down the hill. But then they started comin' our way. I'm lookin' and lookin' and saw one deer had horns. He was the third one back. I said, 'Garth! It's the third one back. Get him!'" Mike starts to laugh again. "He's shakin'. He's lookin'. I said, 'Get him, Garth! Get him!' He's still lookin'. He's still shakin'. The deer start to run down the mountain. Garth knelt down and then—BOOM! Somebody else shot. The deer started around the side of us and the buck slowed down. The other ones took off. He was limpin'. Then there was another shot, and then Garth finally shot and finished him off."

No wonder Garth had been slow to tell about his deer, I think. But every hunter has deer they could have done better on. Once I missed a buck twice because I forgot to aim. He surprised me by running so close I could have reached out and touched him with the barrel of my rifle. I didn't hit him until the third shot when he already was running away from me.

"I was kinda pissed," Mike says then. "Why didn't I wait for that one. But, oh well, whatever."

"You don't know," I tell him. "If you had waited, that eight-point might never have showed up."

"Right," he agrees. "Tell you the truth. I think today was the first time I ever had a chance of seeing a buck in the woods and being able to shoot at him. Because all the other times I usually just see does. But that was an experience, seeing the buck coming and everything. Y'know, I got shook up."

"Hey, only a third of the hunters who go into the woods every year ever get anything," I remind him.

He nods. "Like they say, some people go in the woods and never get a deer."

I remember the hunter who wrote me when I worked for the newspaper. He got his first buck after thirty-four years of hunting. I wrote a special story about him.

■

After Mike leaves the cabin, I sit alone for a few minutes half-watching the Seattle-Raiders' game on Monday Night Football. Then I realize I haven't seen Dad since shortly after Bob said he was going to butcher the deer. I can't recall him going down to the small cabin. Slowly, I push myself up and stick my head into the middle bedroom. It is too dark to see anything, but I can hear light snores rising out of a bottom bunk. I pull the door closed and decide to head for the river.

Bob is working on the last quarter of Garth's buck when I step through the door. Eddie is in the far corner talking about other hunters he knows who got bucks, and Garth is leaning against the wall next to the door. Mike is on the side, fiddling with a screw driver. I exchange greetings with Eddie and congratulate him on his eight-point. I ask him where he got it and then, certain he already has told the story, let it go and lean a shoulder against the door frame to watch.

One of the reasons I enjoy hunting with Bob, Garth, and Mike is that nobody seems to get jealous when somebody else gets a buck. I have been out with a lot of jealous hunters, and I cringe at the idea of ever going with anybody like that again. I hate the way they degrade another hunter's deer and pick on little things until they fester and cast a pall over a camp. And then, when they are successful, they never stop talking.

Although nobody is bragging and I am comfortable enough

standing in the small cabin, I still feel left out. Separate. I am the only one without a deer. Everybody else can relax and joke. But I need to keep my concentration. Tomorrow is going to be a tough day. I cannot afford to let go if I want to be at my best tomorrow. Nor do I have a reason to let go.

When Bob is finished with Garth's buck, we help hang the other deer, bag the meat for the refrigerator under the back porch, and step back to watch as he begins to cut away the hide. Then I think it is time to head back for the big cabin and maybe bed. Not only can everybody else relax now, but they can sleep in tomorrow. Dad and I, though, have a full day of hunting waiting. And I still have that good feeling.

XI

Bearded Bards of Long Ago

If we are indebted to Philip Tome for providing a portrait of deer hunting in northern Pennsylvania during the pioneer period, then we are equally owing to E. N. Woodcock and Henry Shoemaker for preserving a record of hunting during the industrial period, the Golden Age of deer hunting. Woodcock makes his contribution through a 1908 autobiography. *Fifty Years a Hunter and Trapper*, and Shoemaker his through two works of folk history, the slim, little *Stories of Great Pennsylvania Hunters*, published in 1913, and the expanded 1915 work, *Pennsylvania Deer and Their Horns.*[1]

"From time immemorial the chase of the stag has added to the romance of nearly all the nations of the world," Shoemaker writes. "In India, in Japan, in Northern Africa, in Norway, Sweden, Germany, Spain and the British Isles, as well as North and South America, legends have clustered about it and made it a part of the national life. In Pennsylvania, where there was much diversity of race among the early settlers, and such an intimate association with the Indians, the picturesque side of the chase soon became a topic of absorbing interest. The hunters became a class apart, and those whom fortune most favored were linked with the supernatural. Feats of daring, such as climbing bold precipices, following for days the trail of some particularly mammoth Hart, coming out victorious in conflicts with hoof and horn of a wounded quarry, the slaughter of thousands of deer by certain individuals, raised the prestige of deer hunters to an extravagant degree" (p. 40).

■

Ethan Nathaniel Woodcock was born on August 30, 1844, in Lymansville, a small town in Potter County named after his grandfather, Isaac Lyman, who had served as a major in the Revolutionary War, and from whom Woodcock said he inherited "that uncontrollable desire for the trap, gun and the wild" (p. 15).

"In those days clearings were small, woods large and full of game," he writes about his childhood, sounding much like Tome more than fifty years earlier. "Deer could be seen in bunches every morning in the fields and it was not uncommon to see bear's track near the house that had been made during the night. Wolves were not plenty though it was a common thing to see their tracks and sometimes hear them howl on the hills" (p. 15).

Woodcock's first deer hunting experience came at the age of nine, when he took his father's shotgun without permission and hid near a salt lick he knew deer were using. He managed to knock down a buck, but was so shaken when the deer did not immediately die, he dropped the gun and ran home. His older brother was sent out to finish off the animal and drag it back to the cabin. After that day, though, the old shotgun was taken from its place in a corner of the kitchen and hung above the mantle, far out of reach of grabby little hands.

The loss of his father's gun did not stop Woodcock from hunting for long, though. Soon he entered into a deal with a neighbor who owned "two or three guns," and agreed to lend him one in exchange for whatever game he might obtain. Since he could not take home the game he killed without his parents finding out he was hunting, the agreement suited Woodcock perfectly. It lasted until his mother noticed a drop in egg production of the family's hens and discovered the young hunter was selling eggs for the powder and lead he needed for hunting.

Woodcock's mother died when he was eleven years old. His father, being busy with the family mill, did not have the time to watch his son after his wife's death, and the youngster began to hunt openly, ranging further and further afield. By the time he was thirteen, he was hunting with men twice his age and had killed his first deer. But, like Tome, he did not receive his first formal hunting lessons, from an eighty-year-old neighbor named Aleck Harris, until he was eighteen. "We made our camp in the extreme southeastern part of [Potter] County in a section known as 'The Black Forest,'" he notes of his outings with Harris. "It was here I made my first bed in a foot or more of snow with a fire against a fallen tree and a few boughs thrown on the ground for a bed . . . . It was here I first learned to do up the saddles or the carcass of a deer" (p. 16).

While *Fifty Years a Hunter and Trapper* is not nearly of the same literary quality as *Pioneer Life*, it actually provides a more complete picture of the hunter's life. For it describes not only hunting methods, as Tome does, but also ways of "jerking" venison, cooking beans, preserving hides, treating common ailments, and a hundred other camp chores, including building a comfortable hunting cabin. Woodcock and other hunters of the period often entered the woods in October and remained until the season closed in January, only occasionally visiting local farmers to make arrangements to have their deer shipped to New York, Philadelphia, and Pittsburgh. A good "shack" was therefore essential to their survival.

"We selected a spot on a little rise of ground near a good spring of water, and where there was plenty of small yellow birch trees handy to cut logs out of for camp," he says of a cabin he and his partners built near Kinzua Creek in 1865. "We placed a good sized log down first at the end of the shanty that we intended to build the fire place in. Another was placed at the end that was to be the highest, so to give the right slope to the roof. We always kept the large ends of the logs one way, so that when we had the logs rolled up it made the lower or eaves end of the camp about five feet high.

"There was a slope of about two feet for the roof. We felled bass wood trees which split in half, and then dug or scooped them out so as to make a trough. We notched the two end logs down and then placed the scoops or troughs in these notches so that they would lay firm with the hollow side up.

"After placing these scoops across the entire width of the shack we then placed another layer of the scoops (reversed) on the first set. That is to say, the roundings side up. This made a very good roof but required a good deal of chinking at the ends to keep the cold out, but as moss was plenty, it was not a long job. The second day after we got into the woods we had the camp in pretty good shape, well chinked and calked" (p. 69).

As hard as Woodcock and his friends worked on their camps, they worked even harder at deer hunting. "We were seldom in camp until after dark, and we were up early and had breakfast over and our lunch packed in our knapsacks," he writes of another season he spent along Kinzua Creek with William Earl, a hunter from Vermont, or "Varmount," as he called it. "The lunch usually consisted of a good big hunk of boiled venison and a couple of doughnuts and a few crackers, occasionally the breast of a partridge, fried in coon or bear oil. Sometimes the lunch would freeze in the knapsacks and it would be necessary to gather a little paper bark from a yellow birch and a little rosin from a hemlock, black birch or hard maple tree and build a little fire to thaw the lunch. This, however, was quickly done, and was a pleasure rather than a hardship. I have delighted in eating lunch in this manner for many a winter on the trap line or trail, as have many other hunters and trappers.

"Bill and I always had our lunch packed and ready to take up the trail at the first peep of day. Sometimes when we would get in late, tired and wet our clothes frozen, I would suggest to Bill that we shut up camp and take a wood job, just to see what Bill would have to say. He would say that there would be time to take a wood job in the spring or after he killed a certain large buck which is usually called 'Old Golden'" (p. 80).

The "wood job" Woodcock speaks about was that of a lumberman. The oil boom then underway in the Smethport-

Bradford area created a great demand for wood for drilling rigs and homes for new workers, as well as fuel to run the pumps. Many of Woodcock's neighbors would hunt and trap during the fall and winter, then leave their backwoods camps for homes in Bradford, Warren, Port Allegheny, Emporium, and other towns in the region, where they would work in sawmills and on lumber crews throughout the spring and summer. They went back to the woods in the fall despite the fact they could have earned more money at their "wood jobs." But, as Woodcock notes, "won't a man do more hard work to get thirty cents out of a coon skin, or a saddle of venison, or bear, than he would to get thirty dollars in some other way?" (p. 153).

Although *Fifty Years a Hunter and Trapper* contains the usual stories about successful hunts, Woodcock also tells of the less than heroic outings every hunter knows. He frequently comes home empty-handed, and he even admits to twice suffering from "buck fever," becoming so excited when a herd of a dozen deer appears unexpectedly in front of him that he misses them nine times. He calls stories about "blood-curdling and hair-breath escapes from wild animals," something that was prominent in the hunting literature of the period, mostly "pipe dreams" (p. 226). But he does admit meeting "with many queer circumstances while on the trap line and trail," like the deer charmer he encountered during a hunt in wet snow in Cameron County in 1869.

"I was working my way very cautiously along the side of a ridge and down near the base of the hill in low timber, as that is the most natural place to find deer in a storm of this kind. I had just stepped out of the thicket into the edge of a strip of open timber where I could see for several rods along the side of the hill. I had barely stepped into the open when I caught sight of some object jumping from a knoll to a log where it was partly concealed behind some trees, so that I was unable to make out what it was. I was sure that I had never seen anything like it before, either in the woods or out in civilization. I could get a glimpse of the thing as it would pass between the trees, then it would disappear behind a brush or a large tree for a moment, then I would get a glimpse of it as it would move.

"Sometimes it would appear white and then a fire red, I could see that it was coming in my direction. As I always wore steel gray, or what was commonly known as sheep gray clothing, which is nearly the same color of most large timber, I stepped to a large hemlock tree, leaned close against the tree, set my gun down close to my side and stood waiting to see whether the thing was natural or otherwise.

"It was not long before I could see that I had been frightened without real cause, for it was a hunter who had dressed in fantastic array to put a spell on or charm the deer. He had on a long snow-white overshirt and had tied a fire red cloth over his hat and a black sash was tied about his waist. I stood perfectly quiet against the tree until the man was within a few feet of me, I could no longer keep from laughing, and I burst out with laughter. The man jerked his gun from his shoulder as he turned in the direction in which I was standing and gazed at me for a moment and then said, 'You frightened me.' I replied that I guessed that he was no more frightened than I was when I first caught sight of him.

"Well the man explained that he always dressed in that manner when the underbrush was loaded with snow, as the deer would stand and watch him with a curiosity until he was within gun shot" (pp. 135–36).

Woodcock missed only two deer seasons from the time he started hunting at age nine until his death at sixty-nine in 1913. Both of those seasons were lost because the gallon or so of spring water he drank everyday for his "roomatiz" failed to fend off the disease.

■

Shoemaker compares the state's nineteenth-century hunters to "the bards of long ago . . . bearded men, hoary-headed men, with keen, deep eyes, long thin noses and high cheek bones, men of action, probity and decision. Simple as the day God made the first man! "[2] Shoemaker himself, however, was totally unlike the men he writes about.

Descended from a Dutch couple who arrived in the New World in 1685 and settled in Germantown, Pennsylvania,

Henry Wharton Shoemaker was born in New York City on February 24, 1882. His father, Henry Francis Shoemaker, served as a first lieutenant with the 27th Pennsylvania Volunteers during the Civil War and, after the war, became chairman of the board of the Cincinnati, Hamilton, Dayton Railway and organizer of the Hamilton National Bank of New York. The younger Shoemaker attended private schools in the big city and Columbia University, which he left in 1900 to take a job with his father's railway.

After a few years working in company offices in New York and Cincinnati, and construction camps in the Midwest, Shoemaker entered the diplomatic service in 1904 as secretary of the American legation in Lisbon, Portugal. Later he was transferred to Germany where he served as third secretary in the American embassy in Berlin.

Returning to the United States in 1905, Shoemaker and his brother, William, founded the banking firm of Shoemaker, Bates & Company. He stayed with the firm until it was dissolved in 1911 and then purchased the Altoona *Tribune*. Later he acquired the Altoona *Gazette* and *Times*, merging the three into the *Times Tribune* and making himself one of the most prominent newspapermen of central Pennsylvania. At different times, he served as a member of the Pennsylvania Forest Commission, Historical Commission, Geographic Board, the Bushy Run Battlefield Memorial Commission, the Pennsylvania Battlefields Memorial Commission in France, the Huguenot Society of Pennsylvania, the Netherlands Society of Philadelphia, and the Pennsylvania Federation of Historical Societies. He also worked to preserve and develop recreational areas in Pennsylvania'a forests. In 1924, the state Forestry Department named a peak in the White Deer range of Union County, Shoemaker Mountain.

At first glance, Shoemaker's interest in a collection of mostly illiterate or semiliterate backwoodsmen may seem odd. But the old Pennsylvania deer hunters were just part of a general love he had for Pennsylvania and its history. In addition to his deer hunting books, Shoemaker wrote or edited numerous other works of Pennsylvania history and folklore, including *Legends of the Pennsylvania Mountains,* a twelve-volume set published from 1913 to 1922, and books on extinct animals, mountain minstrels, Indian folk songs, and Pennsylvania firearms.

Without Shoemaker's fascination for men "as simple as the day God made the first man," there would be very little known of such hunters as Seth Nelson and John Q. Dyce.

■

Born in Penns Valley in 1809, Seth Iredell Nelson was about thirteen years old when his family moved to Potter County and a spot approximately twenty miles up the First Fork Sinnemahoning Creek from the village of Sinnemahoning. In 1834, he married Elizabeth Keller, the daughter of Dr. Thaddeus Keller of Connecticut. The couple had six daughters and three sons, and, for some reason, gave the daughters all the same middle name—Sally Ann, Julia Ann, Elizabeth Ann, Mary Ann, Rosa Ann, and Lucy Ann.

In 1840, Nelson moved his family south from Potter County to Paddy's Run in Clinton County. They remained there for six years, Nelson working in a local sawmill and gristmill, and hunting whenever possible, before they embarked on a series of moves that eventually took them to Round Island on Sinnemahoning Creek about six miles east of Sinnemahoning at the foot of Altar Rock, a former Indian lookout post where a French scout is said to have shot and killed an Indian sentry. According to at least one source, Nelson's cabin still stands along the creek and is used as a hunting cabin.

As a hunter, Nelson was so renowned that the Seneca Indians called him King Hunter of the Sinnemahoning. He reportedly killed over thirty-five hundred whitetails, five hundred bears, five hundred elk, one hundred wolves, one hundred panthers, and Pennsylvania's last wolverine. He shot the wolverine on a deer hunting trip in 1863 and exhibited its hide with the Maxwell Collection of mounted animals at the Philadelphia Centennial Exposition in 1876. He downed his last buck in Clinton County in 1895 at the age of eighty-six, when the animal was at its rarest in Pennsylvania. He died in 1905 and was buried in the Nelsonville Cemetery atop Karthaus Mountain.[3]

A glimpse of Nelson's character (Shoemaker's books deal mostly in facts and figures), is provided in a biography written after his death by his daughter, Rosa Ann, a portion of which was published in *Amazing Indeed: Strange Events in the Black Forest* by Robert Lyman. "Seth was a Baptist and a firm believer in Christianity," she writes, "and often said that after his death he would live forever and forever. He had psychic ability with many dreams that came true. One foretold the death of a son. At age 80 he gained renewed sight so he could read without glasses. At age 82 he had a severe attack of grip which almost deprived him of speech, which returned a few years later.

"As an athlete he was second to none in his locality. He could jump over a pole held up by 2 tall men. One of his proudest feats was to go directly across the Susquehanna River on a plank or in a tub. No one else could do it. He could do anything required and do it well with no training; blacksmithing, carpenter work, shoe making and even made his own gun."[4]

Nelson, in fact, gained wide fame as a gunsmith. His pieces are still sought by collectors and many are in museums. Deer hunters from all over the East traveled to his shop near Round Island to obtain custom-made rifles. Many of these hunters camped near the shop, "until a specially ordered weapon was begun and finished, so as to supervise every detail of its fabrication. Quaint and full of historic lore was this mystic wayside shire of arms."[5]

Supervision to some of Nelson's customers meant that "the shutters be closed and the smith's work carried on by candle-light lest a passing hex cast a glance upon the barrel, which would ever afterward be deprived of the power to kill. The proud owner of a cherished gun would never leave it near a hex, lest she run her cold trembling hand along the barrel and forever destroy its accuracy. There was also spells or pow-wowing to make a gun shoot perfectly, and these were put on before a foe was to be removed, and more especially with the heavy rifles used at shooting matches. Needles and papers written full of incantations were slipped under the barrels where they joined the stocks to keep away the witches."[6]

Nelson also repaired some famous guns. Among them was a long rifle that once belonged to Indian fighter Robert Covenhoven. It came to him with thirteen notches on it and was accompanied by Covenhoven's knife, which had seven marks on the handle for the Indian scalps he sold at Harris Ferry (Harrisburg).

In an 1899 interview with Shoemaker, Nelson tells of seeing giant deer antlers nailed to woodsheds all across northern Pennsylvania when he was a young man. The sight of a set of moose antlers on Nelson's own shed prompted Shoemaker to question the old hunter about stories he had heard of moose in Pennsylvania. "The magnificent old hunter replied that they were Canadian antlers sent to him some years before by a party who had once hunted with him in Pennsylvania. 'But,' added the old Nimrod, 'there once were moose in Pennsylvania.' Asked if he had ever seen any, he replied that he never had, that the last moose were gone long before his day, but that he had killed at least five hundred elk, sometimes called 'grey moose,' in Pennsylvania forests."[7]

■

Known as the "poet hunter," John Q. Dyce was born in 1830 near McElhattan, a small settlement located roughly halfway between Lock Haven and Jersey Shore. His family was prominent in the Highlands of Scotland and included well-known soldiers, artists, surgeons, and scientists. John was educated in a log schoolhouse near his home and at Dickinson Seminary in Williamsport, which he attended with the intention of becoming a Methodist minister, but he soon found himself at odds with the dogmatic theology of the day—and more and more drawn to the woods and to hunting. Soon he quit the seminary to become a professional hunter.

Standing over six feet tall, with raven black hair and beard, Dyce was said to have more closely resemble a Greek or Roman philosopher than a backwoodsman. This was especially true when he was singing or quoting the poetry he loved so dearly. He kept a violin, harmonica, accordion, and dulcimer in his hunting cabin and would entertain his fellow hunters in the evening by singing old ballads. His favorite song was "All Is Vanity, Saith the Preacher," a tale of what happens when deer hunting collides with religion.

There is a place called Sinnemahone,
Of which but little good is known:
For sinning, ill must be its fame,
Since Sin begins its very name.
So well indeed its fame is known,
That people think they should begin
To drop the useless word Mahone,
And call the country simply Sin!
But to my tale: some years agone
The Presbytery—having heard
Of the sad state of Sin—resolved
To send one to preach the word,
And Mr. Thompson was bid to see then
To the conversion of the heathen.
I shall not linger long to tell
Of all that on the way befell;
How he was lost among the bushes,
And floundered through the reeds and rushes;
Or how, when hungry, down he sat
To corn-cobs fried in 'possum fat!
How his black coat's unusual hue
Caused a grim hunter to pursue
And cock his gun to blow him through,
Believing, as I've heard him swear,
Our missionary was a bear.
'Tis true,' he said, 'I never counted
On seeing such thing as a bear
Upon a good stout pony mounted;
But yet I can with safety swear
That such a wondrous sight
Might we expect by day or night,
Rather than, in our hills, to note
A parson with a rale black coat!'

The news soon spread around the land,
That Parson Thompson, on next Sunday,
Would in the school house take his stand,
And preach to them at least for one day.
The Sunday came, and with it came
All of the ragged population;
Men, women, children, dogs to hear
The tidings of salvation.
The women came in linsey-woolsey,
And tall wool hats increased their stature;
The men in shirts and leather leggins;
The brats and dogs in dress of nature!
Then men who seldom stop at trifles,
Brought tomahawks and knives and rifles.
Service began—the parson wondered
To hear the singing that they made—
Some Yankee Doodle, some Old Hundred,
The hounds, astonished, howled and thund'red,
Until the forest shook with dread.
The singing o'er, the prayer was said,
But scarcely had the text been read
When, panting with fatigue and fear,
Rushed past the door a hunted deer.
Prayer, hymn and text were forgot,
And for the sermon mattered not—
Forth dashed the dogs—not one was mute—
Men, women, children followed suit.
The men prepared the deer to slaughter,
The girls to head it to the water.
None staid but lame old Billy Tench,
Who sat unwilling on his bench.
Nor for the sake of hymn or prayer
Did Billy keep his station there,
But, as he said, with rueful phiz:
"For a damned spell of roomatiz!"
The parson groaned with inner pain,
And lifting up his hands amain,
Cried dolefully; "'Tis all in vain!"
Up starting nimbly from his bench,
"Tis not in vain," cried old Billy Tench,
"When my good hound, old Never-Fail,

Once gets his nose upon the trail,
There's not a spike buck anywhere
Can get away from him, I'll swear." [8]

According to Shoemaker, Dyce once shot nine deer in one day, ninety-eight during a season and, unbelievably, three with one shot. "On the Spring Run Ridge he sighted a buck, a doe and a fawn standing together. He fired, the bullet piercing the brain of the buck, the throat of the doe, and lodging in the heart of the fawn" (pp. 43–44). Dyce also talks of shooting does with antlers, bucks in velvet as late as October and November and with atypical racks, which he believed always had more points on the left rack than the right (p. 89). He died in 1904.

■

In the introduction to *Pennsylvania Deer and Their Horns*, Shoemaker says he "makes no claim for exactness or completeness in these pages; it is a 'pioneer' work, merely 'blazing the way' for future investigations" (p. 11). Possibly because he started his work at a time when the old deer hunters of the nineteenth century were rapidly dying off and wanted to cover as much ground as possible, he provides only names, or names and totals, in most instances. "George Smith, of Elk County, born in 1827, and who died in 1901. Killed 3000 deer in Pennsylvania, including 7 in one day, and 2 at one shot. Nelson Gardner, of Elk County, killed 1000 Pennsylvania deer, including 4 in one day, 125 in one season, and 2 at one shot. Daniel Karstetter was considered by many the greatest deer hunter on the northern border of the Seven Mountains. In his long career he killed 600 deer, including 4 in one day, and 2 at one shot . . . " (p. 45).

Shoemaker's list includes the greatest hunters from each section of the state, the greatest Indian hunters, and the best known "colored" hunters. Unfortunately, however, nobody chose to follow his lead and gather together the hunters' stories while the men—or at least members of their families and friends—were still alive. And, since they were the "average" men of the time and left scant records beyond the usual notations in family bibles, local newspapers, and government records, Shoemaker's information is most of what remains. So, when Pennsylvania's "greatest hunters" are remembered today, it is usually because of their connection with a village, a stream, a road, or a mountain somewhere in northern Pennsylvania: Reuben Tyrrell through the village of Tyrrell in Bradford County; J. P. Hammersley through Hammersley Fork in Clinton County; Nelson Gardner through Gardner Hill in Elk County.

Shoemaker has done more than merely preserving a record of the old hunters, however. He puts a face on that faceless man, the market hunter. For the people he writes about were the individuals who destroyed Pennsylvania's orginal deer herd. Nobody kills one hundred deer a year or three thousand in a lifetime without an eye toward earning a profit by selling the venison.

But if reading the kill totals of Shoemaker's hunters today leaves a hollow feeling in the stomach, or sends a shiver up the spine, or even brings a tear to the eye, his tone makes it clear they were not outlaws in the eyes of their society. Actually, it was sportsmen, not the general public, who found them guilty of wiping out the game they wanted for sport hunting. According to John Reiger: "What the late nineteenth-century sportsmen and their journals had to fight was nothing less than the national myth of progress. An incredible rapidity of physical change, probably unexcelled in world history, was already the single most dramatic fact of the American experience. This impermanence had long been glorified as the essence of 'progress'—that indefinable but inevitable something which was the trademark of the United States. In the words of one observer of the 1830s, 'Americans love their country, not . . . as it is, but as it will be . . . They live in the future, and make their country as they go on.' The truth of those statements is shown by the fact that from 1607 to 1907— scarcely more than four lifetimes by present expectation— America would be changed from a couple of wilderness settlements into the most powerful nation on earth."[9] Pennsylvania, with its abundance of coal and lumber and steel mills, was the ideal place for the myth to become reality—and it left no room for wildlife.

So powerful was the nineteenth-century myth of national progress, that it created a kind of schizophrenia even in the men who launched the conservation movement. "Bill Long, born in Berks County in 1790, died in Clearfield County in 1880, held the marvelous record of having slain 3500 Pennsylvania deer," Shoemaker writes in the same chapter in which he lays out a plan to save the whitetail in Pennsylvania, a plan that states, "one stag to a hunter is right and just" (pp. 44, 59). Teddy Roosevelt, the best-known conservationist of the period, and his son Kermit, could not refrain from shooting 468 game animals while on a safari in Africa at the same time he was establishing the U.S. Forest Service, setting aside millions of acres of woodlands for national forests, and fighting for laws to stop the sale of wild game.[10] A photograph of John Phillips, a founder of the Pennsylvania Game Commission, in *Camp-fires in the Canadian Rockies*, shows him with a grizzly he shot and the caption, "Mr. Phillips Regrets the Impending Extinction of the Grizzly Bear."[11]

A good share of the old hunters did manage to change, however, evolving a code of sportsmanship and becoming defenders of wildlife. William Anneman of Scranton, "for years one of the leading deer hunters of northeastern Pennsylvania," became a game protector. Coleman K. Sober of Lewisburg, "a leading deer hunter of central Pennsylvania," became a member of the state Game Commission. Dr. Joseph T. Rothrock, "an ardent sportsman," was the founder of the Pennsylvania Department of Forestry. Colonel R. Bruce Ricketts of Wilkes-Barre, an "earnest" and "successful" deer hunter, donated the property for Ricketts Glen State Park on the Sullivan and Luzerne county line.[12]

"Now I think that all who are lovers of the woods and fields should join in a general move to protest this wasteful slaughter of all game and game birds," Woodcock writes, "no matter whether we are the so-called 'pot hunter' or the 'gentlemen sportsman,' but none will regret this unreasonable waste of game more than those who are living back in the mountains, where game is most plentiful, when it is gone. Nor none will get more benefit and pleasure from the very fact that they are living in a game section, yet these are the ones who do not seem to care how great the slaughter, apparently never taking it into consideration that the present rate of slaughter will soon leave their game laden section as bare of game as that of the older settled counties.

"Comrades, let us all join in the preservation of what game and fish there is left, whether we may be called pot hunters or gentlemen sportsmen. I would be the last one to wish to deprive any trapper or camper from making good use of game at any time when in camp, but let us be careful about the waste of it" (p. 268).

XII

Fate of the Forest

Damn! I whisper, when I check my watch against the dusky light from the window over the bed. Ten 'til seven! Instantly, I throw off my sleeping bag, pull on my clothes, and climb down the ladder into the kitchen where I find a pot of coffee waiting and Dad working on his lunch.

"I been up since six o'clock," he tells me.

"Why didn't you wake me?" I complain.

"That's all right," is all he says.

But I don't like it. I am more anxious than yesterday. I want to get back in the mountains and try again. Everybody else already has a deer. I don't care what Benoit says about it being okay to enter the woods late. We should be on our stands. Or at least on the tram road. I grab a cup of coffee, take a gulp, and throw together a couple of sandwiches. Damn! I think once more, staring out the windows at the fast fading night. Then I stuff an oatmeal cookie into my mouth and head for the living room.

Bob rolls over when he hears me take my boots from next to the wood stove and sit down to put them on. Usually, he is one of the first people out of bed, but opening day has beaten everybody. Snores are rising in such an off-key chorus I have to smile. Besides, there is no reason for Bob or the others to get up. Dad and I are the only ones going out; a drive with everybody is planned for tomorrow.

As soon as I finish lacing my boots, I hurry back into the

145

kitchen, grab another oatmeal cookie and a banana. Then we collect our lunches, coats, and rifles, and, as quietly as possible on the creaking wood floor, slip out the door.

Outside, melting snow is pouring off the gutterless roof in steady streams that splash noisily on the gravel drive. Heavy cloud cover has held the heat in and kept the thermometer on the porch above forty degrees. The "greenhouse effect" flashes through my mind. I have never known a deer season so warm. Then I notice the neighbor's truck. We are ahead of one person anyway.

■

When we reach the Forest Service road leading back to Baldy, we see only three other vehicles.

"Looks like we'll have some room today," I note, as Dad backs the Bronco off the road.

"I don't know," he replies. "Depends how many guys come from those cabins."

The joy I felt yesterday at being back in the mountains is completely gone when we start down the road. Ambition has robbed the woods of their allure. They are now something to overcome, something from which to wrestle a prize. It is the white man's philosophy. Western philosophy. "Go forth, be fruitful, and conquer." Though I often talk about moving beyond such thinking and becoming more an element of nature than a warrior against her, it is difficult. The Jesuits say, "Give me a boy until his fifth birthday and he is mine for life." I progress in my quest only when my mind is alert to my attitudes. When my subconscious is in control, I am again concerned with subduing the earth, be it dreaming of a cabin in a wild mountain meadow, clearing a campsite, or killing a deer.

■

The farther we move down the road toward Baldy, the more hoof prints and the fewer boot prints we find. As we pass the saplings and cut timber on the edge of the mountain, buck rubs so fresh they look wet catch our eyes. I think about Bob saying the rut is late this year. That's not completely correct. But I can't remember seeing such fresh rubs this late in November.

Rut is the period when the buck's sex drive is at its peak. It consists of several phases extending over three or four months, starting with sparring among rivals and ending after breeding. In much of North America, the rut begins in September and ends by January. Researchers believe photoperiodism, or the shortening of the day, is probably most responsible for triggering rutting behavior. The rutting season in Pennsylvania lasts for about two months in the autumn, reaching its height in November. But we are in the last few days of November, when we expect it to be over.

"Early in the rutting season, whitetail bucks tend to thrash saplings vigorously, often breaking them," according to the Wildlife Institute. "Rubs made later in the rut have greater visibility and may serve more of a signpost function since they characteristically are left standing but with the bark removed. Bucks very deliberately rub their glandular foreheads on debarked saplings. This leaves a scent that may allow other deer to identify the metabolic condition and perhaps the individual identity of the buck that made the rub. However, other bucks and occasionally even does may rub over a scent mark left by an earlier buck."[1]

The bare, white trunks of the saplings would seem to indicate the rut is nearly over, but their freshness makes me think the bucks are still frisky. I file the thought away in the back of my mind.

■

As we did yesterday, Dad and I quickly separate once we are on Baldy. Only this time, he heads for the rock shelf where I opened the season, while I continue on down the mountain. He is hoping to catch the buck everybody missed coming through again. I am playing the numbers, going with the area where I had seen the most deer.

"I'll stay there 'til about nine-thirty," Dad tells me, as we split apart. "Then I'm gonna walk out to the point and work my way back this way."

I nod without saying anything and walk away. The plan is the same one we have been using since my first day of deer hunting. It is meant to drive deer toward me and improve my chances of getting a shot at a buck. It has run a lot of white-tails in my direction, though never a buck. So my expectations are low. But, of course, the situation can change at any time. And the plan gives Dad pleasure, I know, and then I freeze as a flicker of movement behind a deadfall catches my eye. Something tells me it is a bird. But I am not sure. I wait. My eyes strain to catch it again. There is a good dusting of snow on the ground. The air is clear. If it is a deer I should be able to get a look at it with my binoculars as soon as it steps out from behind the branches. But before I can pull my binoculars from my coat, three deer appear from behind the rock next to the deadfall. Then a fourth, who stares directly at me. I do not dare move for my binoculars for fear of driving them, and everything else away, but I sense they are does. At least I don't see any big racks.

Two minutes may pass quickly in conversation. But to the person staring down a deer while propped up on one bent leg, it is an eternity. By the time the fourth deer finally gives up and the herd moves off down the mountain, my right leg is cramped and numb and my back aches from the odd strain put on it. But I have been quiet and gotten a good enough look to feel certain none of the deer carried antlers.

Once the does are out of sight, I stumble over to a tree a few yards away and lean against it to watch the rock from where they had emerged. Then, after about ten minutes when no buck appears, I slowly make my way over to an arrangement of three boulders with a small hemlock growing alongside. I tell myself I will stay there watching the does' route for another fifteen minutes or so. But no sooner do I settle into place than a doe startles me by popping her head up from between two rocks only fifty yards away. I had had no idea whatsoever she was there. And, since the rocks are only about the size of bicycles, I think I caught her on her bed. By her head movements and the fact she is continuously scanning my direction, I also guess she knows I am nearby. Only the dark ness of the hemlock keeps her from focusing in on me. Then suddenly she bolts from the rocks followed by two other deer. Quickly, I unsling my rifle and sight along the barrel at the second two deer until I am sure they, too, are does. Then I wait, my rifle still ready, eyes shifting all around the rocks, for a buck. But none shows. And now the mountain ahead of me is spooked, I think.

■

For more than an hour, I wait and watch from under the hemlock. In place of yesterday's barrage only four or five shots sound during my vigil, and a trace of discouragement enters my mind. All the shooting yesterday had acted as a stimulant, touched some primal root and kept me sharp, expecting a buck to come running in my direction at any moment. Without it, my mind drifts. I notice that the tips of all the branches on the bush in front of me have been nipped off. Then I look around the mountain and notice the browse line, the low, vague ceiling created below the canopy of overhead branches by deer feeding on the lowest limbs of trees. It is a clear sign of an overtaxed land. I remember a talk I had earlier in the fall with Brad Nelson, the biologist who is wildlife program director of Allegheny National Forest.

"Don't get me wrong," he said, "I enjoy deer hunting. I enjoy seeing deer. But I am also quite concerned about what they are doing, from an ecological standpoint, to the forest. We're spending an awful lot of money because of the deer. We're fencing a lot of stands, and fertilizing them to try and get the seedlings to grow faster because the deer are just eating them so fast.

"Most of our forest has a distinct browse line," he continued, "with very few shrubs on the understory. The shrubs we do have are mainly the ones that are unpalatable to deer, or they do well under heavy browsing. The striped maple is a good example. The deer browse very readily on it. But it is tremendously hardy and does real well when it's browsed on. We have other species in the forest that have almost totally disappeared. Many of the viburnums—airwood viburnum, hobblebush, arrowleaf, mapleleaf. Some of the berry-type shrubs that belong to the viburnum family, a lot of them have almost totally disappeared from the forest. And mainly because of the deer."

Game Commission researchers have found similar problems all across the state. The commission's information chief, Ted Godshall, told me that as far back as the early 1970s biologists had found that five species of shrubs had disappeared from Pennsylvania's forests because of overbrowsing by deer.

The range of food the whitetail will consume in Pennsylvania verges on the unbelievable—and even includes a slight amount of meat. Biologists from the Game Commission and Pennsylvania State University's Wildlife Research Unit have identified ninety-eight different plant species in the digestive system of deer killed on the road. Fifty-seven were tree, shrub, or vine species, and forty-one were herbaceous plants. There also was a lot of unidentifiable plant material, mostly herbaceous, that could easily extend the list of species beyond ninety-eight.[2]

Food preference, naturally, depends on the plant species occurring in an area and the time of year. But about 60 percent of the diet year-round consists of woody plants—stems, leaves, or fruit. Green leaves, herbaceous plants, and new growth on woody plants are eaten in the spring and summer. In late summer, fall, and early winter, hard and soft fruits, such as apples, blueberries, and acorns are the major part of the deers' diet. Winter sees the whitetail turning to evergreens and hard browse like bark and dry leaves. Among the wood plants found in the stomach contents were: apple, arbor vitae, aspen, beech, birch, blackberry, black cherry, black locust, blue beech, blueberry, cherry, chestnut oak, coralberry, crab apple, deerberry, dewberry, dogwood, elderberry, elm, grape, gray dogwood, greenbriar, hawthorne, hazelnut, hemlock, hickory, honeysuckle, jack pine, Juneberry, larch, mountain laurel, mulberry, oak, orange, partridge berry, pear, persimmon, pine, pitch pine, privet, red oak, red cedar, red maple, rhododendron, rose, sassafras, spruce, sugar maple, sumac, sweet fern, teaberry, tulip poplar, Virginia creeper, white pine, willow, and witch hazel.

Non-woody plants identified in the study included: alfalfa, aster, bean, bellwort, cabbage, Canada mayflower, cantaloupe, carrot, cinquefoil, clover, club moss, cohash, corn, crown vetch, dandelion, domestic lettuce, goldenrod, ground cherry, Indian pipe, liverwort, Mayapple, milkweed, oats, panic grass, plantain, pokeweed, potato, ragwort, rye, sheep sorrel, soybean, speedwell, spikenard, spring beauty, strawberry, tomato, trefoil, violet, wheat, wild geranium, and wild mustard.

Godshall said the public in general has very little idea of what deer eat. When suburbanites complain to the Game Commission in the winter about starving deer destroying expensive, ornamental shrubs, they want game protectors to somehow take the deer back into the woods and make them stay. But they came out of the woods because there was no food. There were too many deer for the carrying capacity of the woods.

"Well, then, we're supposed to feed them," Godshall said. "They think you can just go to the store and buy deer food. They don't realize that a deer is a browsing animal and you just can't buy deer browse. They think, 'Well, feed them hay or corn,' which is poison to them. Deer live on browse, which is the tender tips between the buds of woody vegetation, trees, and shrubs. Microorganisms in their stomach that aid in digestion are designed to process cellulose. When you throw something like hay or corn at them, it's like throwing black pepper at a starving man. It's too hot, a high protein food their stomach's cannot digest. It doesn't pass through and they can't get it back up. They will starve to death with a belly full of hay or corn. It's quite common.

"They do, of course, eat grains and grasses from time to time," he continued, "but when you sock that to them as their only food after they've been getting by on browse, it'll kill them. Or at least make them sick. Depending upon how much of it they get. If they get a belly full of it and can't digest it, they'll die."

Deer eat browse up to six feet off the ground, and the range of their diet and their numbers have been causing problems for other wildlife in northern Pennsylvania. The shrubs and lower limbs devoured by them have deprived many song bird species of suitable nesting territory; grouse, squirrels, and hares of cover; and put the whitetail in direct competition with the wild turkey for food.

"If there is one thing," Nelson said, "that determines the size of the turkey population, it is winter habitat. Mainly, they eat a lot of shrub berries and vegetation just above the snow line. Because we don't have areas with good shrub cover to produce berries that persist into winter, it has hurt our turkey population. Acorns are another thing turkeys eat throughout the winter. And often times they concentrate in areas of seeps, where you have warm water coming up out of the ground that causes the snow to melt and makes a place where they can pick around and get grit, little insects, and herbaceous vegetation that grows in those seeps. The deer come in and just about wipe everything out of those seeps. So there is a lot of ground cover the deer have eaten that has definitely affected the turkey population."

While Allegheny National Forest still possesses a healthy turkey population, Nelson feels it could be much better and the hunting season on turkey much longer if there were fewer deer. There also could be larger grouse and squirrel populations if deer numbers were cut, according to him. The Forest Service and Game Commission are trying to aid the turkey by planting shrubs with fruit that persists through the winter, on south-facing slopes below eighteen hundred feet elevation, and then fencing those planted areas off to give the shrubs a chance to mature. When the plants are ready, forest workers take down the fences and allow the turkeys to use the areas as winter habitat. Of course, deer feed in those shrub plots, too.

With variables such as forest maturity, the needs of other wildlife, and economic interests in mind, researchers from the Game Commission and the Forest Service have determined that Allegheny National Forest is capable of adequately sustaining nineteen deer per square mile of forest, a figure that probably can be applied to other forested regions of the Allegheny High Plateau. At present, though, for areas within the national forest, Elk County shows thirty-three deer per square mile; Forest, thirty-six; McKean, twenty-eight; and Warren thirty-one. Since Elk County has a whitetail population of about thirty thousand, according to Godshall, numbers per square mile outside of the forest's boundaries, in more open country, are certainly higher.

"We figure we can have nineteen deer per square mile and not affect the number of deer we kill as far as the buck harvest goes," Nelson said. "As a matter of fact, as the deer herd comes down, we start getting healthier deer. We start getting deer with bigger racks. And a lot of hunters like deer with bigger racks."

■

Near midday, six does tumble down off the top of the mountain to stop about thirty yards away. Unable to see me under the dark hemlock or pick up my scent in the motionless air, they mill about for several minutes. Then two hunters appear in the distance. Their ears flick alert and, long before either of the hunters knows the deer exist, they hurry off in the direction of the downed timber and other cover below the end of the road. The sight makes me wonder how many times deer have moved so far ahead of me. More than I care to imagine without injuring my self-image as a hunter, I conclude, and then jump as six shots echo in rapid reports off the next ridge. Somebody has missed. So many quick shots usually mean a miss. I ready myself for running deer, but the shots sounded a little too far off and I do not believe the buck will come near me.

Once the two hunters pass, I reason they have driven everything out of the area and decide it is time to move. Slowly, I start to work my way closer to the face of Baldy, into the rocks where I jumped the turkey yesterday. I settle down to wait once more. I hope a buck has circled behind the hunters and won't be expecting me, but my rational mind, focusing on the six does, tells me the chances are unlikely and everything has been cleared out. My edge dulls and time slips into daydreams. I think how great it is working for myself and being able to arrange my schedule so I can spend an entire week in the woods. I wonder if the freedom I feel is what the Indians knew living by their own devices without clocks guiding everything. If it is, I can understand why they fought so hard and were so confused by the white man's regimentation and never ending need for more.

Indians have been much on my mind since I finished *Son of the Morning Star*, Evan S. Connell's book about Custer and the Battle of the Little Big Horn, a few days ago. I think if more people lived like the Indians, the world could work. But that would require people to trust their intuition, and that is frightening. There is no safety in feelings. But there are no guarantees in the boredom of a safe life either—and so much less satisfaction.

The knocking of a woodpecker on a dead tree a few yards away ends my drifting. The hollow echo fills the mountain and I look up to spot the fireball crest of a giant pileated woodpecker. To me the pileated is among the most beautiful of birds. It always excites me to see one. Just then, the sun breaks through the clouds, luring a half-dozen chickadees to a tree over my shoulder. Hopping from branch to branch, they sing back and forth to each other until another cloud crosses the sun and ends their excitement. But the quiet lasts only a moment before a flock of geese appears overhead, honking their way south.

Every time I see a flock of geese, I am reminded of the old Gary Cooper movie *Sergeant York* and the scene where he compares shooting the kaiser's soldiers in the trenches of World War I to hunting geese: he just started at the of the line and worked his way to the front. Like geese, the soldiers never got "riled up" because most of them did not see the man on the end dropping. I have often wondered if a hunter could down an entire flock of geese in that way. I have no desire to try it, but I think the scene says a lot about blind followers.

As the geese fade into the distance, a red squirrel appears, dancing over the limbs of a downed tree and then up the trunk of a live one. It is the first squirrel I've seen in the two days we've been on Baldy. In other years I've seen three or four a day. This one's appearance brings to mind a friend who talks to squirrels. He drives them crazy with his whistling chirps, halts them in their tracks, and sends them running up and down trees in blinding dashes. The memory makes me wish I had more opportunities to do things like play with squirrels and watch pileated woodpeckers. It would be nice to live in the country again, deep in the mountains. But I know I am fooling myself. Many times the idea of dropping everything and working as a hunting and fishing guide in some place like Montana has crossed my mind. But Montana is so far away from everywhere. And, after I've had my fill of fishing and hunting, I would miss the city. From where I live now, Pittsburgh is only a half-hour drive. I love its theaters and bookstores and the Carnegie Library and lunches with friends in restaurants only locals frequent. It might be nice to move a bit farther out into the country, but I would not care to leave the Pittsburgh area. Not everything about cities is bad. What I need is a cabin of my own in the mountains where I can stay whenever the need arises. Even Thoreau did not care to live far outside of Concord.

In *The Fate of the Earth*, Jonathan Schell talks about what the creation of nuclear weapons has done to the earth. "The Japanese," he writes, "used to call the pleasure quarters of their cities 'floating worlds.' Now our entire world, cut adrift from its future and its past, has become a floating world. The cohesion of the social realm—the dense and elaborate fabric of life that is portrayed for us in the novels of the nineteenth century, among other places, inspiring 'nostalgic' longing in us—is disintegrating, and people seem to be drifting apart and into a weird isolation. The compensation that is offered is the license to enjoy life in the moment with fewer restrictions; but the present moment and its pleasures provide only a poor refuge from the emptiness and loneliness of our shaky, dream-like, twilit world. The moment itself, unable to withstand the abnormal pressure of expectation, becomes distorted and corrupted. People turn to it for rewards that it cannot offer—certainly not when it is ordered to do so. Plucked out of life's stream, the moment—whether a moment of love or of spiritual peace, or even of simple pleasure in a meal—is no longer permitted to quietly unfold and be itself but is strenuously tracked down, manipulated, harried by instruction and advice, bought and sold, and, in general, so roughly manhandled that the freshness and joy that it can yield up when it is left alone are corrupted or destroyed."[3]

Few things can stop the world like time on a deer stand. I decide it is time to move out of the big timber and back toward the saplings.

■

Rounding the bend at the head of the saplings, I catch three deer trotting across the road. They are too far away and too quickly out of sight to identity, but their appearance brings back the edge. I estimate I have seen fifteen deer so far. Then I unsling my rifle, ready for a buck following the three deer, and slowly move down the road to find a stand on the far side of the saplings.

When I reach the spot where the deer crossed the road, I hear two hunters talking. Their voices sound terrible and crude in the silence of the woods. I can only hope the noise they are making might drive a buck my way. But it is doubtful. Probably they already have spooked every bit of wildlife out of the area. I continue along the road until I notice two trees growing close together on a piece of high ground and turn into the woods.

From my new stand I can see far down into the hollow where a branch of Minister Creek rises to life out of a rocky depression blanketed with spongy moss. And almost immediately, I catch a glimpse of distant movement—deer passing through the timber in the wide beginnings of the hollow. But they are so far away I cannot say how many may be in the herd. Or pick them up in my binoculars before they vanish among the trees. All I can do is wait to see if they turn in my direction.

When the deer fail to show after about fifteen minutes, I walk back out onto the road and check up and down it, trying to decide what to do next. It is almost two o'clock. I can either start hunting my way out to the Bronco, get there between four and four-thirty, and make Dad happy, or I can return to Baldy. Heading back would be the prudent thing to do. But the glimpse of the herd has made me feel like hunting again. I think if I walk behind the saplings and into the bottom of the hollow maybe I can catch them coming through. Their pace and attitude had seemed calm and casual. I start back down the road.

On the far side of the saplings, I spot a group of hunters standing around a rock. A man, his wife, and son. We nod at each other and then I ask if they have seen a hunter dressed in orange.

"An old guy?" the woman asks.

"Yeah," I say, and smile at the remark. Dad often calls hunters younger than him old guys, but seldom applies the term to himself.

"He was heading out," the woman says.

I think he probably will stop at the hemlock grove he pointed out in the morning. Then I tell myself I can spend a couple of hours in the hollow and still get back around four-thirty if I hurry. I thank the woman, and then move another fifty yards along the road and into the hollow.

■

Another breeze rustles down the hollow through the dry, brown leaves still clinging to a few trees. Although I know the reason for the noise, it sounds so remarkably like deer bounding over the forest floor that I involuntarily tense and shift my gaze from tree to tree until a chill runs up my spine and shivers across my shoulders. Though it is not quite three o'clock, the steep walls of the hollow have robbed the sun of its last angles of light and warmth and filled most of the hollow with shadow. Each successive breeze is sharper than the last. I shift my weight from one foot to another and rearrange myself among the three small hemlocks under which I am waiting. Then I flip up my collar, hunch deeper into my coat, and start to think about what probably lies ahead.

Everybody had come Up North with the idea of spending a week. But now that Bob, Garth, and Mike all have deer, I expect they will want to leave after we drive the woods for deer tomorrow. Or Thursday morning at the latest. And I can't blame them. I would probably lose interest, too. But I had been looking forward so much to spending a full week at camp and to the rhythm of an extended hunt. Last year, when I took my deer on the third day, I was just beginning to feel that rhythm. Now I want more. The proper way to hunt big game is without time restrictions, coming back empty-handed but knowing the deer are out there as the world grows sharper and more intense with each passing day. I had been so involved with last year's hunt that a sense of depression had come over me when it ended. Or rather that mixture of loss and excitement that comes after finishing something in which a total immersion is required. In hunting, instead of a gradual decline in intensity as the end approaches, everything is over in an instant, with the touch of a trigger and the flash of a barrel. It would be great if a deer did not have to die to complete the cycle of experience and, like a trout, could be released to be taken again. But that's not the way of hunting and I have not as yet grown beyond the need to punctuate the end with a bullet.

As the shadows lengthen to fill the entire hollow, I wonder if I am too close to the road, so I work my way deeper into the bottom, until I come across a large collection of tracks. Something tells me they belong to the deer I had seen off in the distance at the head of the hollow. I think they must have already passed through and are probably on Baldy. But it is getting too late to head back any further. Maybe if Dad was not waiting for me I would try. But I don't want to upset him. Besides, if I were to get a buck on Baldy now, I probably would not get out of the woods until seven o'clock. Reluctantly, I decide to wait out the day between two small hemlocks growing over a rock.

The silence and depth of the woods begin to lull me after only a few minutes on my new stand. My mind drifts to Garth and his belief all deer are supposed to fall where they are shot.

He is such a character. Then I think of how Dad is getting older. He no longer always hears me when I whistle at him in the woods. Some people have said that's sad. But in the mountains, in deer season, it seems perfectly natural. "Only the earth and the heavens last long," the Indians say.

With my foot, I move a few more dead twigs away from the base of the tree against which I am leaning to give me more clean space in which to stand. Then, almost directly in front of me, the woods explode with crashing and snapping, and a herd of deer is running at me. Wildly, my eyes dart from one head to another until I spot a set of antlers. A spike. My heart pounds as I struggle to get my rifle off my shoulder and manage to catch the trigger guard in the game pocket of my coat. Then two of the lead deer, no more than ten yards away, catch my awkward fight with the rifle and begin to run. But the buck is confused. He moves only a couple of steps to a hemlock maybe twenty yards in front of me to assess the situation. He does not see me and gives me a perfect profile shot between the trunks of two trees. Finally, the game pocket releases its hold. I bring my rifle up, bounce the barrel off a nub of branch, level its sights on the buck's shoulder, and fire. He goes down in a pile and leaves me shaking all over.

XIII

The Weight of Success

Usually it takes me about a half hour to field dress a deer. That includes admiring the angle and range of the shot; scanning the woods a half-dozen times to see if anybody is approaching who I might tell about the shot; unloading my rifle, and finding a safe, dry place to lay it; removing my coat and binoculars; rolling up my sleeves; moving the deer to a spot where his head will be higher than his hind end and away from the mess; admiring the rack; running my fingers through the heavy coat; cutting into the soft underbelly and removing the entrails; then cleaning my knife and hands with snow, creek water, puddle water, spring water, damp leaves, moss, a handkerchief or, as last resort, my pants; filling out the tag; searching my pockets for string or a wire twisty from a loaf of bread with which to attach it to an ear; tying the deer's forelegs to his head with the drag rope; rolling my sleeves back down; putting my coat back on, and then slinging my rifle across my back and starting out. This time, however, since I finally ran out of the string and twisties I had put in my coat a mere ten years earlier, I also have to add cutting a piece of boot lace to attach the tag.

Still, driven by the sight of the hollow turning from shadow to real darkness, and the knowledge that at least a mile and a half drag lies ahead of me, at the end of which will be a stomping and swearing father ready to mount a search, I manage to finish the job in just fifteen minutes.

Actually, I might have finished dressing the buck in ten

160

minutes flat except for the brief, awkward moment when the father and son appeared and stared. They came from the same direction as the herd. The father said they had caught a glimpse of the deer jumping far ahead of them and had driven them toward me. In his voice, I could detect a hint of belief that the buck should have belonged to them. But he knew as well as I did that they never had a shot. I was in the right place at the right time. It is the way deer hunting in crowded Pennsylvania often goes.

The son, for his part, could not take his eyes off the opened deer. He looked to be about fourteen, maybe only thirteen, and probably had never seen the interior workings of such a large creature before.

"Look at that!" he told his father, pointing at an exposed muscle twitching above a hind leg. "It's still moving."

"Electricity," I say, volunteering a minicourse on the nervous system.

"Electricity," he laughs, and looks at his father. But his dad isn't interested. He is still contemplating what might have been. Roughly, he motions to his son and they start away mumbling something about maybe catching up to the rest of the herd and finding another buck. Never happen, I say to myself.

■

When I spot the vague remnants of an old oil or logging road about fifty yards above where the buck lay, getting him out of the hollow suddenly looks as though it is going to be much easier than I had expected. The saplings start about a hundred yards up the old road. From there the Forest Service Road leading out is maybe another one-hundred-fifty yards away. Altogether, it looks as if I have about three-hundred yards to go before I am out of the woods—in a manner of speaking.

So, aided by a charge of leftover adrenaline, I pull, tug, yank, lift, crash, strain, grunt, slide, sweat, and puff the buck up to higher ground in what feels like record time. But when I check my watch, I find over forty minutes have passed. It is almost four o'clock. The quick fix dissolves into an endless road. I squat down next to the buck to breathe and steel myself.

Dragging is something that should never enter a hunter's mind, especially if there is much distance involved. Like working in a factory, the only way I have found to handle a tough drag is to numb the brain and bear down. The only goal to set is the dead tree twenty yards ahead. Reach that point and it is rest time. Beyond it nothing exists until the lungs refill with oxygen and the heart slows a beat or two and the cramps loosen in the shoulders, hands, and legs. Then it is time to move on to the dripping rock thirty yards ahead.

Proper handling of the rope is another important factor in surviving a long drag. Until I shot my first buck and had to move him two miles out of the woods, I never would have dreamed there were so many different ways to hold a piece of rope. Grasp the end in the right hand, wrap the slack up the left arm and pull walking sideways. Grasp the end in the left hand, wrap the slack up the right arm and pull facing to the other side. Hang the rope over the right shoulder. Hang the rope over the left shoulder. Wrap it around the right hand and pull walking backward. Wrap it around the left hand and pull some more walking backward. Find a stick, tie it to the end of the rope and pull with both hands behind the back. Turn around, hold the stick in both hands and pull walking backward. Run the rope over the left shoulder, across the chest and tuck the stick under the right arm. Then run the rope over the right shoulder, across the chest from the other side and tuck the stick under the left arm. The possibilities are limited only by the hunter's ability to find another pain-free position.

Seven or eight pounds of rifle, too, never feels so heavy as when dragging a deer. Dad picked up the Model 128 Remington I use at the start of my deer hunting career. He bought it and a box of shells from a friend in the mill for $35. When he gave it to me, I was disappointed. I had wanted a bolt action rifle, and the Model 128 is a pump. I also had wanted a .30/06, and it is a .35 caliber. When it comes to sporting arms and fly rods, there always has been a strong streak of the traditionalist in me. In my youth, a bolt action .30/06 seemed the height of modern hunting tradition and sophistication. It was Teddy Roosevelt, Rama of the Jungle, and Hemingway on safari. Over the years, however, the weathered old Model 128 has earned my respect and affection. Now, I can't imagine hunting with anything else. But on drags there have been more than a few times I would have signed my life savings over to be rid of The Thing stiffening my back or cutting into my shoulder. And times when I have actually thought about dumping it somewhere and coming back later. Though I would never do it.

■

I am kneeling over the deer, concentrating on my breathing, when my attention is captured by a glow of bright orange in the western sky. I check my watch again. It is seven minutes later than the last time I looked. And I still must be a mile from the Bronco. I won't reach it until six o'clock. Or maybe six-thirty or even something 'til seven if I want to be realistic.

"Dad's going to go crazy," I tell myself aloud. Then I stand up, pull the rope over a shoulder, and drag the buck around a bend.

While I was resting, I had half imagined, half hoped, that I might round the bend and look down the road to, if not the Bronco, then at least the diamond markers of the North Country Trail, which are only a hundred yards or so from the Bronco. But what I find is more road—now running uphill. I stop and stare off to the west. In the ten minutes it has taken me to make the bend, the orange on the horizon has changed to pink. Soon that will be gone, too, replaced by a dull glow of pale yellow. And then full darkness. I look back down the road, ready to boost my moral by congratulating myself on how far I've already traveled, when I notice three hunters coming up behind me. Against all my better judgment, I think, "I am saved."

■

Though I would never ask for help—I shot the buck, it's my responsibility to get him out—I cannot imagine that the

163

hunters will not offer to help. I know if I were coming up on somebody dragging a deer so late in the day I certainly would offer a hand. But hunters are not always as congenial as fishermen. I don't know why. Maybe the woods just aren't as soothing as water. But I know other people who feel the same. So, as the three approach, moving slowly, stopping every once in a while to scan the woods for a last minute piece of luck, I continue to drag. I pull until I see the big one has a beard and the other two are the man and woman I had spoken to earlier about Dad.

"Well, you screwed your hunting up," the big hunter says as soon as they reach me. "But I guess you don't mind."

I smile and then, between gasps of breath, answer their questions about the deer. They nod in approval, say they heard me shoot around three and then the big hunter asks:

"Well, could you use some help? "

"Tell you what. I am not going to turn you down," I answer, fighting back an urge to shout for joy.

■

With two men dragging and one resting, it still takes almost a half hour before we glimpse the first twinkle of the street light at the trailer across the road from the Bronco.

During the walk, I learn the man and woman are hunting out of a cabin around Chapman Dam and that they are hoping their friends, including the boy I had seen them with earlier, are already at the truck. The last thing they want to do is go back into the woods at night looking for them.

"Yeah," I tell them. "I know my dad is back at the Bronco right now getting mad because I am late and ready to come out looking for me."

They smile knowingly, and then, as if on cue, Dad appears out of the last light walking down the road toward us. When he reaches me I can see he is ready to start complaining until it dawns on him the buck might be mine.

"Did you get him? " he asks.

"Yeah," I say, and then he breaks into a smile and quickly moves to replace the big hunter on the rope.

"You ever hear the story about the two hunters dragging their first deer out of the woods? " the big hunter steps up to me and asks.

"No," I shake my head.

"Well," he starts, "they tied the deer up by its back legs and they're dragging it along, when this other hunter comes up on them and sees the way they have the deer tied. He says, 'What're you doin'? Don't you know it's easier if you tie the rope around its neck and drag it like that?' The guys look at each other and say, 'Yeah. Lets try that.'

"So, they take the rope and they put it around the deer's neck and start dragging. After a little while, the one guy looks at the other guy and says, 'Hey! Y'know, he's right. It is easier this way.' The other one says, 'Yeah. Except we're gettin' further away from camp.'"

■

In the Bronco, when the deer is finally loaded in the back and we are ready to leave, Dad looks at me and says, "Every time we go out late you get one."

Then he smiles and drives off.

XIV

Monarchs of the Woods

"Like in the human kingdom," writes Shoemaker in *Pennsylvania Deer and Their Horns*, "some stags outstrip and outrank their fellows. Like them, some stags earn immortality, are remembered long after they have passed the scene. Pennsylvania has its full quota of famous stags, about which the old hunters love to tell, and tell again." (p. 71)

Though nineteenth-century hunters may have slaughtered deer with wild abandon, they also enjoyed a more personal relationship with the whitetail than most modern hunters. Generally, they lived in the same mountains as their quarry and suffered through the same harse winters and lean times on the farm. They saw deer more often, understood what they faced in the wild and, since they were dependent on the whitetail for food and profit, better learned their habits and traits.

Without the distraction of satellite television, many of the old hunters also were well versed in the classics, or at least the Bible, and connoisseurs of the art of storytelling. For entertainment, they would spin yarns about bucks who eluded them season after season before finally being brought low by skill or luck. They would give these bucks names—Old Dan, Old Goldy, Big Hoof, Old Mosby, and The River King—endow them with personalities and, in a few instances, even supernatural abilities.

In place of colorful names and stories today, the best a

"monarch of the woods" might expect from the urban/suburban hunter is a bland, generic title, such as "a big one" or "a big buck." Or classification according to antler size, "a big eight-point," or "that six-point." Instead of tales about how difficult a certain buck had been to fell, chased for weeks, or even years, over hill and dale, details of a hunt will now most often focus on how quickly it ended. "Got him at seven-thirty and was back in the cabin by eight o'clock." Nothing like the legend of the White Ghost, a pure white buck of enormous size for whom White Deer Valley in Union County is named, appears in the late twentieth century.

"Again and again he was met point blank in the forest by capable hunters, but no bullet could touch him," Shoemaker writes. "He seemed to bear a charmed life. At length Shaney John, the celebrated Indian hunter from the Juniata Country, then a very young man—was prevailed upon to cross the mountains and slay this defiant stag. He lay in wait for it, a poisoned arrow, a slender dart of bone, in his bow. The magnificent stag, white as a ghost, emerged from the forest into a cornfield, where he snorted his defiance to the whole race of hunters. Suddenly the arrow sped through the air, while the stag stood broadside, catching him in the flank. The animal gave a slight start as he felt the prick of the dart, and looked around, as if searching for the insect that had bitten him. Detecting nothing, he stood still and unharmed.

"All the while Shaney John was watching him from the corner of the woods. At the end of a couple of minutes his head dropped a little, as if he was sleepy. The hunter stepped out in plain sight. The white stag noticed him, and moved forward, as if to do battle, but with unsteady tread. It was a distance of a hundred yards to where the Indian stood, but the deer evidently was determined to reach his foe. As he drew near he lowered his fine head as if to charge, but the splendid crown of royal antlers 'wabbled,' when he was within almost a horn's thrust of Shaney John he dropped dead. The Indian left the carcass lay while he walked to a nearby cabin to bring his friends to the scene. When he returned to the spot, accompanied by a score of comrades red and white, he found that the deer had turned coal black in color. When the animal was opened to be cleaned, the flesh proved to be already rancid. The horns crumbled in the hunter's grasp, when he tried to move the body. All present agreed that the White Stag was a 'ghspook' or ghost. After that occurrence, other white deer were seen in the valley, and it became gradually known by that name. Several white deer were later killed in and about the valley" (pp. 72–73).

■

"Odocoileus americanus borealis (Miller)" was, according to Shoemaker, the "true deer" of Pennsylvania, the "Big Deer" hunters sought so relentlessly for over two hundred years, from the time of William Penn's landing until the days of Andrew Carnegie's steel mills.

During the colonial period, the Big Deer ruled northern Pennsylvania to roughly the Juniata River, where they began to encounter *Odocoileus virginianus,* or the "Little Deer" that hunters know today. The only section of the state where Big Deer were not found, except possibly in passing, was the southern tier counties. "In the Southern counties the 'Little Deer' fought with it for possession of the territory," Shoemaker explains. "Always of a mild disposition, more like the red deer of Europe, than the smaller variety, it would not have yielded ground but for superior numbers" (pp. 16–17).

To the old hunters, the male Big Deer was known first as a "hart," and then later a "stag," names that were carried across the Atlantic from Europe where they had been in use for hundreds of years. Early German immigrants, the Pennsylvania Dutch, called the original deer "harsh" and the male of the species a "harsh-buck." Later hunters often called the original deer "swampies," probably because the last refuge of the animal was in hard to hunt swamps. The first settlers reportedly saw herds of five hundred moving through the virgin forests, usually led by a large stag attended by several younger stags known as "satellites."

"There was a small herd in the Black Forest [Potter County], which refused to be broken up," notes Shoemaker. "It still numbered a dozen individuals in 1900. Cal Wagner, a noted hunter of the Seven Mountains, in 1876, came upon a herd of 30 Big Deer on the high plateau above Zerby Station [Centre County]. There was a herd of at least twenty in Clearfield County in the eighties. The herds were banded together from earliest days for mutual protection from human and animal foes. The old, experienced stags which led them were the 'brains,' though the younger satellites performed outpost duty of no mean nature. But there were too many hunters, and the stately Pennsylvania Hart in his pure form ceased to exist" (pp. 17–18).

Shoemaker estimates the average weight for a mature Pennsylvania Hart at 200 pounds. However, other writers use the figure of 175 pounds for the average "northern deer," but that is still significantly larger than the average 140-pound buck of today. And, whatever the average size of the state's original deer, the records of trophies that have survived are truly impressive, especially because they are for field dressed bucks. William T. Hornaday, director of the New York Zoo, mentions a deer of 278 pounds. Clement F. Herlacher of Clinton County tells of one stag weighing 240 pounds and another 235. Woodcock lists one of 220 pounds; Marcus Killam of Pike County one of 306 pounds; John Swope of Huntingdon County, 225 pounds; and S. J. Pealer of Columbia County, 260 pounds (pp. 18–19).

Of the few Big Deer mentioned by Shoemaker that were weighed before being field dressed, one was shot by Nelson Tyrell of Bradford County. That buck tipped the scales at 350 pounds. "In my boyhood days 200 pounds live weight was not an unusual weight for a buck in Pennsylvania," wrote Dr. Joseph T. Rothrock, the "Father of Pennsylvania Forestry," in a 1914 letter. "Naturally, such deer are becoming very scarce."[1]

Such records leave little doubt that even an average-sized Pennsylvania Hart was a magnificent creature, the trophy of a lifetime for any of today's deer hunters. Especially since the antlers of a trophy Big Deer were every bit as impressive as it size. "It can be assumed that a Big Deer's head reached the following proportions under ideal conditions," Shoemaker concludes. "Length 29 inches; greatest width, 22 inches; tip to tip, 17 inches; circumference, 5½ inches, with 6 or 7 points on each horn. With the 'Little Deer,' now 'the' deer of Pennsylvania, it can be taken as: Length, 18½ inches; widest, 9½ inches; tip to tip, 10 inches; circumference, 3½ inches; points not more than 4 on each horn. And this would be the maximum for *Odocoileus virginianus*. The 'mixed Breed' deer are liable to have large antlers according to preponderance of 'Big Deer' blood. As stated previously no measurements of imported deer or their horns will be given in these pages. It is a great pity that they were ever brought into Pennsylvania" (p. 92).

In a vague sort of way, records seem to support Shoemaker's assumptions, since the biggest trophies measured tend to come from the first half of the twentieth century, when a few of the "Big Deer," or at least their genes, may still have existed. The world record "typical" whitetail, meaning one with symmetrical antlers, was taken by John Breen in Funkley, Minnesota, in 1918. It scored 202 points on the Boone and Crockett Club scale, an international scoring system that awards points based on antler spread, symmetry, diameter and length of beams, and number and length of tines. On Breen's buck, the right main beam measured 31⅛ inches, the left beam 31 inches. There were eight points on each beam and the rack measured 23⅝ inches at the widest spread. The second-place buck scored 198⅜ points and was taken by Roosevelt Luckey in Allegany County, New York, Pennsylvania Hart country just across the border from Allegheny National Forest, in 1939. The right beam was 29⅝ inches long and the left 29½ inches. There were six points on the right beam and eight on the left. Its widest spread was 18⅛ inches.[2]

Pennsylvania's record typical buck (as of 1986) measured 189-0 points on the Boone and Crockett Club scale. It was shot by Fritz Janowsky of Wellsburg, New York, while hunting in Bradford County in 1943. Likewise, the third, fifth, sixth, seventh, eighth, and tenth largest typical bucks all came from the first half of the twentieth century. Two of the remaining top ten Pennsylvania bucks came from the 1970s and one from the late 1950s. Those later deer were taken from Greene, Bedford, and Beaver counties, where there is more farmlands—and so better feed to grow larger deer—and fewer hunters pressuring the animals. All the earlier bucks on the top ten list came from such traditional northern deer counties as Sullivan, Jefferson, Mifflin, McKean, and Clarion.[3]

About the later deer, Small Deer, on the list, it should be remembered that exceptions exist to every rule. And there was no Game Commission compiling records in the centuries when the Big Deer roamed Pennsylvania's forests. The fact that hunters such as Tome and Woodcock were more interested in deer as a source of meat or income than trophies, also makes it likely that practically all Big Deer antlers were left to weather away over woodshed and barn doors, leaving behind only stories like that of the Strohecker Head.

■

Samuel Strohecker was a hunter who lived in the High Valley section of the Seven Mountains of central Pennsylvania. His trophy was a Big Deer taken in 1896 and inspected by Shoemaker two years later. According to the writer's own measurements, the Strohecker rack was 31 inches in length, 21 inches at its widest point and 16 inches from tip to tip. The circumference taken above the brow point was 5½ inches. There were 15 points on the right horn, 11 on the left, a notable exception to John Dyce's belief that the left antler always has the most points on an irregular rack (pp. 88–89).

"Of course the writer, boylike, wanted to own the noble head," Shoemaker notes. "Strohecker was modest in his valuation, offering it for $15. This seemed remarkably reasonable, as the taxidermist, the great Eldon, had done his work well. The expression of the head was most strikingly lifelike. The writer, being at that time a prospective Sophomore in college, had to 'write home' for the money to make the purchase. By the time his indulgent parents, who never refused him anything, forwarded the check other fancies had arisen, and the money was spent elsewhere. Years passed, other scenes and other interests sometimes wavered the writer's fealty to the sport of the chase, during which time many deer heads were seen, and quite a few measured. But no Pennsylvania head, old or recent, had quite the same beauty as the mental image of the Strochecker stag" (pp. 89–90).

Fifteen years later, in the autumn of 1913, the now financially stable and more mature Shoemaker decided to try and purchase the head again. But when a friend of his who was traveling in Rebersburg, Centre County, where Strohecker lived, inquired about the trophy he was told it was gone.

" 'Sam' Strohecker had died 'years before,' as his widow said, and she had married again. At the vendue after his death, the head was sold 'to some stranger,' and that was all that could be learned. The kindly old lady led her visitor out of the rear door to an arbor in the back yard. On it was nailed the ant-riddled horns of a stag, with six points on each horn. 'That's the only trophy we have left of poor Sam's hunting days,' she said. 'You are welcome to it if you wish, but it can't hold a candle to the 'big head' which we sold" (pp. 90–91).

Bob MacWilliams, in *Pennsylvania Game News,* sums up the situation surrounding old trophies: "It's sad to think how many great whitetail trophies have disappeared over the years, simply vanished with no permanent record of their existence to interest and excite sportsmen. Sometimes not even the hunter who took one gave it much thought. More often, though, he gave it a special place in his home or camp. But the years take their toll and eventually conditions change, and a trophy which had great personal value to someone comes to mean nothing to others unaware of its background, and it is tossed into the trash."[4]

What such stories seem to say, and what every real hunter knows, is that it is the quality of the hunt that matters, not the size of the deer or its rack. A good story recorded in a camp log or passed on from father to son will hold more interest and outlast most trophy racks. Take the tale of "Old Dan," a buck who ruled the forests of Huntingdon County from 1885 to

1895. His antlers will never be displayed, but his craftiness must still be admired a hundred years after his passing.

■

"Some years ago," writes C. Lloyd Jones in the *Semi-Weekly News* of Huntingdon, "a party of young ladies and gentlemen while out on Short Mountain, on a beautiful Friday in the month of April when the sun was shining in full glory, and while looking for that most beautiful, fragrant and lasting wildflower, the trailing arbutus, gathering it among the mosses and ferns, they happened to see a large male deer with seven prongs still in velvet, and they looked in astonishment to behold such a beautiful specimen of the deer family so near to them. When they returned home they described this beautiful and stately creature, and an old hunter hearing them speak of its large prongs, its smooth red hide with a stripe along its neck, as pure and white as the fallen snow, and a large scar on its left hind shoulder, said from the description they gave that it was 'Old Dan,' a name given it in remembrance of an old recluse who lived in these parts many years ago and was a great hunter in his time here in central Pennsylvania.

"Old Dan was a quiet and queer old bachelor, with a cunning and craftiness known only to the hunters of those days. He had told that while yet a young man he was a soldier in the German army, and beyond that he said nothing more about his life. Because of its cunning and craftiness, they named this beautiful animal after Old Dan. The scar on his left hind shoulder was caused by a party of hunters who went out on Short Mountain to give chase to this wise old fellow, one of the party asserting that he shot him by following his tracks among the leaves by the blood he lost, but they gave up the chase as night came.

"Old Dan, while a young fawn, was seen first by Trapper John P. Swope while he was visiting his traps, and was lost in admiration to behold such a beautiful young animal. He says it was the most beautiful creature of its kind he ever beheld in the wild state. Trapper Swope said he saw him quite often

173

while out at his traps, but never had the heart to shoot him, as Old Dan was too fine a specimen for him to kill. Hunters at different times saw this animal, but he seemed to bear a charmed life for quite a few years. He was seen one summer by some woodsmen, and they said he had a mate and a fawn with him this time and that his mate and fawn were just as pretty as Old Dan.

"A party of hunters were out deer hunting one autumn, and, as usual, they placed three men of the party at three different deer crossings. Everything being quiet and still, one of them began to feel sleepy and put his gun against a tree. While the hunter was leaning on the tree and almost fallen asleep, he heard a noise back of him on the crossing. He quickly turned his head, and there only a few feet from him stood Old Dan. He was lost in admiration at the beautiful deer before him, and, as hunters say, he got the buck fever and almost forgot about his gun. When he finally reached for his gun, Old Dan saw him move. Up went his tail or 'nag,' as the hunters say, and away he went through the woods. The hunter said he shot at the deer, but is not certain whether he hit him or not. Old Dan seemed to know when they were after him, for he was so cunning that he was seldom seen by men with their powerful firearms that do so much destruction to the denizens of the woods and vales, but was seen quite often by others.

"At last he was shot by one of a party of hunters who went out to try and bring in this wise old fellow. The hunting party was composed of John Patterson, Isaac Chilcoat, George Piper, David McClure and others. They routed seven deer, and the first and only one they brought home they killed just after they routed the seven. Mr. Patterson informed the writer of this sketch that he shot Old Dan and badly wounded him, for they followed his trail on the mountain by the blood until dark. As it snowed during the night, they did not go after him, but the cunning old animal was so badly wounded that he left the mountain, coming through Barree and on down through the farms on the Juniata River which he tried to cross near Warrior Ridge, but was drowned. Sometime during the day he was seen and taken out of Cresswell's mill forebay by John Port, now deceased, but at the time track foreman for the Pennsylvania Railroad Company between Barree and Petersburg. Thus ended the tale of one of the craftiest animals that ever roamed over central Pennsylvania."[5]

■

Among other deer whose names have survived is Old Goldy, a giant buck with "seemingly top-heavy antlers" who supposedly lived in the forests around Roulette and the Allegheny River in Potter County for about fifteen years. He was given his name because in summer he was a light golden bay color and in winter a pale orange. He was downed by a "bold hunter" during the 1913 season "and the press of Northern Pennsylvania teemed for days with the achievement."

Teddy was another large buck from the Black Forest. He was called Teddy, probably after tough old Teddy Roosevelt, "because he could not be drowned." Shoemaker gives no further details, but driving deer into a river or creek where they were most vulnerable was a common practice with many of the old hunters, as well as the Indians. Evidently, Teddy was forced into the water at some point in his life but would not succumb. He was finally brought down during the 1914 season.

Old Mosby was named for the Confederate general John S. Mosby, a noted guerilla fighter during the Civil War, because of the numerous "raids" he led on corn and wheat fields in the Seven Mountains of Centre and Mifflin counties for ten years after the Civil War. He was brought down by Lewis Dorman, a famed panther hunter of the time, and his antlers were said to have been the largest ever taken from the region.

Big Hoof got his name from a "peculiar twisted hoof-mark." He is said to have had a rack of antlers "as big as any elk," an apparently common description during a time when hunters believed elk and deer mated and produced offspring with gigantic antlers. He reportedly escaped Bradford County hunters for twenty years—it was commonly, and wrongly, assumed that a deer lived as long as a horse—before Nelson Tyrrell got him.[6]

■

Along with tales about individual deer, the old hunters also passed on certain superstitions involving the whitetail. Shoemaker recalls that albinos could be killed only by specially prepared weapons—a silver bullet or a poisoned arrow— and their meat was tainted. "The White Deer, despite its symmetry and beautiful color, is generally supposed to contain the soul of some person who has committed the crime of incest. In Europe it is considered unlucky to kill a white chamois; death coming to the hunter within twelve months" (p. 73).

Pennsylvania mountaineers also believed it was unlucky to look upon a dying buck, a European tradition that might have had something to do with the dying animal placing a curse on the killer. On the other hand, they thought it was very lucky to encounter a buck while on a journey. The French even had a proverb: "Qui rencontre un cerf, un loup, ou un ours, c'est très bon signe" ("If you meet a stag, a wolf, or a bear, that's a good sign").

Another belief of the old hunters was that deer could be lured to their camp by music, which may have been part of the reason John Q. Dyce kept his hunting cabin stocked with musical instruments and always entertained his companions with song. Shoemaker reports deer frequently approaching lumber camps and settlers' cabins at dusk when music was being played. "It is related that Fiddler's Green on Potatoe Creek in McKean County, was named for a famous greensward where the deer danced to the music played by an eccentric backwoodsman named Vincent Hogarth." In a related vein, the old hunters thought deer like to play among themselves in open areas in the forest, sometimes chasing each other in a figure eight pattern around a tree. They dubbed the clearing supposedly made from such play "Fairy Parks" (p. 29).

Then there was the belief that the hooves and antlers of

Pennsylvania deer became poisonous from killing venomous snakes. Hunters who survived a battle with the poisonous hooves and antlers of a buck were said to be immune to the bullets of an enemy and made the best soldiers. "If thou be hurt with hart," an English proverb states, "it brings thee to thy bier, but barber's hand will boar's hurt heal; therefore thou need'st not fear." The French counter with, "Après le cerf la bière, après le sanglier le miere" ("After a stag—the coffin; after a wild boar—see a surgeon").

∎

Perhaps because the old hunters lived closer to the white-tail, or because they killed more deer in a single season than a modern hunter will in a lifetime, the hunting literature of the nineteenth century is packed with descriptions of hand-to-hand combat between hunters and stags. Tome, Shoemaker, and Woodcock all relate "heroic battles" in their books, as does Lyman in *Strange Events in the Black Forest.* But the the most famous incident appears in Meshach Browning's auto-biography, *Forty-Four Years of the Life of a Hunter* (1859).

Browning's book, like his contemporary Tome's *Pioneer Life,* is a true classic of deer hunting literature. He was born in Frederick County, Maryland, in 1781 and died in 1859. Although not Pennsylvania born, he frequently crossed the Mason-Dixon Line to hunt in Bedford County, Somerset County, and, particularly, Fayette County. In his book, which is so full of humorous incidents a person sometimes has to wonder how tall are his tales, he describes a vicious fight he once had with a white-tailed buck in the Youghiogheny River, one that was so well known Currier & Ives even produced a print of it, though not a very accurate one.

"On the morning when the first snow fell that season, I rose early, intending to hunt the west side of the Great Yough. river. I went to the river, which, being pretty well up, the water reached about half-way up my thigh. I took off my pants and moccasins, waded over, and after again putting on my clothes, I felt first-rate. I had gone but a short distance, when I discovered the tracks of a very large buck, which had gone into a thicket, as I thought, in search of company, it being then in their mating season. As I concluded he would not stop until he found what he was seeking, I did not think it worth while to follow him; so I passed on, and hunted until toward the close of the day, when, finding the tracks of a large bear, I followed them into a thick laurel swamp. It being very cold, and everything being frozen hard, I knew that he would not feed until the weather moderated; at which time I promised myself to meet him on the same ground, if he should think proper to come out.

"With this on my mind, I left the feeding ground, and directed my course for home, until I came to the buck's track which I had seen on my way out. From what I had seen of the movements of the deer during the day, I knew that he was still in that thicket; of which I took advantage, as he could not run any other way than through the river, or out at me. I went on toward the spot where I thought he lay, when directly out he came, within range of my rifle. But as I saw I would have to fire at him on the run, for he was badly frightened, I let him come as near as he would, when, as he was dashing on, I shot at him. He kept on for some distance, but at length stopped. As soon as I fired, I ran after him with all speed; and when he stopped, I was still within gun-shot. Before I could load, however, he went into a thicket; and in following his trail, I found, by the quantity of blood after him, that he was badly wounded.

"I had a first-rate half-breed greyhound dog with me, which, finding that I was going home, had crossed the river; but when he heard the report of the gun, he returned to me. I sent him into the thicket, when out came the buck, with the dog close at his heels. They passed me like a streak of lightning, and down a steep hill into the river, making such jumps as were really astonishing. When I reached the edge of the water, I could see neither dog nor deer; but, looking down the stream, I discovered them fighting with great desperation. The river was so deep that they could get no foothold, and they had floated down until they came to a ripple, at the head of a fall of at least ten feet. Immediately below where the dog and the deer were fighting, there was a hole in the river, about twenty feet deep, out of which it would be almost impossible to get the buck, if he once got into it; so I concluded to leave my gun against a tree, wade in, and kill him with my knife. I set my gun against a tree, and waded in—the water in some places being up to my belt, and in other places about half-thigh deep. On I went until I came within reach of the buck, which I seized by one of his horns; but as soon as I took hold, the dog let go, and struck out for the shore, when the buck made a lunge at me. I then caught him by the other horn, though he very nearly threw me backwards into the river; but I held on to him, as I was afraid of our both being carried into the deep hole by the swift current. I dared not let him go; for if I did, I knew he would dart at me with his horns. I must kill him, or he would in all probability kill me; but whenever I let go with one hand, for the purpose of using my knife, he was ready to pitch at me. I called and called the dog, but he sat on the shore looking on, without attempting to move.

"After awhile, it occurred to me to throw him under the water, and drown him; whereupon I braced my right leg against his left side, and with my arms jerked him suddenly, when down he came with his feet toward me. Then it was that my whole front paid for it, as his feet flew like drumsticks, scraping my body and barking my shins, till ambition had to give in to necessity, and I was not only compelled to let him up, but even glad to help him to his feet again, though I still held on to his rough horns. From the long scuffle, my hands beginning to smart, and my arms to become weak, I took another plan.

"I threw him again, and as he fell I twisted him around by his horns, so as to place his back toward me and his feet from me. Then came a desperate trial, for as this was the only hope I had of overcoming him, I laid all my strength and weight on him, to keep him from getting upon his feet again. This I found I could do, for the water was so deep that he had no chance of helping himself, for want of a foothold. There we had it round and round, and in the struggle my left boot was accidentally placed on his lowermost horn, which was deep down in the water.

"As soon as I felt my foot touch his horn, I threw my whole weight on it, and put his head under the water, deeper than I could reach with my arm. I thought that was the very thing I wanted; but then came the hardest part of the fight, for the buck exerted all his strength and activity against me, while I was in a situation from which I dare not attempt to retreat.

"I was determined to keep his head under, although sometimes even my head and face were beneath the water; and if I had not been supported by his horns, which kept me from sinking down, and enabled me to stand firmer that if I had no support, the stream might have been called, with great truth, 'the troubled water'; for I know that if it was not troubled, I was, for often I wished myself out of it. I know that the buck would have had no objection to my being out; though he probably thought that, as I had come in to help the savage dog, he would give me a punch or two with his sharp horns, to remember him by. Indeed, that was what I most dreaded; and it was my full purpose to keep clear of them, if possible.

"In about two minutes after I got my foot on his horn, and sank his head under water, things began to look a little more favorable; for I felt his strength failing, which gave me hopes of getting through the worst fight I had ever been engaged in during all my hunting expeditions.

"When his strength was but little, I held fast to his upper horn with my left hand, and keeping my foot firmly on his lower horn, I pressed it to the bottom of three feet of water, and, taking out my knife, when his kicking was nearly over, I let his head come up high enough to be within reach, when at a single cut I laid open the one side of his neck, severing both blood vessels. This relieved me from one of the most difficult positions in which, during all my life, I had been placed for the same length of time."[7]

■

Stories about women appear to be few and far between in nineteenth-century hunting literature. Probably that is because the literature was written by men rather than because women did not hunt. Certainly, women who lived on the frontier picked up rifles and added meat to the family pot whenever they could. Shoemaker, writing just before World War I, says that "an entire chapter could be written about women as deer hunters in Pennsylvania," but only mentions five. Among them was Dorcas Stackpole who, with her husband, kept a hotel on the old pike near McVeytown in Mifflin County. "She could fiddle like a man and could dance with the best, and with it all, including her hotel experience, which she continued to run after the death of her husband, was a good Presbyterian. She loved parties and believed in having a good time and stopped for nothing when there was fun ahead. She lived to a good old age, and as illustration of the love she had for parties we will state that upon a certain occasion in her old age when she was ill a friend inquired of her son James how she was. He answered the question as to her probable recovery by irreverently answering: 'Oh, if it was a good supper she was going to mother would have been off long ago.' It was not meant for unkindness, but as a joke owing to her love of the sociabilities of the time.

"It is related of her that upon a certain occasion she saw a deer crossing the river near her hotel, raced into the river by some hunters. She ran to the water and caught the deer by the horns just as it was emerging from the water, and, after a hard struggle, succeeded in drowning it. As the combat was going on the hunters reached the opposite shore of the river and seeing what was going on they called to her: 'Go it, Dorkey,' and she did 'go it' until she had the deer into venison, which she could probably do, as she was a very large woman and thought nothing of jumping into the pig-pen and killing a hog" (pp. 85–86).

XV

Sparring

Bob is feeding slivers of purplish deer liver into a big skillet of onions and hot bacon grease when I step up behind him.

"Well, that's number four," I smile.

"You get one?" he turns, startled.

"A spike," I shrug.

"What the hell," Garth says from the doorway. "It's still a buck."

"Anybody who gets a buck after the first day, you better shake their hand," Bob adds, and extends his paw.

As we shake, I fight off an urge to box the air and dance. After Bob, Garth, and Mike had returned with deer, I wanted a buck more than I cared to admit, even to myself. Although I believe that competition in the field is wrong, I had felt challenged when I saw their deer. But since I knew it would take concentration to succeed,—and maybe because I feared failing or, worse yet, appearing jealous,—I had kept my control. Now, I suppress my joy because I don't want anyone to see how much getting a buck had meant to me. Then, too, I don't want to offend Dad, make him feel more out of place than he must already. Nevertheless, I cannot keep from smiling, or hoping that someone will ask about my buck. But everybody is busy with dinner and no one seems interested.

"Didn't you see anything, Pap?" Bob asks, when Dad steps into the kitchen.

"I seen deer," Dad answers, "but nothin' with horns on."

"Well, we'll get 'em tomorrow," he tells him, and then motions to the table where a gigantic salad and a plate of liver are waiting. "Grab somethin' to eat."

I pull a couple of cold beers from the refrigerator and hand one to Dad. Then we load up bowls with salad and squeeze into chairs at opposite ends of the table.

"You gotta try this," Garth says, shoving the liver closer.

While I love to sample new dishes, liver is one food my taste buds wrote off long ago. I simply do not like the flavor.

"You gotta try this, though," Garth insists, when I tell him I don't like liver. "This is good. I ate a whole plate myself."

"It doesn't taste nothin' like beef liver," Bob reassures me from the kitchen.

Garth continues to insist, so I give in and take a piece. The taste is surprisingly light and subtle, as different from the thick, heavy beef liver I've attempted in the past as a pound of onions is from a pound of garlic.

"Not bad," I say.

"The best," Garth grins and nods.

The trick to cooking good deer liver, Bob says, is to soak it in salt water to remove the bile and then cut it thin. The thinner the better. Then fry it with a coat of pancake batter and plenty of onions. It is a simple dish, but has increased my respect for the whitetail again. I feel stupid for having classified such an exquisite wild creature with domestic beef. That is like comparing a bland, white-fleshed hatchery trout raised on a variation of dog food to a wild fish whose flesh has grown red and flavorful on a diet of mayflies. I regret leaving the liver from my deer in the woods. I hope a fox dines royally on it, and make a mental note to place a plastic bag for the liver from my next deer in my hunting coat. Then, at last, Garth asks about my buck.

■

We are still nibbling at the liver when John Arva and Joe Minnita arrive from their camp near Chapman Dam State Park. Ronnie Rossetti, another member of their camp, had called earlier in the day to report taking three deer, including

183

an eight-point by John. When Bob told him we also had three bucks hanging, John decided to ride over and see for himself.

Like Bob, John is in his mid-forties and has been hunting Up North for about thirty years. The two met more than fifteen years ago through a mutual friend from West Newton, John's home town. Bob had sought the introduction after hearing about the success John was having with deer in Allegheny National Forest around Chapman Dam and Hearts Content. Since Bob wanted to expand his hunting territory beyond the State Game Lands above the cabin, they began hunting together and have continued to do so on and off. Last year, we gathered together for a drive on the third day of the season.

Although Bob had never said so, and may deny it, it is clear from from the way he talks about their hunts together that John is something of a spur to him, if not a hero of sorts. John seems to stir the competitiveness Bob once told me he enjoys about deer hunting, while also serving as a measuring stick against which Bob judges his own accomplishments as a hunter. The fact that they are about the same age probably plays a part in their relationship, too. As I am drawn to Garth, who is two years younger than me, and Dad to Bob's Uncle Pete, another World War II veteran, Bob and John share a friendship only those of the same generation can know.

"I had a hard time seeing him," Bob says, when John asks about his spike.

"It's those little ones that are hard to see," John laughs. "You can see the big ones a mile away."

"I missed the first shot," Bob confesses then. "I got him with the next shot, about two hundred yards away. He was down in the bottom. You know how that basin is."

John nods with the knowledge of a hunter who knows an area. I notice it is the first time Bob has mentioned missing his deer, and then the sparring begins.

■

Biologists have found that white-tailed bucks are sociable creatures. More sociable, in fact, than does. Yet as soon as the velvet has worn off their antlers, and even though they have no interest in mating, they will start to spar with each other.

Sparring matches are low-level encounters, nothing like the violent antler fights that are so often shown in wildlife films and may occur later when competition for breeding takes place. They apparently establish a hierarchy among bucks prior to the breeding season. The matches frequently begin when one buck lowers his antlers to another buck of similar size feeding nearby. The second buck usually accepts the challenge, and the two join antlers, pushing against each other until one is shoved backward and withdraws from the contest. Sometimes both bucks will stop sparring simultaneously, with no clear winner or loser, and resume feeding side by side as if nothing has happened.

On occasion, smaller bucks will challenge larger bucks. When that occurs, the smaller buck is either immediately driven off, or allowed to test its strength against the larger buck, who will simply stand still while the young buck pushes. These contests can last from a few seconds to several minutes.

Sparring patterns also vary among bucks of different ages. For all but the smallest bucks, however, matches end by the time breeding starts. Probably because they are less certain of their place in the hierarchy, bucks in the yearling stage and two-to-three-year-olds are more active fighters than older bucks who are well established in their positions. Fights among equally large, dominant bucks are uncommon events that usually last no more than fifteen to thirty seconds. Antler size, which closely reflects body size and physical condition, is a good visual indicator of the position of a buck in the hierarchy of an area.

The behavior of deer hunters toward each other is not unlike that of white-tailed bucks. During most of the year, they are friendly and happy in one another's company and exhibit no aggressive behavior about their sport, even when reliving old hunts. But the closer the season gets, the more assertive they become. By the week before opening day, the clubs and bars, factories and offices where they gather and work are hotbeds of debate about buck habits, hunting spots, past mistakes and successes, shell loads, equipment, and a hundred other finer points of deer hunting.

In the mountains during the season, talk and opinions become even more intense. While embarrassment is usually kept to a minimum, and encounters almost always broken off before anyone is deflated, hunters test one another like sparring bucks. Those of similar rank usually do it through respect, those less certain of their abilities through envy. Those who do not take the sport so seriously resort to gentle teasing, especially of older hunters whose bright star has dimmed.

Although there is quite a bit of difference in size between the two men—Bob is more than six-foot tall and barrel-chested, John is thin and somewhere under six feet—they give the impression of two dominant bucks who enjoy testing each other's knowledge and resourcefulness.

"He said you drove down there," John says, about the area where Bob and the others had taken their deer. "I said, 'Ronnie, I'll bet money you can't drive down there.'"

"No, we walked in," Bob says.

"That's what I told him. You can't drive down there."

"Go look again," Bob suddenly says smugly. "You can get down there." He pauses, assessing the affect of his words, and then adds, "If you want to smash your Blazer all up."

The remark catches John off guard and leads Bob to launch an offense. Stories pour out. In short order, he makes Garth's eight-point into one of the most beautiful deer he has ever seen; tells of an even larger buck he saw in the same area when they were scouting on Sunday; lectures on the way deer were keeping to the bottoms; then points out that he, Garth, and Mike were the only hunters on the entire mountain; and finally tosses in the fact I have just returned with a buck.

"No, shit!" John says surprised. "Congratulations."

"That's the fourth one," Bob smiles, and offers the liver.

John declines the meat, which leads Bob to inform him of the proper way to prepare deer liver, a move that costs him the advantage when John agrees with his recipe and brings the conversation around to the existence of trophy bucks in a certain area.

"Hey, Bob. You'll always have big bucks where they're cutting timber," he points out, "because the bucks get good feed in February and March to grow antlers."

"There's another reason for them big bucks over there," Bob quickly answers, sensing the shift.

"What's the other reason? " John demands.

"The reason is the tornado."

"Well, timber's down. Cut down or blown down—it's the same thing."

It is a good hit. But Bob ignores it, countering with a promise of big bucks in the future.

"There's gonna be some four- and five-year-old deer over there. Two years ago we saw a rack over there that would put yours to shame. And he was big. You should have seen the hoof prints."

The remark fails to turn John, though. He surprises Bob by bringing up the three-point Joe took earlier in the day. It was the third for their camp. Bob has forgotten about the buck and tries to parry the thrust by suddenly remembering that Ronnie had mentioned it. Then he buys time by asking for details, not content until he fixes in his mind the exact spot where Joe took the deer.

"I remember that place quite well," he concludes. "There are nice deer back there."

Back and forth the sparring continues, ranging far and wide over stories many hunters can relate to.

■

"Ronnie saw a couple bucks," John notes.

"I can't believe Ronnie saw bucks," Bob laughs, "because I've been with Ronnie already and told him, 'Look at that nice six-point.' He said, 'Get the hell out! That ain't no six-point!' I said, 'Jeez, Ronnie. It's only eighty yards away.' He couldn't even see horn on a deer eighty yards away in a open field. A six-point! And he's seeing them now? You better watch him. He's startin' to see things. Or did he get new glasses? "

"He has new glasses," Joe smiles. "But he says he takes them off when he sees a deer."

■

"I followed these footprints," John starts. "They went up to this guy. He had his back to me. He was only off this hollow thirty-five, forty yards. So I walked over to him and asked if he saw a guy in green pants and an orange jacket. He said, 'Nope, I only saw two guys dragging a buck.' I'd seen those guys down below so I thought Joey was still out in front of us. We're drivin' for him.

"So I snuck out away from that guy about a hundred yards, and all at once here comes a deer up over the bank. Beautiful rack. Beautiful rack. The deer stops right between me and the guy. I can see the buck. I can see the guy. I duck out of the way. I already have my deer. Ronnie already has his deer. I am waiting for this guy to shoot. I am looking at this buck with my naked eye. It's only thirty-five yards. I see he's bleeding from his hind leg.

"So, the buck moved out like there was nothing wrong with him. He walked up and he walked up and he walked up and walked up. And then POW POW! This guy shot twice while the buck was walking. So, I look again and the buck's standing there. I can still see a little bit of blood, the same place it was before. POW! The guy shoots again.

"I didn't know if the buck ran or what. I watch the guy run up to where the deer was. He's running all around up there. So I figure he missed that sonofabitch but I see this blood trail. We'll go out here and find Joey and we'll come back.

"Then here comes Ronnie. I tell him we got to go get Joey. There's a buck hit. It ain't hit bad. We'll follow the blood trail. That guy's not following it. He's up there running around in circles. Ronnie said, 'Let's go up and see if he has it.'

"Well, we went up there and he's all shook up. He has the buck. But he probably knew it was hit because he saw blood going over to the spot where he shot. Ronnie said, 'That buck was hit before you shot.' The guy said, 'No, it wasn't. No, it wasn't. I said, 'Yes, it was. I saw it.' Then he didn't know what to say. He thought we were trailing it and were going to take it off him. He was that type of guy. He was just all shook up. He thought that wasn't his buck because it was hit. Believe me! That buck was fair game."

■

"We followed the tracks and there they were on both sides of the fence," John says about another deer. "And here comes a guy. He says he ain't never seen anything like it. That deer grew wings. He said, 'You should've seen it go over that high fence. And it didn't touch the fence.' We figured it was eight-foot there."

"That's not eight-foot," Bob disagrees. "It might be seven-foot. They might have special mesh on there. I don't think it's much over six-foot."

"Seven or eight feet. That's still a helluva vertical jump," I point out.

"We stood at the fence and looked and said, 'Jesus, good-ness. How did it get over that?'"

■

"I talked to Judy," Bob tells John, about a call from his girlfriend earlier. "She said, 'I want to go up Friday. Maybe I'll get a buck.'"

Everybody starts to laugh.

"Yeah, it's that easy," John says. "One year, my brother-in-law, he never got a buck in his life, he's up Little Run with me and gets a four-point. I mean, he's happy. Never got a buck in his life. My sister sees it. It's only a small four-point. She says, 'You shouldn't have taken it. You could have gone up to Uniontown and got a bigger one!'"

"Just walk into the woods and pick one out," I say.

"Like goin' to the supermarket and gettin' what you want," Joe smiles.

"He said, 'Boy, was she mad I brought that one home,'" John adds, then a blue pickup appears on the cinder and gravel road below the cabin and seems ready to turn into the yard.

"What's he doin'? You better get down there and stop

him!" Bob suddenly shouts at Mike. "He's gonna put ruts in the yard."

But the truck reverses in time and the crisis passes. Then John asks to see Garth's eight-point, and we decide it is time to hang my deer. Everybody heads for the small cabin. Along the way, we meet Mike's friend, Tommy Mollard, and Mike's girlfriend, Sue Burke, who have come north from McKeesport for a day.

■

Few things in life can equal a stay in a good deer camp. Even men who are not hunters have found themselves making annual trips to the cabins of friends after just a single visit. Often they serve as cooks and dishwashers, something their wives may not see them do more than a half-dozen times a year at home. A study by Tom Heberlein, a University of Wisconsin sociologist, found that 60 percent of the deer hunters he interviewed could think of nothing in their lives comparable to the pleasures of deer camp. A full 88 percent indicated that annual trips to camp, with their accompanying reunions of friends and relatives—many who have seen each other only in passing, or not at all, since last season—are of the "utmost importance." In a world that yearly becomes more disjointed, baffling, and artificial, deer camp remains a firm, replenishing oasis.[1]

While camp is always a pleasant place, before deer have fallen it also carries an undercurrent of intensity, of preparation. But once bucks are hanging, the air lightens and becomes joyous. I feel that change for the first time after John and Joe leave and we return from the river to the big cabin. Most of it is me, of course. But the general mood has grown lighter, too. Yesterday everybody was so tired there was little celebration. But now the cabin is full of laughter and teasing. And beer cans popping.

I glance at Dad sitting in the stuffed chair next to the bookcase with a big bag of potato chips on his lap. He is smiling and appears happy. But I can still see the edge in him. Tomorrow is in the back of his mind. He may not say so, and he takes pleasure in my achievement, but I know it must hurt a little to be the only person in camp without a buck. I wish I could help him like he used to help me when I was a boy. I recall him saying he had thought about going down into the gully where I got my deer but decided against it when he saw how rugged it looked. He is getting old, I think helplessly. The only thing I can do is drive deer for him tomorrow. I hope everybody is ready to drive. Seriously drive. Bob wants to work the Hickory Creek Wilderness and a sapling stand above where Garth and Mike took their deer. Then, if we don't get anything there, move to the tornado area where I got my buck last year. It's a good plan. Dad has said he wants to see parts of the forest Bob knows, and I feel certain there is a buck or two left in the heavy cover of saplings and blow-downs. I am glad, too, that Tommy has come along. The chances of success should increase with two sets of eyes watching.

Tommy is another of Bob's conversion projects. Like Garth, he comes from a family of nonhunters and has never hunted deer, or anything else for that matter, in his life. Bob is ready to help, but it is evident his work is cut out for him. Tommy is a twenty-one-year-old stretching his wings and such a novice that he has neglected to fire the rifle he borrowed from an uncle.

Wednesday, too, is far from the best day to start a deer hunting career. All of the easy bucks are gone. But it was the only day Tommy could get off from the muffler shop where he works.

The poor manner in which Tommy is being introduced to deer hunting makes me see again how fortunate I have been in having a father ready to pass on the secrets of the sport. But Tommy should do well under Bob's guidance. Bob has a clear affection for Tommy. He is constantly challenging him, pushing him farther, just like he does Mike. "Listen up now. I am trying to teach you somethin' here," he is always telling him. Or, "The problem with you, Tommy, is you're bullheaded. You think you know everything. Well, you don't know as much as you think you do." The big buck pushing back the little buck.

BUCK FEVER

■

My worries about the seriousness of tomorrow's hunt are somewhat alleviated when Eddie shows up looking for someone to go to Tidioute and everybody turns him down.

"Gonna snow tomorrow," he says, after finding no takers. "It's startin' to rain and snow now. Rain changing to snow up by Erie, but here it might be all snow."

The idea of a snowstorm approaching I know makes Dad nervous, especially since we probably will be heading home tomorrow. He will want to quit early. In a way, though, the idea of being snowed in Up North appeals to me. *The Call of the Wild* flashes in my mind, sitting warm and cozy, eating bacon and beans, while the snow piles up to the cabin windows. The thought makes me feel silly, a boy who has never grown up. I push myself up out of the chair next to the table, stretch and notice Mike and Sue sitting together in the corner. He had put on a tough guy act about helping her do the dishes after dinner, but she had ignored him and before anybody knew it had him next to her with a dish towel in his hand. I smile to myself and start for the kitchen.

Probably a dozen times over the past two days I have tried to call home without any luck. Now, I pick up the phone, dial for a collect call and give the male operator my name.

"Well, did you get your deer, Mike?" he asks, while making the connection.

The question is so out of character from the usual operator's drone, I don't know what to say for a second.

"I take it you've had a quite a few calls from hunters," I finally laugh.

"All day long," he says.

"Well, I got a spike," I tell him.

"Congratulations, Mike," he says.

Once again nobody answers the phone at home, but the call leaves me smiling. I can't imagine such an operator back in Pittsburgh. But that's buck season Up North. I walk back into the living room thinking how much I love the mountains.

XVI

Computer Model

"Most hunters do not really know why they hunt," notes John G. Mitchell in his book, *The Hunt,* "and some would not want to know if it ever occurred to them to wonder. The writer John Madson and his colleague Ed Kozicky once observed in a pamphlet for the Winchester Arms Division of the Olin Corporation that 'hunting is a complex affair with roots too deep to be pulled up and examined. If a hunter is asked to explain his sport, he can no more rationalize hunting than he can describe emotions.'"[1]

Social scientists, psychologists, and sociologists, however, through surveys, interviews, and questionnaires, have produced a portrait of the modern hunter. They have put together lists of motives and attitudes, charted growth, tallied up numbers and figures, and even developed categories of hunters.

Among the most frequently cited behavioral scientist to have focused on the deer hunter is Dr. Stephen R. Kellert of the Yale School of Forestry and Environmental Studies. In a study for the U.S. Fish and Wildlife Service, Kellert described three basic types of hunter (although elements of all three may be present in any individual): the utilitarian, the dominionistic, and the naturalistic.

The utilitarian or "meat" hunter was the most common in Kellert's study, accounting for 44 percent of the persons who hunted during the previous five years. This type is concerned mainly with getting meat and views wildlife as a crop to be

193

harvested. The dominionistic hunter, in contrast, enjoys the sport more for its recreational value, but, to borrow a leaf from the Book of Genesis, believes man should have dominion over the beasts of the earth. This group, 38 percent of the hunting population, regards hunting as a social activity, with competition, achievement, and skill being its predominate goals.

Naturalistic, or nature-oriented hunters were the smallest group pinpointed by Kellert (18 percent). However, they also were the most knowledgeable about wildlife and nature. Desire for an active role in nature and an intellectual curiosity characterize hunters in this group. They find their greatest satisfaction in direct, personal contact with wild places and creatures, and frequently seek such contact as an escape from the assembly line of contemporary life.

On the other side, Kellert identified three basic categories of people again who oppose hunting. These are the humanistic, the moralistic, and the ecologistic.

People in the humanistic group tend to perceive wildlife as kind and innocent. In their anthropomorphic view, hunters inflict terror and pain upon harmless animals. The moralists, on the other hand, consider hunting for recreation and pleasure to be evil, exhibiting a lack of reverence for life. Those in the ecologistic group oppose hunting because they think it is unsound to manipulate natural habitats for the sole purpose of providing selfish benefits to humans.[2]

Though passions often run high between hunters and their opponents, Kellert found the actual degree of antihunting sentiment in the U.S. to be unclear. Most data suggest it varies according to the presumed motives of the hunters. The majority of individuals surveyed—between 59 and 62 percent—said they were opposed to hunting for purely recreational pleasure. But an overwhelming number—between 82 and 85 percent—supported hunting if it was linked to some practical benefit, for example, if the meat was consumed or if the hunters maintained a subsistence lifestyle. "The implication," Kellert notes, "is that the majority of Americans value hunting if some degree of practical or tangible benefit is involved—

an attitude perhaps related to the cultural significance of hunting in American history."[3]

According to a National Shooting Sports Foundation study, much of the opposition to hunting among the general population (not from the diehards), was due to the perception that hunters lack hunting and shooting skills, needed no knowledge to purchase a hunting license, and showed a lack of respect for nature and the rights of others. The conclusion drawn from this study was that hunters need to become more responsible and knowledgeable about their sport and quarry to reduce public opposition to hunting.

■

The reasons people hunt any game animal are as varied as the individuals involved and can shift from one day in the field to the next. Kellert's study for the Fish and Wildlife Service established "nature" as the number one reason given for hunting by most hunters, a concept that included everything from simply being outdoors to becoming a part of nature. "Escapism" was the number two reason, generally defined as needing a break with daily routine, a chance to "get away from it all"; and third on the list was "companionship," the opportunity to gather together with friends and relatives.

Fourth in importance was "shooting." Though stories of successful, or missed, shots abound in every deer camp, this aspect of hunting plays a larger part with small-game hunters, who routinely get more chances to exercise their marksmanship than deer hunters, who may get only one shot a season. "Skill," however, is a close cousin—it involves matching wits with a wild creature, making difficult shots, properly caring for equipment, knowing how to use a compass and map, and so forth. "Vicarious satisfaction," defined as reading books and magazines, watching films, and telling stories about hunting, plays an important role in the hunting experience by extending the season, heightening anticipation, and stirring memories; it becomes more important as the probability of hunting success, or even seeing deer, decreases. "Trophy display" was important to some hunters because of the way a whitetail rack or mounted head on the wall allowed them to exhibit their skills to friends and relatives and remember the hunt.

"Harvesting," the actual killing of a deer, figured only as number eight in the hierarchy of reasons for hunting, which may surprise many people. But the number of hunters in the United States has remained remarkably consistent since the mid-1950s, averaging just over 7.5 percent of the population, despite the fact that only 17 to 20 percent of the deer hunters in the field are successful in any given year. Large numbers of people clearly go deer hunting each year knowing their chances of success are slim.

"Equipment," the ninth most important reason for hunting, involves the pleasure of owning, maintaining, and using fine hunting gear. "Outgroup verbal contact" and "outgroup visual contact," at the bottom of the list, may be translated as the pleasure of seeing and talking to other people with a similar interest. There was a limit to this sociability, however, because seeing more than ten hunters on opening day was found to detract from the enjoyment of the hunt.[4]

■

The most comprehensive data about the modern American hunter are gathered in the U.S. Fish and Wildlife Service's *National Survey of Fishing, Hunting, and Wildlife Associated Recreation*, which has been conducted by the U.S. Bureau of the Census every five years since 1955. The survey produces both a national report and individual reports for all fifty states.[5]

"Since the earliest days of this nation, hunting has provided a source of satisfaction to millions of Americans," the report notes. "In 1985 [released in November 1988], 16.7 million persons hunted, representing a total effort of 334 million hunting days and expenditures of $10.1 billion. Hunters spent an average of 20 days in the field in 1985. Interestingly, hunters spent an average of $603 in 1985—about the same amount that was spent by the average fisherman. Hunting for big game (deer, elk, etc.) accounted for 12.5 million hunters, 131.3

million days, and $6 billion, an average of 10 days and $476 per big game hunter" (p. 4).

In 1985, Pennsylvania had 1,148,000 licensed hunters age 16 and older, second only to Texas with 1,488,000. Of that number, 1,068,000, or 93 percent, were residents, and 80,000, or 7 percent, were nonresidents. Approximately 96 percent of the state's hunters age 16 and older, or 1,102,000 individuals, hunted for big game, namely the white-tailed deer. Hunting days totaled 20,081,000, of which 8,972,000 were spent on big game (pp. 118, 119, 130). In economic terms, hunters spent $714,211,000 for food, lodging, transportation, and equipment in Pennsylvania in 1985. The figure was the third highest in the nation, again behind Texas ($1,074,600,000) and California ($824,960,000) (p. 135). Hunting is big business in Pennsylvania.

Who are the people behind these statistics? The 1985 survey found that 43 percent of the big game hunters hailed from cities and 57 percent from the country. The U.S. population as a whole, age sixteen and older, the segment on which the study was based, was 69 percent urban and 31 percent rural in 1985. No details on the percent of urban and rural hunters were collected for the individual states, but the regional figures show that the Middle Atlantic region, of which Pennsylvania is part, contributed 12 percent of the nation's 16,684,000 hunters, or 1,976,000 individuals. (p. 66).

At a time when men and women participate equally in most types of work and leisure activity, hunting remains a highly segregated sport. In 1985, female hunters constituted about 9 percent of the U.S. hunting population, and only 2 percent of the women in the country hunted, compared to 18 percent of American men sixteen years of age and older. Despite this low percentage, the actual number of females who hunt has greatly increased from just under 418,000 in 1955 to almost 1.5 million in 1985 (p. 31).

Likewise, few blacks or members of other minority groups are hunters. Though blacks made up 10 percent of the U.S. population over sixteen years of age in 1985, only about 3 percent, or 457,000 hunted. And of that number, only 229,000 hunted big game. All other minority groups accounted for just 1 percent of the nation's hunters, a total of 213,000 individuals, of whom 164,000 hunted big game, again about 1 percent of the total. White men and women comprised 96 percent of the hunting population (p. 66).

Why women and minorities are greatly underrepresented in the hunting world certainly involves a number of factors, but among the most important would seem to be tradition. Women, blacks, and other minorities have never had the same strong hunting traditions and hunter role models—Daniel Boones, Davy Crockett, Hawkeye, Jim Bridger, and the rest— as the white male.

Both the U.S. Fish and Wildlife survey and a study by Robert Jackson, a social psychologist at the University of Wisconsin–La Crosse, also found hunting to be a family sport. According to Jackson, 68 percent of male hunters he interviewed were introduced to the sport by their fathers and 52 percent of the women by their spouses.[6] The U.S. Fish and Wildlife survey showed that 82 percent of all male hunters age 16 and older, and 87 percent of all female hunters age 16 and over, were introduced to the sport by a relative. Of the remaining hunters age 16 and older, 12 percent of the males and 10 percent of the females became hunters because of friends of the same age. Only 6 percent of the males and just over 2 percent of the females started hunting because of someone outside the family circle (p. 95).

The U.S. Fish and Wildlife survey also found hunting to be a sport primarily practiced by young adults and those in early middle age. The figures for 1985 show that 17 percent of the nation's hunters were between eighteen and twenty-four; 49 percent were between twenty-five and forty-four; 13 percent were between forty-five and fifty-four; and 14 percent were fifty-five or older. The skills these hunters need are acquired early in life. Although a few claimed to have started hunting before the age of seven (3 percent), most began between nine and fifteen (60 percent). They do not generally come from wealthy families. Only 12 percent of hunters in 1985 had an annual household income over $50,000. Twenty-six percent earned between $30,000 and $49,999; 16 percent earned between $25,000 and $29,999; and 42 percent earned less than $25,000 (p. 95).

Figures on education level reveal that 7 percent of the nation's hunters in 1985 had eight years or less of schooling; 17 percent had nine to eleven years; 41 percent had a high school education; 27 percent attended or graduated from college; and 7 percent had some post graduate education.

Sociologists and psychologists probably can draw numerous conclusions from these figures and follow many leads for further study. But it seems clear that although the urge to hunt can be found in every social class and age group, at every education level, and among all race and both sexes, hunting in America is by and large a white, male, lower-middle- to middle-middle-class sport, something that a ride through the mountains on opening day certainly appears to support.

■

Throughout history, or at least since 360 B.C., when the Greek Xenophon wrote *Cynegeticus*, the first book on hunting, men have hunted for all of the same reasons as the modern hunter pictured by the social scientists. Even Xenophon talks of sportsmanship and the joys of the hunt. "Among the many pleasures to which youth is prone, hunting alone is productive of the greatest blessings."[7] But hunters do go through various stages in their hunting life as their goals and motivation evolve.

According to another study by Robert Jackson, the "shooting stage" occurs mostly among youngsters and those individuals who are just learning how to shoot. To these beginners, firearms and shooting skills are of the utmost importance. In the "limiting-out stage" which follows, success in killing the maximum legal amount of game is important. After that, in the "trophy stage," a hunter chooses to specialize in difficult or trophy animals. During this intermediate stage, an individual wants to show off how well he has learned the lessons of the first two stages by bringing in exceptional animals.

The final passages of a hunter's life are "methods" and "mellowing-out." In the methods stage, technique becomes the most important part of the hunting experience. Hunters in this fourth stage characteristically seek to limit the advantage they have over their quarry by scorning the use of gadgets and technology. Frequently, they hunt with a muzzle-loading gun or with bow and arrow. Or they stalk or still-hunt deer alone, instead of taking part in drives. Understanding the animal and its habits plays a very important role in the success of a hunt for an individual in the methods stage. When at last the hunter mellows out, success becomes less and less important with every passing season. What matters is the timelessness of it all.[8] James Kilgo says it beautifully in *Deep Enough for Ivorybills*, a story about his years of hunting deer on a Georgia farm.

"During the years that I have been hunting at Groton, seven members of the club have been divorced, four have changed professions, three have dropped out, and Jack Bass is dead, but the Savannah River Swamp remains the same, observing the changing light from one season to the next, year after year. With the conclusion of each hunting season I wonder if I will go again, for I think I have noticed lately a growing disaffection for killing deer. But I was back again this year to watch the reluctant summer give way to autumn, and to smell once more the stirring musk of rutting buck. Whether or not I really wanted to kill the buck, I am not yet willing to forego the company of men who hunt. So I take some comfort in the old dispensation and tell myself that what we have between now and the coming of the Day of the Lord is river swamps."[9]

And the mountains of northern Pennsylvania, I would add.

XVII

The Last Bite

It is already past eight o'clock by the time everybody has had their fill of greasy pancakes and sausage, and we are finally packed into Bob's Blazer. Though it is only a little over two miles from the cabin to Tidioute, the Blazer stinks of burning antifreeze by the time we pull into the gas station on Main Street.

"It's really bad today, Bob," Garth says, and then jumps out and raises the hood.

"Yeah," Bob says. "I think this is definitely the last year for the old Blazer."

From their casual demeanor, it is clear they have dealt with the problem in the past. To Dad and me, however, it is a bit disconcerting. The last time we were in the Blazer, it was rickety, but the air was not toxic. I look at Dad in the front seat and his apprehension is visible. He is used to the purified atmosphere of his well-kept Bronco. But then he won't take his $18,000 Bronco where Bob will take his $500 Blazer.

"That should fix it," Garth says, when he climbs back in. He has done something to a hose. Then Bob jumps behind the wheel and we are off, with Mike, Tommy, and Sue following in Tommy's truck.

"We'll be okay as long as we keep the windows up," Bob says, as we rumble through town, which strikes me along the lines of a death wish. It seems only logical to open the windows so the fumes can escape. "If we put them down that just draws the fumes in," he explains, when I mention my thoughts on the subject, adding for reassurance, "We don't have that far to go anyway."

But Bob's confidence does not keep Dad from stirring uncomfortably in his seat. Or me from deciding the best course might be to take as few breaths as possible.

■

We are barely beyond the sign announcing the Hickory Creek Wilderness when Bob spots a deer standing under the hemlocks on the lower side of the road and slams on the brakes. The unexpected stop carries us forward and then back, and we miss seeing the deer before it ducks under the lip of the mountain. Then Bob says he thinks it might be a buck and quickly formulates a plan. We will run Dad and Tommy a couple of hundred yards up the road, drop them off and then come back to the sign and drive toward them.

"Show him what to do, Pap," he tells Dad, when we stop to let them off, and then jams the Blazer into reverse and whines the transmission all the way back to the sign where Mike and Sue are waiting.

"Okay. This is what we're gonna do," he announces, and lays out a plan that calls for him to follow the creek along the base of the mountain while the rest of us spread out toward the road. Then, before anybody can say a word, he is heading down the mountain and out of sight.

"He gets too excited," Mike says when he is gone.

Bob's enthusiasm is usually a joy to witness for the life it gives off, but I have to agree with Mike this time. I look at Garth. He smiles back, and then says:

"Sasquatch."

■

Since the creek runs closer to the road with each step we take, the folly of such impulsiveness quickly becomes apparent. Somebody down the mountain is forever calling for the person above to "move up." Anchoring the upper end of the line, I soon find myself walking almost along the berm of the road.

"I can't go any further," I finally yell back.

Garth shrugs his shoulders, and we pause to listen to Mike and Bob arguing, one shouting we need to "move up" more, the other pointing out we can't "move up" any further.

By the time Dad's orange outfit comes into sight the line has shrunken to a width of about twenty yards. We shake our heads at the silliness and watch as Bob dashes up the mountain with Tommy in tow, complaining he found Tommy watching the wrong direction.

"That buck probably snuck passed him," he complains, and then sends Mike and Tommy hurrying back for the vehicles.

■

Diving out of the Blazer the way we did makes me recall a list of the most common complaints nonhunters have about hunters. "Use of automobiles while hunting to spot game or to shoot from the automobile" was number eight on a list of eighty complaints collected by the Wisconsin Hunting Ethics Committee. A "lack of an appreciation of the esthetic values of hunting," was number forty-six.[1]

Technically, we had not violated any game laws. We had not been "riding the roads," purposely trying to catch a buck in the open. Bob had simply glimpsed a deer and slammed on the brakes. It was a reflex action. I doubt many hunters could have resisted the urge. But being in the majority does not stop me from feeling embarrassed. What we did left much to be desired in the spirit of the hunt. If I was one of the people with a big game tag still on my license, I would have felt cheated taking a buck in such a cheap manner.

"You Americans make good soldiers when you have an Eisenhower to lead you. But good hunters? Never!" one German hunter is quoted as saying in Robert Wegner's *Deer and Deer Hunting*. "You are too intent on getting your bag limit in the shortest time possible," add another. "The essence of the hunt is thus lost in the process."[2]

The ethics of hunting are as complicated as life and death. As I have grown older and far beyond the small rural world of

my childhood, my attitudes toward hunting and the death of a
game animal also have evolved. As a boy, success in killing
deer or rabbits or pheasants was important in order to keep up
with my friends, to prove my abilities, to make my father
proud of me—or a hundred other reasons that had more to do
with my own insecurities than any true enjoyment of the
sport. As I grew older, went away to college, immersed myself
in Thoreau and Tolstoy, Hemingway, D. H. Lawrence, Her-
man Hesse, and James Joyce, watched the senseless slaughter
of Vietnam, and learned for the first time that some people did
not see life as a simple battle to reach the next economic level
or social class, I began to wonder about hunting. What right
had I to mete out death to another one of the earth's creatures? The thought never troubled me enough to give up hunting. But it nagged at me. My world was no longer so clear or so
certain.

Though ambiguity may be the way of the world, it is not
the nature of humans to long exist in disorder. So, I began to
search for answers. Or maybe comfort is a better word. I pon-
dered the thoughts on hunting of Ortega y Gasset, Aldo Leopold, Hemingway, and, of course, that lanky New Englander,
Thoreau. I looked back over my history at what had moved
me in boyhood and found figures like Daniel Boone, Lewis
and Clark, Teddy Roosevelt, the mountain men, and Davy
Crockett. At the age of five, inspired by Walt Disney's Davy
Crockett, I brought home a dead rabbit I found in a neighbor's
field for my grandmother to make me a Davy Crockett hat. I
thought about stories that excited me: Africa's white hunters.
Jack London in the Yukon. Tarzan in the jungle. The Eskimo
in his igloo. Natty Bumpo with the Indians.

Eventually, I stored up enough intellectual and emotional
justification to fend off any attack on hunting. "A fascinating
mystery of Nature is manifested in the universal fact of hunting: the inexorable hierarchy among living beings," says Ortega y Gasset. "Every animal is in a relationship of superiority
or inferiority with regard to every other. Strict equality is
exceedingly improbable and anomalous. Life is a terrible con-
flict, a grandiose and atrocious confluence. Hunting sub-

merges man deliberately in the formidable mystery and therefore contains something of religious rite and emotion in which homage is paid to what is divine, transcendent, in the laws of Nature."[3]

"Alone with the pain in the night in the fifth week of not sleeping," Hemingway writes of a time he spent in bed with a broken arm, "I thought suddenly how a bull elk must feel if you break a shoulder and he gets away and in that night I lay and felt it all, the whole thing as it would happen from the shock of the bullet to the end of the business and, being a little out of my head, thought perhaps what I was going through was punishment for all hunters. Then, getting well, decided if it was punishment I had paid it and at least I knew what I was doing. . . . Since I still loved to hunt I resolved that I would only shoot as long as I could kill cleanly and as soon as I lost that ability I would stop."[4]

Anybody who explores the hunting issue can find endless material to support any view—for or against the sport. To approach it with an open mind (though no mind with a history is entirely free of prejudices), to explore both sides of the issue, as I tried to do, led me through an endless maze into a hopeless muddle. I floundered there until I realized the only thing to do was trust my intuition. When I did that I came full circle back to my boyhood in the country when I lived much closer to nature. I felt hunting once more to be completely natural. I saw I seldom have been so alive as when I have been hunting, and all the doubt disappeared into the landscape. At least for a time. Since, as Thoreau writes, "no humane being, past the thoughtless age of boyhood, will wantonly murder any creature which holds its life by the same tenure that he does."[5]

■

When we reach the Queens area, we turn onto a side road and take Dad and Tommy down to the bottom of the mountain. Then we return to the top and form a line through the saplings, spacing ourselves so we can occasionally glimpse the person next to us. We begin to move through the brush and young trees.

I move only about fifteen yards when a grouse flushes almost at my feet. I shout at Garth, who is on my left, as the bird rises straight ahead through a clearing before veering off toward him. Watching it, I think how I always come across such perfect shots when I am not hunting grouse. Then I take another step and a second bird goes up almost from the same spot. It too follows a straight flight path out of the clearing before slanting off to the right. I call to Garth again and imagine downing a double. I've never even come close to a double on grouse.

Fighting my way through the saplings—bending, twisting, squeezing—I notice how hot the day is turning. Sweat trickles down my sides. Almost all the snow of the past two days is gone. I find a matted-down circle of grass in one of the remaining patches of snow, a deer bed, and then several buck rubs. I start to count the rubs, but quit after six. Everywhere I look there seems to be another one, but with a deer already hanging, my interest in such signs has faded. I wish only to push something toward Dad. Then I wonder if we have made a mistake, if he might have wanted to go back to Baldy. But driving is a good way to hunt on the third day, and he has said he wants to see new parts of the forest. So I think it is all right and that the location won't matter at all if he gets a deer.

Quicker than I expect, we are out of the saplings and into the high grass and brush that separate the stand from the mature forest at the bottom of the mountain. Dad and Tommy are posted between the brush and the stream, and we soon reach them. Nobody has seen a thing. Bob begins to lay out our next drive. It will cover another stand of saplings up the mountain to the right.

As Dad heads off alone to post, Bob shows Tommy where to watch for deer. Then we spread out and wait ten minutes until everything is set and start in.

No grouse flush in front of me this time, but buck signs are everywhere again. A well-worn trail follows the remnants of the fence I am walking at the upper end of the line. Deer are certainly in the area, I think, and hope we can drive one out. Then I hear Mike shout that a deer has jumped in front of him.

I watch to see if it is coming my way and get ready to try and turn it down the mountain. But nothing shows and soon we are out of the saplings and gathering to assess the situation. Mike thinks he saw a flash of antlers when the deer jumped. But it had surprised him and moved so fast through the saplings he is not absolutely sure. Then Tommy says he saw the deer. It ran past him. But he is evasive when it comes to the question of whether or not it was a buck.

"Well, didn't you see it?" Bob demands.

"I saw it. It went down that way," Tommy says, pointing along the face of the mountain.

"Was it a buck?" Bob asks.

"I don't know," Tommy answers.

"You don't know and he ran that close!"

"I was waitin' for him to get in the open," Tommy answers.

Everybody immediately glances around the area. We are standing in the middle of big timber, about as open as it gets in the forests of Pennsylvania.

"Waiting for it to get in the open," Bob laughs, relishing having the upper hand. "It don't get any more open that this!"

Though Bob is only trying to show Tommy, as he is always telling him, "you don't know everything," I still feel sorry for him. It is his first time in the woods. I think Bob should be easier on him. The deer, as Mike thought, was probably a buck and had completely surprised him. Further teasing might turn Tommy off hunting. What he needs is someone to explain things to him.

"You better pay attention and learn something, boy," Bob says.

Tommy doesn't answer.

■

As we start to walk back to the Blazer, Tommy recovers enough from his confusion and embarrassment to begin his usual sparring with Bob.

"I'll take you to a place a half-mile from here and get your ass lost, boy," Bob tells him.

Tommy repeats the words, mocking him.

Bob stops and feints going after him, making Tommy jump back.

"One of these days, boy," he smiles.

"Yeah. You better watch so you don't get hurt, old man," Tommy answers.

"Oh, boy!" Bob laughs. "That'll be the day I quit when I can't handle you guys."

As Bob and Tommy continue to needle each other, my mind drifts once more to the problems facing hunting. Tommy cannot change the fact that he grew up without anyone to teach him how to hunt. And I am sure if he stays at it under Bob, no matter what they sound like when they are together, he eventually will do well. But his ignorance of the woods and deer points out the inadequacy of the two-day hunter education course a new hunter must pass before purchasing a license in Pennsylvania.

Americans love to think of themselves as having a grand hunting tradition. The image of the pioneer hunter pushing back the frontier and carving the greatest nation on earth out of the wilderness still plays well with the national psyche. As does the manliness of it all. The rugged individual surviving, even prospering, in a harsh land through the use of his wits and courage. We love to look at ourselves in such a way.

But how different we appear to the German hunter. "You Americans make good soldiers when you have an Eisenhower to lead you. But good hunters? Never!" It almost sounds blasphemous. But the German hunter who made that remark is ignorant of our myths and traditions. He is criticizing what he sees before him: a nation of hunters with comparatively little respect for the sport, untrained and ignorant of the woods and the quarry, and concerned mainly with filling out a game tag as quickly and conveniently as possible.

An old soldier and military history buff I know once told me a story about a British general from World War II who was asked to rate the best jungle fighters in the world. The question led the officer to expound knowingly on the various strong points—hiding, tracking, and so on—of the Japanese, the British, the Australians, and other troops who fought in the South Pacific and southeast Asia. When asked why he had nothing to say about the Americans, he answered, "The Americans aren't jungle fighters. They come in and clear the damn jungle out."

The propensity of Americans to overwhelm a situation with money and technology, to bend nature to their will rather than adapt, is all too readily apparent in hunting. A person needs look no farther than a sporting goods catalogue or hunting magazine to pick up the scent. Electronic deer and predator calls. "Simulates buck grunt to bring challengers in close." Cross-hair illuminator. "Eliminates the problem of seeing dark cross-hairs on game during low-light conditions such as right at daybreak and sunset—just when game animals are most active." Scent line. "Creates mock trails that will have your trophy coming to you."

Aldo Leopold saw the attitude and problem in the 1930s, long before the era of high tech, when he wrote in *A Sand County Almanac:* "Then came the gadgeteer, otherwise known as the sporting-goods dealer. He has draped the American outdoorsman with an infinity of contraptions, all offered as aids to self-reliance, hardihood, woodcraft, or marksmanship, but too often functioning as substitutes for them. Gadgets fill the pockets, they dangle from the neck and belt. The overflow fills the auto-trunks, and also the trailer. Each item of outdoor equipment grows lighter and often better, but the aggregate poundage becomes tonnage. The traffic in gadgets adds up to astronomical sums, which are soberly published as representing 'the economic value of wildlife.' But what of cultural values?"[6]

Of course, there are exceptions. Some hunters know the deer. Some know the woods. Some, usually the older ones, appreciate the quality of the hunt. Certainly, though, we are vastly inadequate on the whole when compared to hunters such as the Germans. Every year I realize once more how much I do not know or appreciate about deer hunting, a world I might have understood better sooner if American hunters were required to undergo more formal training before entering

the field. In Germany, a hunter must attend a mandatory series of classes on every aspect of the sport before he can obtain
a license. He must learn to identify local game animals and
predators and know their life histories, diseases, and feeding
habits; be versed in game laws, trespass laws, and game management principles; and know how to field dress different
game species, handle their carcasses, and measure trophies.
He practices shooting and studies ballistics, hunting techniques, customs, and ethics. By the time he is ready to obtain
a license, he has invested approximately one hundred hours in
the classroom and countless other hours at home studying his
Jägerprufung, the 550-page hunter examination book. He then
must pass a three-hour written and three-hour oral examination and prove his marksmanship before a panel of judges.
Fifty percent of the candidates routinely fail.[7]

The German system has been in effect since 1936 and,
soon after its initiation, Leopold was recommending it as a
model for use in a United States that was becoming ever more
industrialized and urbanized. The German "system of law,
administration, ethics, customs, and procedures," he writes,
"is incredibly complete and internally harmonious." Like the
Indian, the German hunter even has a cherished custom that
pays homage to a fallen deer. Observing the rite of "der letzte
Bissen" (the last bite), he takes a twig from a native tree and
places it crosswise in the deer's mouth. He then dips another
twig in the blood of the deer and places it in his hatband.
Then, standing over the animal, he offers a prayer to St. Hu-
bertus, patron saint of the hunt.[8]

Most American hunters, still captivated by the fairly recent past when buffalo roamed the plains in the millions and
a hunting license was unheard of, undoubtedly would fight
such strict regulations. They would shout long and hard about
the freedom of the individual and government interference
(though it is the German hunter, through the German Hunter's
Association, and not the government, who has imposed the
system on himself). Or maybe they would claim the Germans
have a desire for orderliness and rules that no red-blooded
American could tolerate. A hundred other arguments oppos-

ing more restrictive training surely would blossom. But we forget one important thing. Hunting is a privilege, not a right. And it has been that way throughout history. Even in primitive times the privilege of the kill was often reserved for certain members of the tribe, be it by social standing or ability.

In Europe, hunting was a privilege reserved for the nobility—and so craved by the commoner that after the fall of the Bastille at the beginning of the French Revolution in 1789, the very next walls to crumple were those around the nobility's game lands. In the "endless" wilds of North America, hunting became available for the first time in history to anybody who owned a gun. Among the greatest joys the New World afforded the poor immigrant was the opportunity to hunt.

From America's wilderness roots, too, has grown the belief that hunting is a right. Perhaps that was true when a settler needed the meat to survive, but most of us have never experienced hunger. And the result of that belief was to push countless species of wildlife to the brink of extinction—or beyond: clouds of passenger pigeons, a living sea of buffalo, and the whitetail. Now, in an age when the East Coast of the United States has grown almost into a single city, and the West Coast is choking in the exhaust of automobiles more numerous than the buffalo at its peak, and a smaller and smaller percentage of people grow up in the country, the only way to save hunting is to view it as a privilege. "Society has the ability to prohibit hunting behavior with appropriate legislation and enforcement," Wegner quotes a sociologist as saying. "The value of hunting is a value that is socially determined by the attitudes and behavior of (all) people who live in that society. A social decision can be made to prohibit hunting just as a social decision can be made to enhance it with public programs."[9]

America has been described as "mankind's great second chance," a final opportunity to rectify the mistakes of the past. Our national literature is a reflection of our successes and failures in that regard. With hunting we almost failed completely when we allowed game to be sold in the marketplace. If it were not for the efforts of a few men who were finally able to change the public attitude toward wildlife, hunting, and conservation, (though not until the majority of the public had its full pound of flesh), there would be no hunting today. The woods would be barren and lifeless and the world immeasurably poorer. Every time we break a game law, abuse someone else's property, or act in a less than sportsmanlike manner in the field, we are risking everything again. Society at large will not allow the whitetail to be driven to the edge of extinction a second time. In an urbanized America, it will be the hunter who is made extinct. It is the responsibility of every person who loves hunting, for whatever reason, to make certain that does not happen because of his, or her, behavior.

■

I am well into the rhythm of the day when we reach the tornado area. We feel certain a few bucks, faced with the disruptive pressure of the past two days, have sought refuge among the blow-downs. If ever there was a best place to hide, the tornado area, with countless tangles impossible to penetrate, is it. Success is doubtful even for the young and adventurous who are willing to fight their way into some of the tough spots because the noise they make keeps the deer moving ahead of them. The only way to approach the area is with a group of hunters, at least a half dozen, sneak along until an impasse is reached and then stand and watch for five, ten, fifteen, twenty minutes, depending on the feel of a stand. The tactic stirs the deer up and keeps people moving and people watching all the time. And a moving deer is the one most liable to make a mistake.

As we enter the fence and scatter through the area, I am drawn to the spot where I took my buck last season. Only a couple of hundred yards in from the Blazer, off the remains of an old tram road that once provided access to lumber and oil men, it is easy to find. But not to confront. Though that buck will stand head up, proud and alert, on the spot for as long as I am alive, the grass and logs on which he fell bear not the slightest indication that anything extraordinary ever occurred. Nothing. But even with my conscious mind laughing at the ridiculousness of finding a sign, I cannot stop myself from glancing around in search of something. Maybe the antler my shot knocked off. But it was surely devoured for its minerals long ago by a porcupine or some other rodent, or maybe it just rotted.

As I stare at the ground, a longing grows in me. I actually begin to miss that buck. He becomes a friend who has passed. Someone with whom I share a wonderful memory, the most precious thing we can leave another. Silently, I stand and remember the Indian prayer: "I am sorry, brother, that you must die." Then I look down the mountain at the dead tree trunks where I had been standing when the buck stepped into the open. The shot was longer than I ever imagined in my excitement. I am pleased and impressed with myself, but I also recall I had not hit where I was aiming. I could have just as easily missed the other way and gut-shot the buck. The thought sends a shiver up my spine.

■

From the spot where my buck fell, I make my way along the top of the gully that runs diagonally through the blow-downs almost to the fence on the far side. Then I start to pick my way into the gully. I plan to make a big circle and hope to push a buck back toward either Dad or Tommy, both of whom should be somewhere along the fence near the head of the gully.

The going is tough and full of dead ends. By the time I reach the small stream at the bottom, I am sweating and out of breath. I can hear people shouting somewhere. I think it must be Bob or Tommy at each other again, but the voices stop before I can make them out. As I start to cross the stream, I slip off the log I have picked as a stepping stone and go down. Fortunately, I am close enough to the fence so I can grab the wire and keep all but one leg from getting wet. But the fall leaves me swearing at my own stupidity. I climb through the standing hemlocks on the other side of the gully with one boot squishing.

About halfway up the gully, I find a patch of space paved with deer tracks. It is a relatively open place, with a good, wide view across the broken timber. I settle down on a high stump and scan the area with my binoculars, hoping just as much to find an unusual woodpecker or other bird as deer. Then Bob, Mike, and Sue appear along the opposite rim. Bob is leading and setting a rapid pace. I watch them move along the same line I had taken earlier until they disappear behind a wall of broken hemlocks. Then I smile to myself and feel a little sorry for Sue. She has come north only to see Mike. She has no license and was probably expecting a nice walk in the woods with her boyfriend. Instead, she's being run up and down mountains, over deadfalls and through briers. Young love.

■

For what almost seems a selfish, or indecent, amount of time, since we are supposed to be moving deer for Dad and Tommy, I remain contentedly perched on the stump, thinking about and expecting nothing. I watch clouds passing in the blue sky; stare at the sharp splinters of a snapped tree trunk; feel the breeze on my face; listen to the brook at the bottom of the gully. I am tempted to close my eyes. And do for a moment, so far has my hunting edge dulled, until my guilt nudges me and I know it is time to move, to circle up out of the gully toward Dad and Tommy.

But my resolve lasts only a few minutes, until I stumble across a debris-choked spring and, in a pool no more than two feet wide and maybe four feet long, I see a tiny native brook trout patiently finning near the center, waiting for his next meal. He looks to be barely four inches long. He spots me and quickly disappears under the dead brush piled at the head of the pool, leaving me totally in awe. I can see no way he could have entered the spring from a larger stream. There are just too many obstacles between the pool and the stream at the bottom of the gully, the only direction from which he could have come. So, he must have hatched in this pool, and considering how slowly wild trout grow in Pennsylvania's infertile mountain streams, I imagine him alive as a fry when the tornado hit three years ago. The pressure of that storm probably sucked the spring dry. Yet, somehow, he had survived. The thought boggles my mind. Now, he will spend his life trapped in the pool, until a raccoon or bird catches him on a slow day. All I can do is shake my head and walk away.

Above the spring, I pick up more deer tracks and follow them into a sapling stand. Buck rubs are scattered throughout the stand. But I have seen so many of them over the past three days they hardly catch my eye. Then I hear Bob talking and move toward the fence to find everybody gathered on the trail that runs along the wire. Nobody has seen a deer and I can feel the hunt has left everybody. We decide it is time to head out, but just to make sure I step over to Dad.

"What do you want to do?" I ask him. "You want to hunt tomorrow? I'll stay with you and hunt. It's up to you. You're the one who hasn't gotten anything yet."

"Aaaaaaah," he sighs. "It's supposed to snow. We might as well leave, too."

NOTES

BIBLIOGRAPHY

INDEX

NOTES

Of Mountains, Deer, and Lenape

1. Quoted in William A. Turnbaugh, *Man, Land and Time* (Williamsport: Lycoming County Historical Society, 1975), pp. 31–32.
2. Quotes in Paul A. W. Wallace, *Indians in Pennsylvania* (Harrisburg: Pennsylvania Historical and Museum Commission, 1981), pp. 36–37.
3. Lowell K. Halls, ed., *White-tailed Deer: Ecology and Management* (Harrisburg: Stackpole, 1984), p. 40.
4. W. N. Fenton, "Northern Iroquoian Culture Patterns," in *Handbook of North American Indians*, vol. 15 (Washington, D.C.: Smithsonian Institution, 1978), p. 19.

Pumpkin Army

1. Joseph S. Illick, *Pennsylvania Trees* (Harrisburg: Department of Forestry, 1923), p. 26.

To Sell the Sky

1. Halls, *White-tailed Deer*, p. 57.
2. Ibid., p. 66.
3. Ibid., p. 67.
4. Wilbert Nathan Savage, "Slaughter Unlimited," *Pennsylvania Game News*, May 1967, p. 29.
5. Ibid., p. 30; Halls, *White-tailed Deer*, p. 68.
6. William T. Hornaday, *Our Vanishing Wildlife* (New York: New York Zoological Society, 1913), pp. 67–68.
7. Savage, "Slaughter Unlimited," p. 29.
8. David A. Marquis, *The Allegheny Hardwood Forest of Penn-*

sylvania, U.S. Forest Service Technical Report NE-15 (Washington, D.C., 1975), p. 11.

9. *Where to Hunt American Game* (Lowell, Mass: United States Cartridge Co. 1898), pp. 222–25.

10. Halls, *White-tailed Deer*, pp. 70–72.

Big Bucks, Falling Pants, and Carbohydrates

1. Quoted in Robert Wegner, *Deer and Deer Hunting* (Harrisburg: Stackpole, 1984), p. 193.

2. Henry David Thoreau, *Walden* (New York: New American Library, 1960), p. 144.

Recoil

1. Quoted in Halls, *White-tailed Deer*, p. 69.

2. Ibid.

3. Ibid.

4. The following account of John MacFarlane Phillips is based on: Paul L. Failor, "Division of Law Enforcement," *Pennsylvania Game News*, July 1970, p. 29; Frank C. Harper, *Pittsburgh of Today: Its Resources and People* (New York: American Historical Society, 1931), vol. 4, pp. 461–62; William T. Hornaday's *Vanishing Wildlife*, pp. 378–81, *Camp-Fires in the Canadian Rockies* (New York: New York Zoological Society, 1906), and *Camp-Fires on Desert and Lava* (New York: New York Zoological Society, 1908); and articles in the Pittsburgh *Post* (May 18, 1923, and February 29, 1924), the Pittsburgh *Post-Gazette* (October 28, 1932, and June 15, 1937, the Pittsburgh *Sun* (May 27, 1922, and the Pittsburgh *Sun-Telegraph* (September 8 and December 29, 1953).

5. Seth Gordon, "How Pennsylvania Won Wildlife Leadership Role," *Pennsylvania Game News*, January 1974, p. 5.

6. Failor, "Division of Law Enforcement," p. 28.

7. Ibid., pp. 29–30.

Leatherstockings

1. Philip Tome, *Pioneer Life; or, Thirty Years a Hunter* (Harrisburg: Aurand, 1928). Citations will be given in the text.

2. Quoted in Wegner, *Deer and Deer Hunting,* book, 2, p. 43.
3. Ibid., p. 39.

Counting Coup

1. John F. Reiger, *American Sportsmen and the Origins of Conservation* (New York: Winchester, 1975), p. 16.

Bearded Bards of Long Ago

1. Henry W. Shoemaker, *Pennsylvania Deer and Their Horns* (Harrisburg: Faust Printing, 1915), and E. N. Woodcock, *Fifty Years a Hunter and Trapper* (Columbus: Harding, 1941). Both will be cited in the text.
2. Quoted in Wegner, *Deer and Deer Hunting,* book, p. 45.
3. Ibid., pp. 44–46.
4. Quoted in Robert R. Lyman, ed., *Amazing Indeed: Strange Events in the Black Forest,* vol. 2 (Coudersport: Potter Enterprise, 1973), p. 16.
5. Quoted in Wegner, *Deer and Deer Hunting,* book 2, p. 45.
6. Ibid.
7. Ibid.
8. Quoted in Henry W. Shoemaker, *Mountain Minstrelsy of Pennsylvania* (Philadelphia: McGirr, 1931), pp. 103–06.
9. Reiger, *American Sportsmen,* pp. 26–27.
10. Theodore Roosevelt, *African Game Trails* (New York: Scribner's, 1910), p. 466.
11. Hornaday, *Camp-Fires in the Canadian Rockies,* p. 279.
12. Shoemaker, *Pennsylvania Deer,* pp. 55, 59, 19, 21.

Fate of the Forest

1. Halls, *White-tailed Deer,* p. 153.
2. See Stephen Liscinsky et al., "What Do Deer Eat?" *Game News* reprint, Pennsylvania Game Commission, n.d.
3. Jonathan Schell, *The Fate of the Earth* (New York: Knopf, 1982), pp. 158–59.

Monarchs of the Woods

1. Quoted in Shoemaker, *Pennsylvania Deer*, pp. 19–20.
2. Leonard Lee Rue III, *Sportsmen's Guide to Game Animals* (New York: Harper & Row, 1969), p. 466.
3. Bob Bell, Betsy Maugans, and Bob Mitchell, eds., *Pennsylvania Big Game Records: 1965–1986* (Harrisburg: Pennsylvania Game Commission, 1988), p. 53.
4. Bob MacWilliams, "Story of Disappearing Antlers," *Pennsylvania Game News*, February 1987, p. 34. The article concerns Perry Kinley's number five buck (177–0 on the Boone and Crockett Club scale), which was taken in Jefferson County in 1920 but not measured until 1986.
5. Quoted in Shoemaker, *Pennsylvania Deer*, pp. 74–77.
6. Ibid., pp. 77, 78.
7. Meshach Browning, *Forty-four Years of the Life of a Hunter* (Philadelphia: Lippincott, 1928), pp. 250–53.

Sparring

1. Quoted in Wegner, *Deer and Deer Hunting*, p. 190.

Computer Model

1. John G. Mitchell, *The Hunt* (New York: Knopf, 1980), p. 21.
2. Quoted in Halls, *White-tailed Deer*, pp. 709–10.
3. Ibid., p. 710.
4. Quoted in Wegner, *Deer and Deer Hunting*, pp. 208–18.
5. U.S. Department of the Interior, Fish and Wildlife Service, *1985 National Survey of Fishing, Hunting, and Wildlife Associated Recreation* (Washington, D.C.; 1988). Hereafter the report will be cited in the text.
6. Robert M. Jackson et al., "Developing Wildlife Education Strategies for Women," Psychology Department, University of Wisconsin–La Crosse, n.d., p. 5.
7. Quoted in Robert M. Alison, "Cynegeticus—The First Book on Hunting," *Pennsylvania Game News*, July 1983, p. 31.
8. Wegner, *Deer and Deer Hunting*, pp. 208–18.

9. James Kilgo, *Deep Enough for Ivorybills* (Chapel Hill: Algonquin, 1988), p. 181.

The Last Bite

1. Listed in Wegner, *Deer and Deer Hunting,* pp. 252–54.

2. Ibid., p. 251.

3. José Ortega y Gasset, *Meditations on Hunting* (New York: Scribner's, 1972), p. 98.

4. Ernest Hemingway, *Green Hills of Africa* (New York: Scribner's, 1935), p. 148.

5. Thoreau, *Walden,* p. 144.

6. Aldo Leopold, *A Sand County Almanac* (New York: Ballantine, 1970), p. 214.

7. Wegner, *Deer and Deer Hunting,* pp. 249–51.

8. Leopold, *Sand County Almanac,* pp. 211, 222, 271–72.

9. Wegner, *Deer and Deer Hunting,* p. 249.

BIBLIOGRAPHY

Books and Pamphlets

Bell, Bob; Betsy Maugans, and Bob Mitchell, eds. *Pennsylvania Big Game Records: 1965–1986.* Harrisburg: Pennsylvania Game Commission, 1988.

Benoit, Larry. *How to Bag the Biggest Buck of Your Life.* Duxbury: Whitetail Press, 1974.

Browning, Meshach. *Forty-four Years of the Life of a Hunter.* Philadelphia: Lippincott, 1928.

Buck, Solon J., and Elizabeth Buck. *The Planting of Civilization in Western Pennsylvania.* Pittsburgh: University of Pittsburgh Press, 1939.

Caras, Roger. *Death as a Way of Life.* Boston: Little, Brown, 1970.

Connell, Evan S. *Son of the Morning Star.* New York: Harper & Row, 1985.

Elliot, Lawrence. *The Long Hunter: A New Life of Daniel Boone.* New York: Reader's Digest Press. 1976.

Elman, Robert, and Seybold, David, eds. *Season of the Hunter.* New York: Knopf, 1985.

Halls, Lowell, K., ed. *White-tailed Deer: Ecology and Management.* Harrisburg: Stackpole, 1984.

Handbook of North American Indians. Vol. 15, edited by Bruce G. Trigger. Washington, D.C.: Smithsonian Institution, 1978.

Harper, Frank C. *Pittsburgh of Today: Its Resources and People* New York: American Historical Society, 1931.

Harpster, John W., ed. *Crossroads: Descriptions of Western Pennsylvania, 1720–1829.* Pittsburgh: University of Pittsburgh Press, 1986.

Hemingway, Ernest. *Green Hills of Africa.* New York: Scribner's, 1935.

Hornaday, William T. *Our Vanishing Wildlife* New York: New York Zoological Society, 1913.

_____. *Camp-Fires in the Canadian Rockies.* New York: Scribner's, 1906.

———. *Camp-Fires on Desert and Lava.* New York: Scribner's, 1908.

Illick, Joseph S. *Pennsylvania Trees.* Harrisburg: Department of Forestry, 1923.

Kilgo, James. *Deep Enough for Ivorybills.* Chapel Hill: Algonquin, 1988.

Leopold, Aldo. *A Sand County Almanac.* New York: Ballantine, 1970.

Lyman, Robert R., ed. *Forbidden Land: Strange Events in the Black Forest.* Vol. 1. Coudersport: Potter Enterprise, 1971.

———. *Amazing Indeed: Strange Events in the Black Forest.* Vol. 2. Coudersport, Potter Enterprise, 1973.

Marquis, David A. *The Allegheny Hardwood Forests of Pennsylvania.* U.S. Forest Service General Technical Report NE–15. Washington, D.C., 1975.

———. *Tree Regeneration and Deer.* Pennsylvania State University Pamphlet 61, November 1978.

Mattis, George. *Whitetail.* New York: World, 1969.

Merritt, Joseph, F. *Guide to the Mammals of Pennsylvania.* Pittsburgh: University of Pittsburgh Press, 1987.

Mitchell, John G. *The Hunt,* New York: Knopf, 1980.

Ortega y Gasset, José. *Meditations on Hunting.* New York: Scribner's 1972.

Pennsylvania's Wildlife Conservation History. Harrisburg: Pennsylvania Game Commission, 1976.

Pratt, Richard, Bruce Sundquist, and Peter Wray, eds. *A Hiker's Guide to Allegheny National Forest.* Pittsburgh: Allegheny Group, Sierra Club, 1977.

Reiger, John F. *American Sportsmen and the Origins of Conservation.* New York: Winchester, 1975.

Roosevelt, Theodore. *African Game Trails.* New York: Scribner's, 1910.

Rue, Leonard Lee, III. *Sportsmen's Guide to Game Animals.* New York: Harper & Row, 1969.

Schell, Jonathan. *The Fate of the Earth.* New York: Knopf, 1982.

Shoemaker, Henry W. *Pennsylvania Deer and Their Horns.* Harrisburg: Faust Printing, 1915.

———. *Mountain Minstrelsy of Pennsylvania.* Philadelphia: McGirr, 1931.

Thoreau, Henry David. *Walden.* New York: New American Library, 1960.

Tome, Philip. *Pioneer Life; or, Thirty Years a Hunter.* Harrisburg: Aurand, 1928.

Turnbaugh, William A. *Man, Land and Time.* Williamsport: Lycoming County Historical Society, 1975.

U.S. Department of the Interior, Fish and Wildlife Service. *1985 National Survey of Fishing, Hunting, and Wildlife Associated Recreation.* Washington, D.C., 1988.

Wallace, Paul A.W. *Indians in Pennsylvania.* Harrisburg: Pennsylvania Historical and Museum Commission, 1981.

Wegner, Robert. *Deer and Deer Hunting.* Harrisburg: Stackpole, 1984.

———. *Deer and Deer Hunting.* Book 2. Harrisburg: Stackpole, 1987.

Where to Hunt American Game. Lowell, Mass.: United States Cartridge Co., 1898.

Woodcock, E. N. *Fifty Years a Hunter and Trapper.* Columbus: Harding, 1941.

Works Progress Administration. *Pennsylvania: Guide to the Keystone State.* New York: Oxford University Press, 1940.

Magazine Articles

Alison, Robert M. "Cynegeticus—The First Book on Hunting." *Pennsylvania Game News,* July 1983.

Atwill, Lionel. "Pennsylvania Deer." *Sports Afield,* October 1987.

Butler, Robert L. "Forests and Animal Life in Colonial Pennsylvania." *Pennsylvania Game News,* March 1976.

Butt, John P. "Deer and Trees on the Allegheny." U.S. Forest Service reprint from *Journal of Forestry,* August 1984.

Eveland, Tom. "Of White Men and Wildlife." *Pennsylvania Game News,* February 1985.

Failor, Paul L. "Division of Law Enforcement." *Pennsylvania Game News,* July 1970.

Fergus, Chuck, and Shope, Bill. "White-Tailed Deer." *Wildlife Notes,* Pennsylvania Game Commission, n.d.

Gordon, Seth. "Hits and Misses in Deer Management." *Pennsylvania Game News,* November 1974.

———. "How Pennsylvania Won Wildlife Leadership Role." *Pennsylvania Game News,* January 1974.

———. "Pioneer Game Protectors. . . . Unsung Heroes." *Pennsylvania Game News,* March 1974.

Bibliography

Jackson, Robert M., et al. "Developing Wildlife Education Strategies for Women." Psychology Department, University of Wisconsin–La Crosse, n.d.

Liscinsky, Stephen, et al. "What Do Deer Eat?" *Game News* reprint, Pennsylvania Game Commission, n.d.

MacWilliams, Bob. "Story of Disappearing Antlers." *Pennsylvania Game News*, February 1987.

Randolph, John. "Deer Camp." *Outdoor Life*, October 1979.

Roberts, Harvey A. "Decades of Deer Damage," *Pennsylvania Game News*, April 1964.

Savage, Wilbert Nathan. "Slaughter Unlimited." *Pennsylvania Game News*, May 1967.

Weiden, Saul. "Pennsylvania's Ice Age Hunting." *Pennsylvania Game News*, April 1984.

White, Joseph B. C. "Pennsylvania's Natural Resource Problems—An Historical Perspective." *Pennsylvania Game News*, July 1976.

Pittsburgh Newspapers

Post
Post-Gazette
Sun
Sun-Telegraph

Interviews

Adovasio, James. Pittsburgh, September 1988.
Brohn, Paul. Warren, October 1988.
Burnett, Bob. McKeesport, September 1988.
Burnett, Mike. Tidioute, November 1988.
Godshall, Ted. Irwin, October 1988.
Indyk, Garth. Tidioute, November 1988.
Nelson, Brad. Warren, October 1988.
Palcsej, Peter. Tidioute, September 1988.
Sajna, Mike, Sr., Mt. Pleasant, September 1988.
Shaffer, Dan. New Bethlehem, October 1988.

INDEX